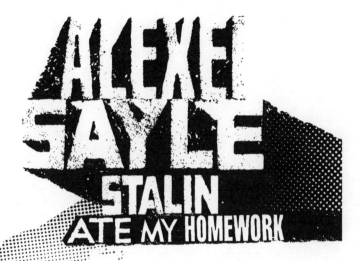

ALEXEI SAYLE

STALIN ATE MY HOMEWORK

SCEPTRE

First published in Great Britain in 2010 by Sceptre
An imprint of Hodder & Stoughton
An Hachette UK company

1

A CIP catalogue record for this title is available from the British Library.

Hardback ISBN 9780340919576
Trade Paperback ISBN 9780340919583

Typeset in Sabon by Hewer Text UK Ltd, Edinburgh
Printed and bound in the UK by Clays Ltd, St Ives plc

Hodder & Stoughton policy is to use papers that are natural, renewable and recyclable
products and made from wood grown in sustainable forests. The logging and manufacturing
processes are expected to conform to the environmental regulations of the country of origin.

Hodder & Stoughton Ltd
338 Euston Road
London NW1 3BH

www.hodder.co.uk

To Molly

Contents

1 Bambi the Counter-revolutionary   1

2 Uncle Willy   4

3 Little Maxim   10

4 Uncle Willy's House   14

5 Cinzano, Comrade Khrushchev?   19

6 In the Front Room   23

7 Once More unto the Front Room   29

8 Open the Second Front Now!   33

9 Milk Marketing   40

10 A Piece of Tin   42

11 To the Atomium   49

12 Disarmament Talks   52

13 The Great Annual Boiled Egg Panic   58

14 A Night in Montmartre   66

15 Saved by the Party   73

16 Emil the Terrible   77

17 Little Zátopek Wins the Big Race   81

18 The Rivals   84

19 The First Delegation of Comrades   90

20 Known Problems with the Sten Gun   98

21 Where's Alf?   104

22 Deadman's Hill   108

23 A Communist Christmas on Merseyside   115

24 At This Moment in Time   121

25 Flight Officer Sayle   126
26 The Shores of Lake Balaton   133
27 This Might Be It, People   139
28 The Undoing of Pemberton   141
29 An Inside Man   146
30 A Smell in the Air   150
31 Making a Profit from Nuclear War   159
32 Sticks and Stones and Sticks   163
33 Lurking in the Rectory   170
34 A Week in Southport   182
35 Odd Behaviour   191
36 'Do You Want a Kiss?'   195
37 Rockin' the Kremlin   200
38 Too Many C2s   207
39 Bicycles to Vietnam or Somewhere   212
40 The Brightest Heaven of Invention   216
41 Morning Assembly   223
42 I Was a Teenage Maoist   228
43 The Unknown Vacuum Cleaner   235
44 But I'm a Member   240
45 1968, a Year of Upheaval   248
46 Highway 61 Reevoosottid   256
47 Beneath the Pavement, More Pavement   262
48 Allen Ginsberg's Whippet   272
49 Someone Else's Sandwiches   276
50 Alexei's Complaint   282
51 A New Revolutionary Era Dawns   285
52 I Wouldn't Call This Paradise   291
53 Molly Gets into Art School   298

—1—
Bambi the Counter-revolutionary

The rumour went round the kids in the neighbourhood like a forest fire: *Bambi* would be coming to the Gaumont cinema in Oakfield Road. It was a brilliant piece of marketing. Every ten years or so the Disney organisation would relaunch their major cartoon movies so that a whole new generation of children became hysterical with anticipation. Whenever a group of us six-year-olds came together, in the playground at break-time or running around the streets after school, we imagined what the film would be like, conjecturing deliriously and inaccurately on the possible storyline. More than anything else there was some collective sense, some morphic resonance that told us all that seeing *Bambi* was going to be a defining moment in our young lives.

Usually I was at the centre of any wild speculation that was going on, dreaming up mad theories about the half-understood world – the year before, I had successfully convinced all the other kids that peas were a form of small insect. But on this occasion there was something lacking in the quality of my guesswork, a hesitation, an uncertainty which the others sensed, because for me, getting in to see *Bambi* was going to be a huge challenge.

I

The lives of other children, when they were away from their families seemed to be entirely free from adult interference – there was a range of activities such as purchasing comics, seeing films, games of hide-and-seek and tag, buying and playing with toys, that were regarded by both sides as 'kids' things'. For my friends, going to see *Bambi* would simply mean their mum or dad buying them a ticket and then crossing over Oakfield Road to the cinema in a big, noisy gang. My life wasn't like that. It was subject to all kinds of restrictions, caveats and provisos, both physical and ideological. I was never entirely sure what was going to be forbidden and what was going to be encouraged in our house, but I suspected that something as incredible as *Bambi* was certain to be on the prohibited list and I knew that if I was going to see this film it would be a complex affair requiring a great deal of subtle negotiation, possibly with a side order of screaming and crying.

It wasn't just seeing the film, fantastic as that was likely to be, that obsessed me – it was that the whole event represented a dream not exactly of freedom but of equality. I had begun to suspect that we weren't like other families. There were things we believed, things we did, that nobody else in the street did, things that inevitably marked me out as different. What I really longed for and what I thought going to the pictures to see *Bambi* would give me was a chance, for once, to be just one of the crowd. I was convinced that, by taking part in such a powerful cultural event as the first showing for a decade of this animation masterpiece, everything that was confusing about other people's behaviour would become clear and all that was strange about my own would somehow magically vanish. I would be exactly like everyone else.

My parents needed to understand that they had to allow me to see *Bambi*! But they didn't. Whatever pleas I made, whatever tantrums I threw, they steadfastly refused to let me go. They had two reasons. My parents disapproved of most of the products of Hollywood but they had a particular dislike for anything made by the Walt Disney company. 'Uncle Walt' had been an enthusiastic supporter of Senator Joseph McCarthy and his anti-Communist witch-hunts of the early 1950s, so they hated him for that. But even if he hadn't been a semi-fascist they would still have had an aversion to his gaudy cartoons and sentimental wildlife films. More significantly in this case, my mother had the idea that I was a sensitive, delicate, artistic boy and she was worried that I would be distressed by the famously child-traumatising scene in which Bambi's mother is killed by hunters in the forest.

Yet they didn't wish to be cruel. They understood that I was missing out on seeing an important and culturally significant film, so as a consolation the three of us took the 26 bus into town to attend a screening of Sergei Eisenstein's 1938 film *Alexander Nevsky* at Liverpool's Unity Theatre. In *Alexander Nevsky* there are several scenes of ritualistic child sacrifice and a famous thirty-minute-long sequence set on a frozen lake beside the city of Novgorod in which Teutonic knights in rippling white robes, mounted on huge snorting metal-clad stallions, only their cruel eyes visible through the cross-shaped slits in their sinister helmets, charge the defending Russian soldiers across the ice-bound water. When they are halfway over, the weight of their armour causes the ice to crack and the knights tumble one by one into the freezing blackness. Desperately the men and their terrified, eye-rolling horses are dragged beneath the deadly water, leaving not a trace behind them.

As I sat in that smoky, beer-smelling room, stunned and disturbed by the flickering black and white images on the screen, it began to dawn on me that all my efforts to be one of the crowd, to be just like the other kids in the street, were doomed to failure. That no matter how hard I tried, I was always going to be the boy who saw Sergei Eisenstein's *Alexander Nevsky* instead of Walt Disney's *Bambi*.

Uncle Willy

My maternal grandfather, Alexander Mendelson, the *shamas* – a combination of caretaker and secretary – of the Crown Street Synagogue, died not knowing that his daughter was married to a non-Jew, was expecting a child, had joined the Communist Party and was living in a terraced house in Anfield at the opposite end of Liverpool. My mother experienced a great deal of conflict over not telling her father about her new life and her baby, but if a girl married out of the Jewish faith the common practice amongst devout families was to 'sit shiva' for them, to mount the week-long period of grief and mourning held for a dead relative and then to treat the errant daughter as if she was in fact dead. She may have wished to

4

be open with her family, to tell them all about her new circle of friends, this new faith she had found and her new husband, but she convinced herself that it was safer to lie. My mother informed her parents that she was leaving the family home, also in Crown Street, and moving across to the other side of the city to, as she told them, 'live in a flat'. Once the patriarch was dead she felt able to tell her mother, brother and sisters her true situation. It is a testament to their good nature, and perhaps a little to their fear of my mother's furious temper, that they didn't then cut her off.

My parents met in 1947 at a discussion group called the Liverpool Socialist Club which assembled for talks, debates and lectures of a left-wing nature at the Stork Hotel in Queen's Square. Notions of social justice, equality and the communal ownership of the means of production were so fashionable that the owner of this smart city centre venue let them have the room for free, even though they were planning, at some point in the future, to take his hotel off him.

At the time of their marriage my father, Joe Sayle, was forty-three years old and my mother, Malka (also known as Molly) Mendelson, was thirty-two. Molly was the oldest child in a family of nine who lived in the heart of Liverpool's poor Jewish quarter. Her mother had been born in the city, but her father was an immigrant who had fled Latvia, then under Russian jurisdiction, as a teenager fearing conscription into the tsarist army. During the nineteenth century the Russian authorities would sweep up any Jewish male, some as young as twelve, and not release them from military service for twenty-five years, when they would be dumped, worn out and confused and often thousands of miles away from their home.

According to Molly her father looked like a lot of the inhabitants of the Crown Street ghetto – men and women who had brought their way of life intact from the old country. His face was covered by a flowing black beard, and winter or summer he dressed in a long dusty coat and big black hat. Not one of my mother's many sisters or her brother ever deviated the tiniest bit from the path laid down for them – they remained throughout their lives devout Jews, staying within the faith, unquestioning and placid. That life was never for Molly. Until she was eleven her father treated her, his first-born, like an equal, encouraging her to learn and to read, chatting to her about his activities during the day, Jewish law and life back in Russia. Once her brother was born, however, all the attention suddenly stopped: now he had a son, her father was only interested in talking to him. But by then her curiosity had been awakened.

Before the Second World War Molly had worked as a seamstress in the tailoring trade, then during the war she had been employed sewing flags for the armed forces – Union Jacks and Red Ensigns. But she left not long after VE Day following her involvement in an industrial dispute. When she met my father Molly was working at the Littlewood's Pools company along with thousands of other women, combing through the weekly football coupons looking for people who had suddenly become rich. Molly was short-sighted and always wore glasses, had a head of luxuriant, bright red hair and, in one of her few acts of conventionality, a temper to go with it. She was capable of going from serene equanimity to incandescent rage in a split second.

As a small child, dressed in flannel shorts, socks, sandals and my best knitted tank-top, my glossy black hair slicked down with water, I would visit the house in Crown Street with my mother. I felt as if I too had been swept up by the tsarist authorities and dumped a thousand miles from home, because though it was only a bus ride away from our house, it seemed as if we had skipped backwards in time by a century or two. The Mendelson family home was a big, black building of three floors and a basement, up the road from the synagogue and next to a yard where my grandfather had operated as a coal merchant. The house appeared very bare, with large stretches of worn linoleum in the hall; everybody seemed as pale as a ghost, and there was always the smell of poor people's soup. The only things that shone brightly were the oddly shaped religious artifacts on the sideboard, their polished brass flanks decorated with strange foreign writing that looked like it had come off the side of a flying saucer. During these calls it felt like we were visiting the embassy of a very poor and distant country – Molly and her five sisters always seemed to treat each other with remarkable brusqueness, as if my mother was applying for some sort of mining permit.

Like Molly/Malka, each of the sisters had both a Hebrew and an anglicised name, so I was always confused about exactly how many sisters there were and what they were called. Who was Rosie? Who was Ester? Was Celia the same woman as Kranie? She certainly looked the same, with identical waxy skin and a skittish manner, but then why did she have a different name? At least the only brother was simply called Uncle Monty.

During the day Monty worked in the kosher section of the big slaughterhouse in Smithdown Road, but in the evenings he was a cantor at the Fairfield Orthodox Synagogue where cruel children in the congregation would laugh at him behind his back because he gave his sermons, not in the normal Mittel-European of the old-world rabbi, but in the same flat, nasal Scouse/Jewish accent that all the Mendelsons had. It was an accent that was at its best when expressing distress, anger, anxiety or confusion. One dark autumn evening in Crown Street I wandered out into the back yard to find Uncle Monty sitting in a rough, temporary shed with a roof made out of palm leaves, eating two fried eggs with his hat on. I thought my uncle had decided to live like a castaway on a desert island, like you saw in cartoons – but in his own back yard, which seemed like a brilliant idea to me. Disappointingly, Molly told me on the bus home he was celebrating the feast of Sukkot, where just after Passover, extremely devout Jews recreate the open-air shelters they'd built while wandering in the desert.

Perhaps that house on the edge of the city centre possessed an odd atmosphere not simply due to the Mendelsons' religious exoticism but also because it sat at the direct epicentre of a network of bizarre, complex and mysterious underground tunnels. These subterranean passages form a labyrinth radiating out from Crown Street, covering a vast area and built during the early part of the nineteenth century under the direction of an eccentric businessman named Joseph Williamson.

Brick-arched, they burrow beneath the entire neighbour-hood with no clear plan, like the meanderings of a gigantic, deranged worm. The passages vary in size as frequently as they change direction, from the vast 'banqueting hall', about twenty-one metres long, eight metres wide and six metres high, to the 'ordinary' tunnels which are only just big enough for a man to walk upright in. Nobody knows for certain quite why Joseph Williamson built them. Some held that he was a member of a religious sect, and that the tunnels were built to provide refuge for himself and his fellows when the world ended. But the most likely explanation is that it was an unhinged scheme to give unemployed men something to do – an early attempt to alleviate the terrible suffering of the labouring masses. And so, in a way, it was. The inhabitants of Crown Street, such as the Mendelsons, would dig a hole in their back yard and tip all their rubbish in, rather than going to the trouble of putting it in the bin – as if it was the most natural thing in the world to have a network of secret passages underneath your house.

Sometimes I would be taken up to the attic where under the eaves lay a strange, wraith-like figure whose connection to the Mendelsons was unclear. This man with his long grey beard, thin bony arms and reedy voice was known as Uncle Willy, and he never left the big brass bed that he rested in. Monty told me, when I asked him what was wrong with Uncle Willy, that he had been attacked by a tiger in India – but even at the time I didn't think that seemed likely. Still, I thought Uncle Willy must be really important to be allowed to stay in bed all day.

My father never came with us on these trips, and when we

9

returned to Anfield our neighbourhood seemed extremely normal and dull. The most exotic thing about Anfield was us.

Little Maxim

Joe and Molly Sayle had their only child on 7 August 1952, the day that egg rationing finally came to an end. Joe wanted to call his son Joe, but Molly insisted that he was called Alexei – Alexei David Sayle. She named me partly because her father had been called Alexander, and partly because while pregnant she had been reading the works of Maxim Gorky. But that didn't mean she wanted to call her child Maxim. That name was an alias used by the author to hide his true identity from the tsarist secret police. He was really Alexei Maximovich Peshkov, and so that's what she called her only son – Alexei.

Although eggs might now be freely available, names remained firmly on the ration. In Liverpool in 1952 there were plenty of sturdy and serviceable British Stanleys and Colins and Davids and Freds and Jims and Philips being born, but there was only one Alexei David Sayle. And if being called Alexei didn't make me feel special, as a back-up David, of course, was King of the Jews.

After going out together for three years my parents had got married in 1950, which came as a surprise to many. Nobody had ever expected Joe to marry, and when his family found out that his bride, who would be coming to live with them and taking over one of the downstairs living rooms, was Jewish they asked each other, 'What will we eat? What will we eat?'

Joe had lived for many years in Tancred Road, Anfield, in a room at the very top of the house, with his stepmother and his niece Sylvia. When she came in from school Sylvia would often hear the sound of Joe tapping away on his typewriter. He had ambitions to be a proper writer, but the work he was doing was more mundane – reports for his trade union, the National Union of Railwaymen, or articles on transport for the Communist Party newspaper, the *Daily Worker*.

Joe's father had been, like so many in Liverpool, a seaman. His mother, who came originally from Jersey, died when he was five. He was left with few memories of her – just a ghostly image of an unhappy woman in white gloves who refused to do any housework. Later the father remarried and Joe, along with his two brothers and three half-brothers, lived with their stepmother.

Though they moved a lot, the family mostly stayed within the Anfield area. Several of Joe's brothers had jobs on the railways, and when he left school at fourteen he too went to work for the Cheshire Lines Company, which served Liverpool, Manchester, Lancashire and Cheshire. To work on the railways in the 1920s and 1930s was to be relatively fortunate. Unlike the docks or the building trade, where men were little more than slaves taken on from day to day, it was a steady job – as a railwayman you were part of a uniformed workforce with a solid sense of identity and represented by strong unions. At the top of the hierarchy were the engine drivers. I was taught to regard engine drivers with distrust, to see them as temperamental, arrogant men who took too much pride in mastering their snorting steam engines. The drivers' union, ASLEF, was often in conflict with the NUR, which spoke for the rest of the workforce, the signalmen, porters, cleaners and guards. Joe was a goods guard, in charge of the cars that carried freight. He rode at the end of the train in his own little wooden wagon known as the brake van. When we watched American cowboy films on the TV they referred to this carriage, more excitingly, as the caboose. The brake van looked like a small Swiss chalet on wheels, a creosoted wooden shed made of planking with a narrow verandah at each end and a chimney poking out of the curved roof. A few times I rode with my father to mysterious-sounding destinations such as Stalybridge and Altrincham Junction. Inside his van there was a coke-burning, black pot-bellied stove that warmed the air with such ferocity that I would become sleepy and have to be taken out on to the gently rocking verandah, to be jolted awake by the cold air rushing by.

Joe's main job was to keep a close eye on the freight wagons, either from his verandah or from a little projecting side window in each wall through which he could see the whole length of the train, and to apply the brakes manually in the event of an imminent disaster. If the train stopped on the line for some reason such as fog the guard had to walk back up the tracks placing explosive detonators on the rails to alert following trains. It seemed heroic work. In our family the guard was clearly the most important member of the train's crew.

But it was the tools of Joe's trade that really fascinated me. Each night he would come home and give me his leather satchel, which held a battered and scratched black paraffin lantern with red and green filters that could be placed over the clear glass lens to warn of danger or give the all-clear, a red and a green flag, squares of linen stitched to a thick wooden baton for the same purpose. In his waistcoat he carried a metallic-tasting whistle and a big fob watch like a miniature station clock.

The most important thing that came with my father's job was free rail travel. Every railway worker and his family could go absolutely anywhere in Europe for twenty-five per cent of the normal fare, and they were in addition entitled to six free passes a year, which meant you could travel right up to the borders of the Soviet Union for nothing. All ferries – to Ireland, the Isle of Man, the Scottish Isles, across the Baltic and over the English Channel – were also included in the deal. A lot of those who worked on the trains didn't seem to have the imagination or the desire to do more than make the odd free trip to Blackpool, but Joe enthusiastically took advantage of these concessions to roam across Europe. Sometimes he would do Communist Party work, attending labour conferences or helping volunteers for the International Brigades travel from neutral Ireland to fight for the Republicans in the Spanish Civil War, occasionally he would write articles on foreign affairs for the Communist *Daily Worker,* but often he would go abroad on his own, simply travelling and falling in with strangers.

As soon as they met, Joe invited Molly to join him on his travels – he loved showing her the world that she had never seen before. In 1947 they joined a group of my father's friends, mostly couples, some married, some unmarried, all members of the same left-wing drama group – Unity Theatre. They had rented a villa together on the shores of Lake Como in northern

Italy. This was extremely bohemian behaviour, associated more with groups of artists like the Bloomsburys than with railway workers. Working-class society remained extremely conservative, and unmarried couples did not go away to stay together in Italian villas – in many homes a girl risked social exclusion if she even talked to the postman without a chaperone. But then to outrage convention was part of the purpose of the holiday. Joe and Molly and their friends revelled in their difference, their love of foreign food and foreign wine and foreign ideas, and had little concern for what society thought.

Uncle Willy's House

Unconventionally for working-class people at that time, and very unusually for left-wingers, once they were married my parents bought their own house. Just before I was born they acquired 5 Valley Road, Anfield, Liverpool 4 for the price of one thousand pounds. Molly borrowed two hundred pounds from bedridden Uncle Willy to make up the deposit – a sum which she never paid back. The terraced house in Anfield was not, however, the home she wanted. There had been another in the more sylvan setting of West Derby Village, but at the last minute she and Joe had been gazumped. So Valley Road was Molly's second choice, and there persisted a sense that she regarded our little house with a degree of disappointment.

There was also something of a problem with the next-door

neighbours at number 7, a family by the name of Blundell. According to Molly these quiet and self-effacing people had wanted our house for their own daughter to live in, but for some reason, perhaps due to the buying power of Uncle Willy's two hundred pounds, we got it. Molly always felt that because of this they bitterly resented us. This might not have mattered if the two houses hadn't shared a water pipe, so that the Blundells were able, if they so wished, to interfere with the flow to our home. My mother was convinced that they would turn off our supply from time to time – in fact she was certain that they somehow knew when she was preparing a bottle of baby formula and would choose that exact moment to strike. One of my first memories is of my mother at the kitchen window screaming over the back yard wall at the neighbours that her child was dying of hunger because they had cut off our water supply.

We lived two miles from the docks in one of the world's greatest ports, 'Liverpool that terrible city whose main street is the ocean', as the novelist Malcolm Lowry described it. A sense of the sea and of infinite horizons was pervasive, though I don't remember anybody actually remarking on it – no one ever said, 'Don't you find a sense of the sea and of infinite horizons is always pervasive?' There always seemed to be a parrot or a terrified monkey which had escaped from some seafarer's house that needed to be chased up and down the back entries by a gaggle of over-excited kids, and sometimes you might see a 'Cunard Yank', a seaman who worked on the North Atlantic run, operating the great liners that ploughed the grey seas between Liverpool and the United States. He would be easy to spot, dressed as he was in the bright blue, yellow or red beebop, zoot suit with handpainted tie that he had bought in a clothes shop in Harlem, Galveston or one of the Mexican barrios of Los Angeles.

Oakfield Road was the main shopping thoroughfare of our neighbourhood and Valley Road, the street we lived on, ran off it at a right-angle. While you could go from one day to the next without a motor vehicle going down our street my parents, particularly my mother, were convinced that Oakfield Road was a continuous stream of thundering traffic that would mow a delicate child like me down as soon as he stepped off the pavement, so I was forbidden to cross it on my own. There was certainly some traffic. Highly polished steam lorries in the blue and gold livery of the Tate and Lyle company chuffed up and down, travelling from the refinery near the docks to the toffee factory where Uncle Joe's Mintballs were made, white clouds of smoke streaming from their chimneys. There were freighters in the dark green of British Road Services pulled by their own strange three-wheeled Scammell tractor units. Buses too, of course: the numbers 26 and 27 in smart green and cream Corporation livery, their destination boards both showing 'Sheil Road Circular', ran in a loop in and out of the town centre. Apart from that, though, you could set up a fruit stall in the middle of Oakfield Road and only have to move it a couple of times an hour. This was another reason why I had wanted to go and see *Bambi* with a gang of kids from the street – it would have been the first time I had crossed over to the other side of Oakfield Road without my mum or dad.

Over Oakfield Road, everything seemed better and more enticing. There was a toy shop called Fleming's with all kinds of colourful stuff stacked up to the ceiling – footballs, puppets, dolls, toy guns and teddy bears. There was a delicatessen run by two men both of whom appeared to be called Dickie, equipped with a giant chromed meat slicer whose spinning, razor-sharp wheel reduced stocky salamis and burly hams to tame, paper-thin slices. Further along the parade there was a cave-like general store which seemed like it had been transported from the American Wild West and sold paraffin, sacks of seeds and slabs of pet food in jelly that you purchased wrapped in news-paper that became damp and evil-smelling by the time you got it home. A large branch of the Co-operative store, three storeys high, dominated the smaller shops. Inside there were separate meat and dairy counters, and people's change went zinging around in brass cylinders suspended on wires above the shoppers' heads as if their money was travelling about by cable car at a ski resort. And next to the Co-op stood my objec-tive, the Art Deco Gaumont cinema, part Egyptian, part Aztec, part brick blockhouse, the current film displayed on a neon-lit awning above the doors, coming attractions advertised by lurid posters along the face of the building and the crowds managed by a uniformed commissionaire dressed like he was a soldier in a very neat war.

The shops on our side of Oakfield Road, shops that I was free to visit on my own, seemed dull and tawdry by compari-son. There were only two that I was even mildly interested in: the newsagent's where I went to get my comics and the women's clothing shop on the corner of our street. Behind the dusty plate glass of this emporium there were arranged the strange items of underwear women wore beneath their dresses – flesh-coloured foundation garments adorned with hooks, clasps and straps like the uniforms of some sort of bizarre paratrooper regiment. These items of intimate apparel were displayed on female torsos made of pink plaster, torsos that had truncated stumps where their arms, legs and heads should have been, as if they had been modelled on the victims of a pre-war railway trunk murder. When I got a bit older this window provoked some very complicated feelings in me.

In Valley Road, even a kid like me with an overly anxious mother was free to run semi-wild. All the children played out in the street during daylight hours, swinging from the gaslamps that stood like watchtowers every twenty yards along the pavement. The children of the street – the Noakeses, the Haggarty girls – came to our house to play with toys and I went to theirs, even if we were having a feud with their family. We ran in and out of the identical yellow brick terraced houses, jumped on and off the low front walls and played the same street games that children had played for hundreds of years.

One of the differences between me and the other kids, which I was highly appreciative of, was that as an indulged only child I was not required to do much around the house. I heard horror stories from my friends about being asked to wash the dishes, tidy up their bedroom or polish their own shoes. Sometimes even I would be sent to the dairy at the opposite end of Valley Road to 'get the messages'. Resentfully I had to walk right to the other end of the street, a journey of over three hundred yards, then hand over money and a note and return with milk or butter from the white-tiled shop. Occupying an awkward triangular site the dairy, unlike the terraced houses, was built of red brick and through its frosted glass windows you could dimly see the hindquarters of the cows shifting uneasily, lined up facing away from you as if they were watching a football match.

❨ 5 ❩

Cinzano, Comrade Khrushchev?

We got a telephone quite early on. I can still remember the number: ANF (for Anfield) 7874. But unfortunately, due to a shortage of lines we were at first forced to accept something called a party line, which meant you were essentially sharing with another subscriber. There were several disadvantages to this arrangement: true, the joint subscribers were charged less for the line rental, but if the other 'party' was using the phone then you couldn't make a call, and while it meant you could listen in to their conversations they could also listen to yours. You would lift up the telephone only to find your neighbour was already on it talking at great length about their hernia operation, and then you would have to wait and keep lifting the phone until it was free. Of course, in our case the other party were the long-suffering people at number 7. We weren't that bothered about them listening in to our conversations since we believed as a matter of course that our phone was tapped by the security services. I was taught from an early age to maintain rigorous telephone security, never to use real names or give specific times, locations or details of meetings. This sometimes meant that me, Molly and Joe went to places where we thought we had arranged to meet people, only to find that they weren't there.

But just as with the shared water supply, Molly was convinced that the neighbours somehow knew when we wanted to make a call and would choose that exact moment to ring their aunty in Shrewsbury. This time, however, she didn't have to shout over the back yard wall to make her feelings clear – she could do it right in next door's ear, at high volume. So we were supplied with our own private line remarkably quickly, at a time when you could often wait years for one.

It still wasn't easy to make a call, though, because in our house vital phone numbers were stored in an arbitrary number of locations. At the same time as the phone arrived we had bought a device, an arrangement of alphabeticised pages inside a spring-loaded plastic box, where by sliding a toggle to, say, the letter C you would get all the people you knew whose name began with the letter C. Provided, of course, that you had written their name and phone number down on that page in the first place. Unfortunately, if they were in there at all most numbers were written on pages that bore no relation to the surname of the person they were attached to, so the Smiths would be under N and the Noakeses under XYZ. More than that, though, Molly tended to store the majority of vital numbers in any location other than our spring-loaded phone book. The most popular places, apart from random scraps of paper that blew around the living room, were the pages of defunct NUR diaries. If you urgently wanted to find the number of Anfield Road Junior School, Auntie Dorothy or the doctor, for instance, you had to know to look under 27 April 1954 (Anzac Day Holiday, Australia).

Apart from the odd overheard phone call we had no clear idea what the neighbours thought, but this didn't stop us making a number of assumptions. One area where we were convinced our life was superior to anybody else's in the street was in the food we ate. The tastebuds of most British people had been destroyed by six years of war and another eight years of rationing, so to the neighbours food had become fuel, plain and simple, to be shovelled down the gullet without ever being tasted.

In our house we basked in the fact that we enjoyed our meals – our dinners were healthy and delicious, not the boiled stodge that everybody else ate. Molly cooked chicken soup and matzo balls, gefilte fish, salmon cutlets and roast lamb. One year we had a goose for Christmas, though it wasn't really a success. At lunchtime on a hot summer Sunday in Anfield Molly would say proudly, 'Look! Everybody else in the street's eating roast beef, roast potatoes and horrible gravy. But We're Having a Salad.'

The telephone with the almost empty phone book beside it sat on a sort of shelf in the front sitting room balanced on a most enigmatic piece of furniture. It was a substantial thing, a highly polished mahogany cabinet with glass cupboards at either end, and in the top half of the centre section there was a fold-down writing desk with a secret compartment where precious papers were stored. In the lower half the flat front pulled out to reveal a drinks trolley on castors with holders for your bottles of Cinzano, Advocaat and Crème de Menthe. It had castors so you could take it round the room on the off-chance that the Lord Mayor or, in our case, Nikita Khrushchev ever came round for cocktails. As far as I knew, it was called a 'Secatrol'. My mother would say, 'Lexi, go and get some glasses out of the Secatrol', or 'I think I left my copy of Maxim Gorky's *My Universities* on top of the Secatrol.' I presumed that everybody had one. A kid in the street would say, 'I've lost my mittens' and I'd suggest, 'Perhaps you left them in your Secatrol' – I assumed this might be the case since ours was always swallowing vital documents and never returning them. After being met with complete incomprehension I was forced to ask my mother about our mysterious cabinet. She told me that it had been bought from the Co-op in 1951 when furniture rationing was still in place. The make-do-and-mend mind-set of the period meant that it was more or less illegal to sell domestic furniture and people were expected to manage with what they had, but if an item could be categorised as being of use in an office and thus part of the export drive then it could be sold. So our cabinet was supposed to be an article of furniture for the workplace – the 'Sec' bit was meant to refer to 'secretary' while the 'trol' came from 'trolley'. In theory somebody's secretary was meant to work at our drinks cabinet, her knees banging against a trolley full of Martini Rosso. As my mother told me about our drinks cabinet I thought that even our furniture had a secret identity and was not what it pretended to be. It remains a mystery as to why my parents felt the first item of furniture they should buy was a gigantic multi-purpose cabinet rather than, say, some comfortable chairs.

In the Front Room

Our house had been built in the late nineteenth century exactly for the type of man Joe was – skilled or semi-skilled working class who kept the freight flowing to and from the docks. It was one level up from the poorest style of terraced house meant for the most impecunious type of family, the kind that faced directly on to the street and had a door that opened straight into the front room. 5 Valley Road had a low front wall behind which was the canted bay window of the front sitting room and an unruly privet bush. A narrow corridor led from the front door to a back living room with the kitchen off it. Below ground was a coal cellar, and on the second floor three bedrooms. Most houses still had an outside toilet in the back yard, but ours had been connected to the rest of the house by demolishing the wall between it and the tiny bathroom that led off the living room. Our stone-flagged back yard had a rockery with alpine flowers dating from the previous owners that Joe tore up and then lost interest in, so it remained a pile of rocks, and a wooden door that led to the narrow cobbled back entry. My bedroom was the small rear room next to my parents', from which I could look out on the back entry and the long back wall that ran the length of the street and acted as a sort of Ho Chi Minh Trail for cats.

When I was four years old I got my own adult-sized single bed, bought inevitably from the Co-op. It had a conventional metal frame with springs, a mattress mounted on these springs and a wooden headboard that, in a rare moment of innovation, had had a little side shelf built into it. The headboard flexed with any movement of the bed frame so that when you got into it or even turned over everything on the shelf fell off on to the floor. I never fully accepted that every time I put something on the shelf it would eventually fall off, so I persisted in using the shelf for glasses of water, fragile toys, pens, pencils and books, and so for years, indeed until I left home, my sleep was accompanied by the gentle sound of things smashing on to the unforgiving linoleum.

Quite early on, when I was a bit too young for it really, I got a toy train set – it seemed like an act of solidarity with the railways that I should have one. It was a Hornby Dublo three-rail set-up. At that time there was an ideological war going on between supporters of two-rail and three-rail model railways. I don't know why we opted for three-rail, but I do know that the set I was given was a goods train with an exact replica of my dad's brake van at the end of it. Maybe the two-rail people didn't do goods trains, or they might have been considered fascists by my parents, perhaps for some reason connected with their behaviour during the Spanish Civil War. Maybe they had supplied toy trains to Franco's forces. Sometimes you never knew. I played with my Hornby Dublo happily enough but never expanded it much from the basic layout. I never felt the need. To me the world outside our front door, the world of 1950s' Liverpool, embodied all those qualities that others found in train sets – a sense of order, a sense of perfection, the feeling that things would remain as they were for ever. In the mornings most of the men went off to work. Joe worked shifts, so sometimes he would be sleeping or coming home when the others were going out, but there were plenty like him and that only added to the general sense of bustle and ordered endeavour. The fathers in our street worked in the building trades, clerked in insurance offices or stood behind the counter in banks, while others attended to the production lines of the modern factories springing up on the edges of the city. Buses and trams and electric trains took them from our street to the workplace, or else they walked or rode black bicycles with rod brakes and creaking leather saddles, and a very few got rides in cars. After they had seen the men go off to work the mothers did the housework and then took their children to the verdant parks dotted with freshly painted shelters, palm houses, floral clocks, boating lakes and open air theatres where there were concerts and Punch and Judy shows in the summer. The city's streets were lined with shops right into the city centre where they were replaced by massive mercantile buildings. All along the river the docks teemed with shipping – cargo boats and giant liners bound for the USA and South America, West Africa and the Isle of Man, while green and cream ferries bobbed back and forth across the river, and green and cream electric trains ran in tunnels beneath it and sometimes me and Joe would lay out my small circle of track in the front room and solemnly watch the train go round and round, a faint, acrid smell of lightning coming from the transformer which brought power from the mains. The front or 'sitting rooms' of most of the houses in the street were reserved for sombre occasions such as this and therefore most of the front rooms in the street went unused for the majority of the year, kept only 'for best' – 'best' being a euphemism for a visit from somebody unpleasant such as the vicar, the police, the doctor or relatives that you didn't like much.

Ours got more traffic, because apart from the phone and the Secatrol this was where Joe's books were kept. My father seemed to have given up buying books once he had a family, as if this was something only bachelors did, because the hundred or so volumes housed in two wooden bookcases in the front room all dated from before the war and provided a vivid picture of the life of a working-class radical of the 1930s. Though Joe never got to speak much about what he felt even in the brief silences when Molly wasn't shouting at the neighbours, these books were like geological rock strata that revealed the evolving layers of his personality. There was a burning curiosity about the future, represented by the collected works of H.G. Wells in a uniform edition. There was an interest in the mind: *An Outline to Psychology* and the works of Emile Coué, the French psychologist and pharmacist who believed you could cure yourself of illness and depression by saying every morning and evening, 'Every day, in every way, I'm getting better and better.' There were hints of another life in that many of the books seemed to be gifts from women, with inscriptions like 'Merry Christmas for 1946 from Betty'. And there was the closest thing we had to a religious object, the book that had made Joe a Communist – Jack London's *The Iron Heel*.

When he was still a teenager, Joe had taken part in the General Strike called by the Trades Union Congress on 3 May 1926 'in defence of miners' wages and hours'. But though the railwaymen and the dockers brought the country to a total halt, elements in their unions, the TUC and the Labour Party were always fearful of revolution and so, nine days after it began, the TUC General Council visited 10 Downing Street to announce their decision to call off the strike. The miners fought on alone for many months before going back to work on worse terms than before. For just over a week it must have seemed like a revolution was indeed possible. In Joe's part of the world warships hovered in the Mersey, their guns trained on the city, troops camped in the gardens outside St George's Hall, while a Council of Action, a sort of primitive People's Soviet, controlled the day-to-day activities of the strike. Over the other side of the river in Birkenhead, a group of strikers attacked the trams and brought them to a halt. Despite the odd fight with the police, by and large throughout those nine days the strike remained solid on Merseyside. Then suddenly it was all over and things went back to the way they were, only now poisoned by a brief glimpse of what might have been.

I don't think I ever heard the story of Joe's conversion to Communism from him but rather it came from Molly, who would relate formative incidents from my father's life, when he wasn't there, as if she was his official biographer. So Joe might have remained simply a left-wing-inclined trade unionist if he hadn't, at the height of his anger and shame over the collapse of the General Strike, encountered a book written twenty years before which seemed to predict exactly how the dispute would collapse and the terrible fate which awaited the working-class when it did.

Jack London was an extremely popular writer known for his action-packed tales of the wilderness, gold prospecting, wild animals and the high seas – novels such as *The Call of the Wild*, *White Fang* and *The Sea Wolf*. But the futuristic *Iron Heel* was something entirely different, and at first Joe was stunned simply by the form it took. The book is supposedly written by an academic, Anthony Meredith, in the year 419 BOM (Brotherhood of Man), which is around AD 2600 in our time. Professor Meredith's book is a commentary on the 'Everhard Manuscript', 'ancient' documents written by a woman called Avis Everhard and hidden by her in the year 1933 only to be discovered centuries later. Avis is the leader of a resistance movement fighting a giant capitalist oligarchy – the eponymous Iron Heel which rules huge parts of the planet. The manuscript itself covers the years from 1912 to 1932 and details the rise of the Iron Heel, the failed First Revolt against it and preparations for the Second Revolt. The manuscript ends with Avis certain that the revolution will succeed but with the reader being aware that, from the historical perspective of the professor in 419 BOM, it was in fact betrayed. In the Second Revolt the revolutionaries are crushed and the capitalist tyranny endures for centuries more.

Joe was spellbound by the sheer cleverness of it: to write a book that worked on so many different levels, to comment on the real world of the present by writing about an imaginary future, to evoke the poignancy of Avis's hopes for the revolution through the reader knowing things that she could not, such as that the uprising fails and she is killed, all seemed astonishing to him. Joe was particularly responsive to the way in which Jack London, a self-educated working-class man like himself, mocked overly intellectual scholars such as Professor Meredith by having the academic get details of life in the early twentieth century completely wrong.

In the world of *The Iron Heel* workers in certain essential industries such as steel and the railways are bought off, allowed a sort of favoured status which brings with it decent wages, adequate housing and reasonable education for their children while the rest of the working masses are left to face centuries of grinding poverty and exploitation simply because in a crisis the treacherous and corrupt union leaders side with the authorities.

As soon as the General Strike collapsed Joe, who was already a member of the British Labour Party, secretly joined the Communist Party of Great Britain.

7

Once More unto the Front Room

Joe's 'dual membership', remaining in the Labour Party while keeping the fact that he was now a Communist secret, was a policy that came to Liverpool all the way from the Kremlin. In the 1920s the Comintern, the department of the Polituro of the Communist Party of the Soviet Union tasked with controlling foreign Communist parties, had despaired of fomenting revolution in western Europe in the short term. So they changed their plans and ordered Communists in the West to join or maintain membership of other more powerful left-wing parties. In this way they hoped to gain influence in the world of politics while at the same time, if they could, sabotaging their rivals.

Members of the Labour Party were supposedly not allowed to be active in any other political group, but the rule was never enforced. Indeed the higher-ups in the organisation were happy to make use of the energy and commitment of those, like Joe, who came to be called 'Entryists'. At the same time they made sure that these Communists didn't rise too high in the Labour Party without first clearly renouncing their revolutionary beliefs. The same was true in the trade unions. Members of the Communist Party were expected to work their way up in their particular union, to fight their employer at every opportunity for higher wages and better working conditions. But, oddly enough, the party also demanded that they be exemplary employees, the logic behind this diktat being that the rank and file wouldn't respect somebody who didn't pull their weight on the job. This meant that Communists were often in the contradictory position of being the best and most profitable employees of firms they were sworn to destroy.

The rank and file too were delighted, up to a point, to have a Communist representing them – they knew that he would fight harder and longer than some less ideologically motivated shop steward. On the other hand, as soon as the Communist tried to politicise any struggle – to take the fight beyond trying to earn a few more pence a week or knock a few minutes off the working day and instead attempted to point out the larger iniquities of the capitalist system – the workers rapidly lost interest and became mulishly resistant to any entreaties. According to Molly, Joe's refusal to dilute his political beliefs cost him dear. Less able men in the union were appointed over him to lucrative and powerful full-time posts, while others in the Labour Party were elected as city councillors and went on to become chairs of powerful committees or even Lord Mayor.

My mother told me this with indignation in her voice but what I saw for myself was that, where another person might have become bitter or disillusioned, Joe seemed to become cheerier and cheerier over the years. Bustling about, a little man with his trilby hat permanently on his head, he always seemed to be laughing. Though everybody understood that here was a man who was dedicated to introducing a one-party state in which government terror was a central tool for ensuring the dictatorship of the proletariat I would hear people say, 'You couldn't meet a nicer bloke than Joe Sayle.'

Various examples of Joe's election literature were stored in the Secatrol. In 1938 he had stood in the municipal elections as Labour candidate for the Kirkdale ward, promising '. . . the demolition of slums and every insanitary house, large-scale replanning of built-up areas with provision of open spaces, children's playgrounds and school development'. He also seemed to have developed a great resentment of trams. Under a section headed 'Transport' my father promised '. . . the gradual substitution of Motor or Trolley Buses on all routes, no further expenditure on new tram cars or new tracks.' Joe stood for the council twice but neither time was he elected. When Molly informed me of this I dwelt on it for a long time, turning this rejection over and over in my mind. It made me wonder what was wrong with the people of Liverpool. What was up with them? Why didn't they vote for my dad?

When he was home in the evening Joe would come to my bedroom, sit on the bed which caused stuff to fall off the shelf, and tell me stories that he'd make up on the spot, inventing characters like Freddie the Frog. Too often though, he was out, either working or at a union meeting. And sometimes, even though he was home, I would have to compete with the Communist Party for his attention. Meetings were not held frequently at our house but there were times when from my position on the floor of the front room I would look up, the air around me wreathed in smoke, staring into a forest of political men's trouser legs.

Though I was only three or four the men who were at those meetings are clear in my mind, not because I recall them directly but because when Molly and I were together in the house or on a visit to Stanley Park, me in my little red pedal car, Molly would provide a judgemental commentary on the meetings and particularly on the members. When she spoke about Joe and his past she employed a valedictory tone, as if making a speech at a meeting, but when she talked about other people in the party I could never tell if Molly was even really speaking to me or to herself. Yet, silent and watchful, I took it all in. In this way I learned that this comrade was a terrible disappointment to his father who was a leading figure in the party, that that comrade was a drunk, that this one spent all his time working for the betterment of the working-class but left his own children and wife cold and hungry, and that I should never let myself be left alone in a room with that one.

One year one of the members told me he would make me a toy fort for Christmas. I think it was just something said on the spur of the moment, and he might have forgotten all about it if I hadn't badgered him repeatedly over the next few months. 'How's the fort coming along?' I would ask him. 'Will it have an electric light bulb?' and 'Perhaps a working portcullis?' and 'Do you think a proper drawbridge would be a good idea?' It took a long time to arrive but finally, wearily, right on Christmas Eve he deposited it at our house – and it was magnificent. It had all the things I had specified: a drawbridge you could wind up and a working portcullis and a little light bulb that worked off a battery. Then he stopped coming to the meetings and I never saw him again. That was one problem with having a family that wasn't based on blood ties – people often inexplicably vanished and you weren't supposed to miss them.

Open the Second Front Now!

Joe and Molly had one Communist Party friend who they were particularly close to. His name was George Garrett, and he had been something of an inspiration for Joe. At the age of fourteen Garrett had run away to sea, then jumped ship in Argentina. He travelled north to the United States and became a hobo, riding the rails around the USA. After a while he returned to seafaring and in 1914 his ship, the SS *Oswald*, was captured by the German navy, but the crew were rescued. In 1918 he married, but remained unemployed for long periods due to his membership of the Communist Party. He returned to New York, where he became a member of the Syndicalist trade union, the Industrial Workers of the World, also known as 'The Wobblies'. On his return to Britain he took part in the first hunger march and the founding of the Unemployed Workers' Movement. Garrett also became a founder member of the Left Theatre, which in turn became the Unity Theatre. All the time he wrote short stories about the sea, working-class life and the battles that poor families had with the repressive institutions of church and state. He was also a literary critic, and his essays on Shakespeare's *The Tempest* and Joseph Conrad's novel *The Nigger of the Narcissus* were published in literary journals. These brought him to the attention of George Orwell.

In 1936 Orwell was in the middle of writing *The Road to Wigan Pier* and so it was natural that, being in the area, he came to Liverpool to stay with George Garrett. Though he was again unemployed and had a large family to feed, Garrett gave Orwell a place to stay and never asked him for any money. The two men would stay up all night drinking and talking about the novels of Dostoevsky, Melville and Jack London, and the plays of Ibsen, Strindberg and Eugene O'Neill. The way I heard the story from my parents, Garrett was happy to entertain his friend for as long as he wished to stay, but they couldn't understand why he allowed this Old Etonian, this poverty tourist, to keep hanging around. They felt that their George was the real thing, a working-class man who had been forced into his life on the road by a desperate desire to escape a terrible life, not because he thought it would make a good book.

The Communists' dislike of Orwell was confirmed when later that year he went off to fight in the Spanish Civil War and on his return, in his book *Homage to Catalonia*, accused Communist factions of waging internecine war on their left-wing allies instead of fighting the true enemy – Franco's fascists. Molly also said that Orwell had promised to give George Garrett a big dedication in *The Road to Wigan Pier* but had gone back on his word. The *Daily Worker*, the Communist Party's newspaper, gave *The Road to Wigan Pier* a really bad review when it was published. Over the years, of all the many people my parents despised – J. Edgar Hoover, Winston Churchill, Hitler and Walt Disney among others – it was Orwell's name that came up most frequently and was spoken with the most venom. I thought he must be the most evil man in the world. On the other hand, while my parents wanted the story to show their friend George Garrett in a good and noble light, it actually gave me the impression that he had been a bit of an idiot to allow himself to be taken advantage of in this way.

Some Communists like George Garrett tried to have as little as possible to do with consumer goods, but around about 1957 we bought the flashiest thing you could possibly purchase – a television set. It was the Co-op's own brand, which was called a Regentone. It had a brown walnut cabinet with a tiny murky grey screen, and a little metal badge of a knight carrying a pennant mounted on a horse fixed to the cloth covering of the speaker grille. The TV was our second big purchase. Molly had made sure that she got a sewing machine first, a heavy black metal thing bristling with wheels and needles that stabbed rapidly up and down, with a stencil of flowers down its flanks to try and hide its murderous intent. It took years before the sewing machine was paid for. Compared to the sewing machine, our TV was a friendly thing.

We had always thought that the families who bought televisions were consumerist members of the working-class who had allowed themselves to get caught up in the bourgeois notion of trying to impress the neighbours. But after the Regentone came into the house that idea was quietly dropped and, like everyone else, we soon made the TV the centre of our lives. Though, to be fair, in our house watching the television was more of a two-way process than in other homes. It seemed we had bought a television mostly so we could argue with it, a response which became particularly violent when a news report came on. Right away one or other of my parents would begin shouting, 'Nonsense!' 'Lies!' or 'Capitalist propaganda!' at anything they disagreed with, which tended to be nearly everything that was shown on the news.

I was surprised at what could be considered capitalist propaganda. Obviously anything criticising the Soviet Union or the People's Republic of China fell into that category, but any item that was congratulatory about the British army's performance during the Second World War inevitably brought shouts of 'Don't forget Stalingrad!' or 'What about the second front?'

'Don't forget Stalingrad!' was a reference to the notion my parents had that the whole turning point of the war was the Battle for Stalingrad in which the Soviet armies under Zhukov defeated Paulus's 6th Army, sending the German invaders fleeing west. As far as they were concerned, such supposedly pivotal moments as the Battle of Britain, El Alamein or the sinking of the *Bismarck* had been completely insignificant and pointless little skirmishes. I don't know if my parents ever mentioned these feelings to our neighbours, people who had fought in or lost relatives during several of these encounters. I expect Molly did, but the Regentone certainly got to hear about them.

'What about the second front?' harked back to the behaviour of Communists before the war and in its early years. Throughout the 1930s the party had been a beacon of resistance to Nazism both at home and abroad, when many others had ignored or tried to accommodate the growing threat. CP members had confronted the British Union of Fascists in street battles up and down the country. More importantly, while all the major powers had been intent on appeasing German and Italian fascism the CP had consistently campaigned against it, going so far as to forego their instincts and join in a broad front with other left-wing parties. In 1939, with war imminent, any party member such as Joe could console themselves with the thought that they had done all they could to warn of the dangers of fascism. Then in August of that year the Soviet Union suddenly signed a non-aggression pact with Nazi Germany. The order came down from party headquarters that the conflict was now an 'Imperialist War', and for nearly two years the Communist Party of Great Britain actually tried to sabotage the war effort by encouraging strikes and denouncing the government for its pursuit of the conflict. In the Soviet Union, along with many other measures the anti-German film *Alexander Nevsky* was banned. After Germany invaded the USSR in 1941 the party flipped again and its members spent the next two years being rabidly pro-war and demanding 'Open the second front now!' By this they meant that the Allies should invade continental Europe right away, without any preparation or planning, simply to take the heat off the Russians in the East.

Another phrase that would often be shouted at our TV when there was any mention of espionage or a court case was 'Remember the Rosenbergs!' Ethel and Julius Rosenberg were Jewish American Communists who were vindictively executed in 1953 after having been found guilty of passing information about the atomic bomb to the Soviet Union. My mother frequently got terribly upset about the execution of the Rosenbergs, with tears rolling down her cheeks at the very mention of their names, so that I thought for a long time they were people we knew. Once I understood they had lived in the United States rather than Anfield the idea grew in me that the authorities in America were likely to whip you off the streets and send you to the electric chair for no reason at all, and that likelihood increased more or less to a certainty if you were black, Jewish or Communist. This gave me a funny attitude towards the United States. I was already aware that there were many amazing things that came from this country – animated films, brightly coloured clothes, comic books – but obviously if you went to the place there was clearly a good chance that you would be electrocuted.

There was, however, a surprisingly long list of programmes, by no means all of them on the BBC (higher-toned than its new rival, ITV), that we felt an obligation to watch. Molly and Joe were both involved with the Unity Theatre. Afterwards Molly joined too and made costumes for some of their productions. Though it was essentially an amateur group Unity pioneered a lot of the techniques which would become standard in fringe theatre, and introduced a number of writers who were subsequently staples of the professional theatre. Even before the war they were improvising agitprop plays from events in that week's newspapers, and the London branch put on the first production of a Brecht play in Britain as well as promoting the work of Clifford Odets, Sean O'Casey, Jean-Paul Sartre and Maxim Gorky.

Over the years many successful actors had graduated from Unity, so when they appeared on the TV we felt it was our socialist duty to watch them. In this way I got to see some of the early work of Lionel Bart, David Kossoff and Warren Mitchell. Alfie Bass, another Unity graduate, was in a hit ITV comedy all about mismatched conscripts called *The Army Game*, and since he was left-wing and Jewish and had been in Unity I was able to enjoy this sitcom of army life with my parents laughing at it rather than them shouting 'Remember Stalingrad!' or 'Open the second front now!' every five minutes. We were also very keen to watch what might have been regarded as populist trash on ITV – historical adventure shows such as *Robin Hood* and *Ivanhoe*. My parents had the idea (partly true) that these shows were written almost entirely by American refugees from Senator McCarthy's anti-Communist purges, and thought they might contain subliminal or subtle messages of an anti-capitalist nature (also partly true).

We also felt it was our duty to watch the Harlem Globetrotters whenever they were on. This was partly because they were black, so we were identifying with and supporting their struggle for equal rights, and partly because we read some sort of anti-establishment message into a man using a stepladder in a comedy basketball game.

(9)

Milk Marketing

On our first-ever day of school our mothers walked us to Anfield Road Primary. Though it was built in a firmly rationalist, red-brick style Anfield Road School possessed a big ventilation spire, mostly for show. It was a striking landmark that, oddly, bore a very strong resemblance to the Soyuz rockets that the year before had blasted the Soviet Sputnik satellite into space, stunning the West and causing much celebration in our house.

At the school gate, my mother gave me a Corgi model of a Le Mans D-Type Jaguar. This is my first clear and unclouded memory – getting that car with its single seat for the driver and huge stabilising fin in British racing green. This might have been the moment when I became obsessed with cars. Most days the only vehicle going up and down Valley Road was the little red pedal car I owned. So the automobiles I saw seemed miraculous, rare and beautiful. It also occurred to me at an early age that they were not all different, but were in fact classifiable. There were models from one company and models from another company, there were new models and old models that they didn't make any more but were still driving around, so it became for me a way to impose a form of order on the world by tabulating them all.

I was certain there was absolutely no chance that we were ever going to own one. Both my parents were pretty unmechanical, and I had also heard that cars cost a huge amount of money – hundreds of pounds, other children told me – and in any case the free rail travel we got made the prospect of owning a motor vehicle economically pointless. From this the idea grew in me that driving was probably about as complicated as making a steam engine go along, that it would require constant attention to all kinds of gauges and dials, the endless manipulation of levers and pedals and probably a large amount of coal. Perhaps my parents' dislike of cars was ideological, too. After all, in the Soviet Bloc the authorities weren't at all keen on their citizens having their own vehicles, going about and seeing things they weren't supposed to see.

My mother needn't have worried about me not liking school, I thought it was great. There were a sandpit and a wigwam, and as an only child it was a pleasant novelty for me to be spending so much more time with kids my own age. It also meant I was able to bring my ideas to a larger audience. At break-time in the first week our teacher, Miss Wilson, said to the assembled class, 'All right, class, now let's bow our heads in prayer and thank God for this milk we're drinking.' At which point I stood up and said, 'No, Miss Wilson, I think you'll find that the milk comes to us via the Milk Marketing Board, a public body set up in 1933 to control the production, pricing and distribution of milk and other dairy products within the UK. It has nothing to do with the intervention of some questionable divine entity.' I think Miss Wilson must have had a word with the rest of the class about me, telling them I was 'special' or something, because I don't remember ever getting picked on. Which you could see as a religious miracle, really.

10
A Piece of Tin

After they were married, had a child and bought a home Joe and Molly had not, as many couples might have done, stopped their travelling. In this post-war period there was one very powerful incentive for anybody, no matter what their political views were, to take part in foreign travel. The Labour government that had been elected in 1945 in a landslide of post-war utopian longing possessed a certain puritanical instinct. The austerity of the life they imposed on 1940s' and 1950s' Britain was to some extent forced on the country by the United States maliciously calling in all their war loans the moment the fighting ceased, but there still seemed to be something dreary, life-denying and over-zealous about food, drink and clothes being so severely rationed up to a decade after the conflict ended.

By contrast, countries such as France and Italy that had been over-run, looted and pillaged by the Nazis were quickly awash with cheap food and wine, rabbits, chickens, fish and wonderful fresh vegetables which overflowed from shops and street markets. And because the Republic of Ireland, just across the Irish Sea from Liverpool, had remained neutral throughout the war it had never experienced any shortage of bacon, butter, cheese or eggs. So while the people back home were being forced to eat omelettes made out of powdered eggs and pies of turnip tops and whale blubber my parents, at least for a few weeks a year, were dining on *schiacciata alla fiorentina* and *langoustine au cognac avec sauce beurre blanc* washed down with a decent Pouilly Fuissé or just having a nice chicken sandwich.

By the age of five I must have been the most travelled child in Anfield. I had been to Normandy twice, Paris, Holland, Belgium, Ireland and the Swiss Alps as well as on numerous trips to London, the Lake District, Devon and Cornwall. Because of all our foreign travel, our exotic backgrounds and our internationalist outlook my parents were convinced that the three of us were really fluent in foreign languages. Joe was thought to have an excellent command of French and something called Esperanto, a language invented by a man called L.L. Zamenhof in the 1920s which was intended to foster peace and international understanding by everybody being able to talk to each other in the same tongue. At home Molly had conversed in

Yiddish with her family, so she insisted that she spoke German like a native, and I was supposed to have inherited Joe's fluency in French. Molly certainly did speak some German. I remember my mother screaming, '*Mein Kinder! Mein Kinder!*' at a man on a train just outside Stuttgart who had tried to open the window of our compartment on a hot summer night and in so doing was threatening the health of her child by creating a bit of a draught.

Before the age of five my memories of overseas travel are fragmentary, a collage of alien smells and images and the sound of somebody yelling, possibly a red-haired woman, but in the summer of 1958 we caught the ferry from Folkestone not to Boulogne but the longer passage to Ostend in Belgium, an often rough four-hour crossing. Once we were out of the harbour the waves were endless rows of scallop shells, grey and flecked with foam, and the boat, though it was bigger than the French ferries, still pitched and rolled in the swell.

Customs and passport control at any Channel port was a lengthy process. After reading from a card you had to answer convoluted questions asked by a man in a strange uniform, there was the use of elaborate seals and stamps, and sometimes you had to remove items of clothing. Going abroad was nearly as complicated as joining the Freemasons. At Ostend we had the usual interrogation, got our passports stamped and our luggage searched. We hated having to open our baggage, not because we had anything to hide but because the Sayles were early experimenters with the concept of wheeled luggage. Each of us had an L-shaped metal contraption with big rubber wheels secured by numerous straps to a corner of our suitcase – straps that had to be undone before the case could be opened. The idea behind this was that you could wheel your luggage along using a handle attached to the other end of the strap. In practice, no matter how tightly you secured them, the case always seemed to work its way free from the straps and would fall off its wheels generally while you were running for a train, either tripping you up and sending you sprawling or, at the very least, stabbing you in the ankle and drawing blood.

Once through customs we needed to get further up the Belgian coast, so we hauled our luggage on to a tram that ran through the sand dunes and the trim little towns to the resort where we were staying. Though the voters of Kirkdale hadn't elected my father in 1938, his dislike of trams seemed to have been widely shared and since the war there had been a steep rundown of the city's network. The year before our trip to Belgium Joe had taken me to see Liverpool's last tram outside St James Street Station. Decked out in strings of light bulbs it had seemed lumbering and sad, like a sickly elephant in a down-at-heel circus. By contrast these single-deck trams that raced up the Belgian coast appeared swift and confident. The Liverpool ones had swayed from side to side on metal grooves in the cobbled streets and, with so many different lines cut in the street, often seemed confused as to where they were going. But here there was only the one line going north, and once out in the countryside these Belgian trams ran swift and sure.

The reason we were staying in this particular small hotel in this particular town was that the woman who owned it advertised in the *Daily Worker*. She wasn't a Communist herself – this was simply a smart piece of business. As Communists were so used to being reviled, when somebody was nice to them party members could often be absurdly grateful for even the tiniest bit of attention, and if somebody was prepared to welcome them into their establishment or try to sell them the products they made they could be ridiculously loyal. There were only about three places that regularly advertised in the *Daily Worker*. One was the hotel we were staying in, another was a shop that sold sub-standard Soviet consumer goods in Shepherds Bush, and the third was a Greek restaurant in Tottenham Court Road confusingly named 'Au Montmartre'. When we were in London we sometimes ate there. It seemed to be full of veterans of the Spanish Civil War, grizzled men in berets and leather jackets despondently eating their way through kleftiko, sheftalia or moussaka, served with chips, peas, sliced bread and butter and a cup of tea.

We checked into the hotel, with its long glassed-in sun terrace facing the beach. After dinner we sat in wicker chairs and stared out to sea as the storm that had been brewing during our crossing finally broke. For the first time I saw forks of lightning explode like cracks in a window, spearing downwards in jagged lines to the black water while a man swam towards the storm, seemingly unconcerned in the electric sea, and my parents debated whether he was doing the right thing. Was floating in the sea during a thunderstorm a bad idea or in fact the safest place to be? They thought on balance it was probably the latter, that swimming towards the tempest was a brilliant strategy to avoid injury by lightning bolts.

The weather was sunny and breezy, we sat on the beach, we ate all kinds of food you couldn't get in Britain and we rode about in four-seater pedal-karts. Molly and Joe didn't just stay at the seaside – here was another thing that was different about us and our holidays. When those few working-class British people who did so travelled abroad they stayed at some tourist hotel on the Italian Riviera or the Spanish Costa Brava, and if they socialised they socialised only with other British holidaymakers. But the Sayles were different – the Sayles knew people who lived abroad, real foreign people!

In 1945, soon after the war ended, Joe had attended a Communist Party conference in Paris at which he had met a couple of Dutch comrades called Ank and Ayli. They were journalists who throughout the war had run an underground newspaper for the resistance. In the aftermath of the conflict there was wide-scale famine in Holland, since the majority of the Allies' relief effort was, ironically, going to feed the defeated Germans. Joe befriended the Dutch couple and, seeing that they were poor and hungry, he helped them out. Now, thirteen years later, they wanted to repay his kindness. We were going to spend the weekend with them in Amsterdam.

Early one morning the three of us took a tram back to Ostend and from there caught a train that travelled inland from the Belgian coast, crossing the border into Holland and terminating in Amsterdam where the once starving couple met us at the Centraal Station. Perhaps reflecting the way our two countries were diverging, or maybe just how their fortunes had improved, Ank and Ayli now seemed to be doing much better than us. They even had that most extraordinary of things, a car, a black Volkswagen Beetle with the oval rear window, and we spent the day driving with them in the Dutch countryside. We took a long straight road that was only for motor vehicles – I didn't know it,

47

but this was my first trip on a motorway. The needle on the VW's speedometer touched 90 kilometres an hour and, not knowing there was a difference between kilometres and miles, I thought we were going at an unbelievable speed.

Later in the day, this being Holland we went for a walk along a canal. As we strolled along this strip of water lined with thin trees I noticed something lying on the ground by the side of the towpath, half buried in the mud and masked by a clump of scrawny grass. I picked it up and brushed the dirt away. It was a square of rusted and pitted metal, mostly flat but bent over along the top and bottom edge, and about the size of a big box of Swan matches. The outer metal was the colour of dried blood, but the middle, a raised crest in grey pewter, remained unaffected by corrosion. It was an emblem, oval in shape, a motif of laurel leaves and at the centre an eagle holding in its talons a swastika. I had found the belt buckle of a German soldier.

'I bet he was shot!' I said, 'Or he was blown up by a hand grenade from a British commando and his guts went everywhere. . . . Or he was knifed in the back by the resistance and as he fell he tore off the. . . .' Later on Molly gave me a little talk, telling me that the Dutch had been through a lot during the war and they might not feel the same way as me about my find. I thought it was just plain rude of them not to be impressed by my discovery.

Molly wanted me to get rid of the horrible thing, but I put the Nazi buckle in my pocket, brought it back to England and kept it in a shoebox under my bed. During the autumn term I took it into school one day to show our teacher and the class, but when my prized possession was passed around nobody showed any sign of being particularly taken with it. I had been looking forward to a big reaction, but there was only polite interest. I couldn't figure it out – the belt buckle had made people edgy and uncomfortable in Holland and here it was doing no business at all. This seemed very odd. Molly had told me that that little square of pitted metal was imbued with evil, yet none of my classmates were able to see it. It appeared that the power of things wasn't fixed: a belt buckle could only make you feel unwell if you had been fighting the Nazis for years, and if you hadn't it was just a piece of tin.

To the Atomium

In the second week of our holiday, we took another train from the Belgian coast – this time to the capital, Brussels. We were to become just three of the forty-two million people who visited the 1958 Brussels World's Fair, otherwise known as Expo '58. The central landmark of the Expo site was called the Atomium, a gigantic depiction of a cell of iron crystal magnified 165 billion times. Rising high above the exhibition site were nine shiny spheres, each representing an atom and each connected to the next by silvery tubes with escalators in them, escalators that you could travel up or down, from one sphere to the next. Eight of the spheres contained displays of the wonders of the modern world and the ninth, the topmost, provided a view over Brussels and the surrounding countryside.

The atom, and particularly the destructive power of the atomic bomb, was permanently at the back of everybody's mind in 1958, so it probably made sense to put a giant one in the middle of the first World's Fair to be held since the Second World War.

From the top of the Atomium I could see the distant domes of the city, the green of Heysel Park and, beneath us, hundreds of national pavilions. It was impossible to visit all the exhibits, so we had to make a choice. Obviously we steered well clear of the British and US pavilions, but, oddly, we avoided the Soviet exhibition too. Maybe we thought all the wonders contained within it would be too much to absorb in only a few hours, but from the second our family entered the Czechoslovak pavilion I could see that Joe sensed he was in the presence of something truly special. Others obviously felt the same way, since it had won the best pavilion award and many other prizes for individual displays. Rather than the weapons, heavy engineering, rockets, wheatfields and big science that dominated the USSR's presentation, at the heart of the Czech display there was something that was still Communist but softer and more human. Apart from the anticipated exhibitions connected with history and geography, the ancient cities of Prague and Brno, the verdant forests and the wild Tatra mountains, there were so many surprising things – friendly colourful films featuring hilarious marionettes from the Puppet Theatre of Prague and case after case of glass, china and textiles designed in a remarkably modern avant-garde style, almost Italian but retaining a subtle socialist sensibility. There was much use of pastel colours, geometrical forms and modern materials – plastic, metal, glass and concrete. At the heart of the pavilion was an entire living room complete with the finest in Czech design, angular but comfy-looking chairs, swirly-spouted coffee pots, bulbous coloured drinking glasses, a coffee table and a sofa.

And there was one more marvel we had to see. After queueing for half an hour or so we shuffled into a small purpose-built theatre, within the exhibition hall, for one of the first performances of the Laterna Magika or Magic Lantern Theatre. If we had been awestruck by the coffee pots and the globular flower vases, then the Magic Lantern Theatre was the final proof that Czechoslovakia was a country like no other, one that seemed able to combine the humane rationalism of the Soviet system with a lyrical, magical spirit all its own.

There was little language used in the show, but most of it required no words as it was a combination of film projection, dance, sound effects, modern music, light and pantomime. In that dark room people from every land sat amazed, bemused and astonished. We had come in footsore and tired, many of us bombarded with images of nationalistic bluster, massive displays of jet engines and drilling machines, but we were now united by an enchantment that was both more ancient and more contemporary than anything at that vast, sprawling exposition. A man in a crazy wig played jazz with filmed projections of himself while clowns battled spiteful, inanimate objects – kettles, chairs and plates flew through the air as if they were alive – and at the high point of the show a man, on film, walked down a street in Prague towards the camera and then nonchalantly stepped over the edge of the screen and suddenly he was there in front of us, in person, on the stage in Brussels! Joe resolved right there that he wanted to visit this incredible place where the Communist way of life could be presented in such a colourful and friendly manner.

Years later I learned that at the core of the Laterna Magika was something called 'black-light theatre', a technique of illusion that takes advantage of an imperfection of the human eye which means it cannot distinguish black on black. It was actors dressed in suits of black moving against a black background who had made the objects appear to fly through the air. The audience had the impression that they possessed free will, but in reality they were being manipulated by unseen hands.

We also didn't know it then, but most of the items in the Czech pavilion, such as the shoes and the furniture and the coffee pots, were only prototypes that were never actually produced.

Disarmament Talks

Back home in Liverpool I began to get the sense that there was something up with our doctor, a neatly dressed man with black hair and a moustache by the name of Cyril Taylor. On the one hand we would make these huge trips right across town, from Anfield in the north end of the city to Sefton Park in the south, to see him when there were plenty of perfectly competent doctors on our side of Liverpool. But as soon as we got to his surgery there seemed to be some indefinable tension in the air. Travelling this far to see somebody usually meant that they were in the party, yet once we were seated in his consulting room he always behaved as if there was something funny about us, as if me and Molly were a pair of droll characters in a play. And from the way Molly talked about him on the bus home I got the clear impression that there was some sort of black mark against our doctor's character, some quality in him that didn't quite measure up.

As I grew a little older it became clearer what was going on. Up until the age of five or six I had thought there were only two specific types of people in the world, those who were 'in the party' and those who weren't. But I now learned that there was a third category. Cyril Taylor was one of those people who my parents dismissively referred to as having 'left in '56'. These were members of the British Communist Party who had resigned after the Soviet Union had violently crushed an uprising of workers and students in Hungary in 1956. Even though Stalin was dead, the Russians showed themselves to be intolerant of any opposition within their empire – during the invasion nearly three thousand Hungarians were killed and two hundred thousand fled as refugees. Mass arrests, executions and denunciations continued for months afterwards. Disillusioned, many like our doctor quit the party.

But others, such as my parents, took the events in Hungary in their stride – indeed, in some ways they welcomed them. Marxism-Leninism was, after all, a theory of compulsion. What Communists longed for was equality, a society in which all people would be the same, but they didn't have any faith that equality would just come about gradually by itself. Rather, they believed that people had to be forced to be equal. For every proletarian who understood right away the benefits of the worker state there were fifty who had to be cajoled or even compelled to see what was being done for them. Then there were all the class enemies, factory owners and policemen and the self-employed who couldn't be allowed to spread their poisonous opinions unchallenged. My parents welcomed Hungary as a test of their faith: it allowed them to show that they would stand steadfast with the party while others like Cyril Taylor, who didn't understand that the march towards liberty, peace and freedom couldn't be held up by a load of people demanding liberty, peace and freedom, joined the Labour Party and became well-known city councillors.

One thing that my parents didn't seem to understand was that, though they were sending a clear message to the world with their stance on Hungary, they were giving confusing messages to their son by entrusting his precious health to a class traitor. If those who left in '56 were renegades and weak-minded back-stabbers, how could one of them look after me? How could somebody who was a traitor be a good doctor? Surely a person who was an evil revanchist would be useless at their job? Something here didn't add up.

Fortunately my teeth, unlike the rest of me, weren't considered important enough to become an ideological battleground in the class war. Our dentist, a man called Savitz who had a surgery nearby in an old house next door to the Astoria cinema in Walton Breck Road, wasn't in the party or anything so he didn't cause me any confusion while painfully hacking my gums about.

* * *

There was, however, a war of ideas which affected me on a more basic level than my parents' attitude to healthcare, and that was their peculiar stance on certain toys. Although Molly and Joe were Communists dedicated to the dictatorship of the industrial proletariat, my mother in particular held opinions on daily life that were closer to those of the more avant-garde elements of the upper classes than to those of our neighbours in Valley Road. My parents had to work for a living, didn't have any servants and didn't know any archbishops or ambassadors, but a lot of the ideas they harboured concerning food, travel and child-rearing would have been familiar to Leonard and Virginia Woolf, Isadora Duncan or Lady Ottoline Morrell. One of the ways in which Molly differed from the majority of parents in our street, though Bertrand Russell would have heartily approved, was in her attitude to toy guns.

There was a theory, prevalent in liberal circles, that giving children war-like toys could awaken in them aggressive, anti-social and overtly male tendencies which were unsuited to the modern world. My parents subscribed to this idea, despite the fact that, as Marxist-Leninists, they believed in the violent armed overthrow of capitalism. If they had been consistent they would have purchased a .22 rifle or a shotgun and booked me shooting lessons. Instead, they refused to purchase any kind of replica firearm.

At first this wasn't too much of a problem – during games of war or cowboys and indians, all the boys in the street just ran around pointing their fingers at each other and shouting, 'Ack, ack, ack!' or 'Kerpow!' But soon their parents began buying them plastic or metal toy guns which usually fired a paper roll of percussion caps, and this left me pretty badly outgunned with just my fingers. Yet no matter how much I pleaded with her, Molly refused to buy me a toy gun. In the end, out of desperation, tired of spending every evening lying dead on the pavement, I started making my own imitation weapons out of bread. I would chew an L-shape into a slice of Hovis, then smuggle it out of the house so I could run around the streets shooting other kids with my wholemeal pistol. I brought such conviction to my play-acting that the other kids were persuaded that my bread gun possessed a degree of firepower, and as long as it didn't rain I was fine.

After a while, though, my parents could see that I was being made to look a little bit too eccentric shooting children with my edible pistol. So, in an echo of the UN Disarmament Commission, which was formed under the Security Council and which met intermittently from 1954 to 1957, we held our own arms limitation talks. After furious bargaining the final outcome, which was agreed by all parties, was this: I would be allowed toy firearms but they would be limited to non-automatic weapons, a restriction which basically meant I could only own revolvers with a Wild West flavour. No automatic pistols, rifles or sub-machine guns would be allowed, though after a while I did get something called a Range Rifle which was essentially a Colt .45 revolver with a stock and long barrel.

Though I now possessed toy guns, an unbridgeable arms gap had opened up between me and the other kids in our street. For instance, there was a gadget that several of the local boys owned called a Johnny 7. This was less of a gun and more of an integrated weapons system, combining multiple grenade tubes, an automatic rifle and a rocket launcher, and my small stock of revolvers was never able to compete with that. I consoled myself with the thought that in the jungles of Vietnam, Cambodia and Laos the lightly armed Communist Vietcong were at the same time taking on and beating the United States army, Range Rifles versus Johnny 7s, but on a larger and more lethal scale.

I also faced a weapons gap in terms of toy soldiers, but the reasons for that are less clear – as far as I can recall, my parents had no policy on little plastic men in uniform. The way toy soldiers worked in our street was that you took all your soldiers round to another boy's house in a box or they came round to yours with their soldiers in a box. Then you fought a battle, and if you lost the other kid technically owned whatever room the battle was being fought in. This was a male-only thing, of course. Boys had soldiers, girls had dolls, so the girls would take their dolls round to each other's houses and maybe they fought each other with them – I don't know. For some reason my toy army seemed to have a large number of non-combatants in its ranks – soldiers carrying minesweeping equipment, endless columns of stretcher-bearers, bandsmen armed only with trombones and a complete plastic ENSA troupe – while the other kid's army usually comprised a massive phalanx of machine gun crews, bazooka teams and infantry, equipped with rifles and sub-machine guns all supported by aircraft, artillery and armoured formations.

I think the pacific make-up of my army might have had something to do with unarmed soldiers, for some reason, being cheaper to buy in the local shop, so I had purchased them without giving a thought to whether they would be useful in battle or not. I also seemed to have in my army a whole mixed regiment of Red Indians with bows and arrows and knights in armour who had become detached from their horses. The outcome of all these childhood battles was that theoretically other boys owned most of our house, though this was never tested under international law.

\||| 13 |||/
The Great Annual Boiled Egg Panic

Over the years my family had evolved a number of rituals which took place every summer, on the morning that we went on our holidays. Firstly there was the getting up far too early, stumbling about in the darkness and bumping into the furniture. This was followed by the ritual cooking of and then failure to eat six boiled eggs. It's unclear why it was felt that on days of travel we didn't require a full breakfast, when you would have thought it was then that we needed it most. But for some reason every summer holiday began with six eggs being boiled, two each for me, Joe and Molly. These eggs would never be consumed because eating them would inevitably be interrupted by the second ritual, which was the running backwards and forwards to the taxi office.

The old black Austin taxi that was going to take us to Lime Street Station had been ordered weeks before from a family firm with an office a couple of streets away, but perhaps because my parents were Communists and the taxi firm were representatives of the petit bourgeoisie – that class which in Marxist terms 'owned their own means of production' and whose political allegiance could therefore switch between the ruling and the working-class depending on self-interest – we didn't trust them to turn up. Lord Harmsworth, Dame Margot Fonteyn, Cole Porter or the Duke of Edinburgh might ring the taxi firm asking for a cab to take them to the dog track, a cocktail bar or a grouse shoot, and they would inevitably bend to the will of the aristocrat or the celebrity rather than an ordinary working-class family such as ours. So I would be sent at ten-minute intervals to remind them that a taxi had been ordered to take me and my family to Lime Street Station, and in between my visits Molly would telephone them with a slightly different version of the same message. From the other room I could hear her begging them to swear that a taxi would be coming and reminding them that our money was as good as the Duke of Edinburgh's, alternating her entreaties with screaming at me, 'Eat your eggs, Lexi! For the love of God, eat your boiled eggs!' Then, as like as not, we would run across the road and get a bus.

In August 1959 there was a particular hysteria attached to our preparations because this year was extra-special. Molly, Joe and Alexei were going to Czechoslovakia – we were travelling eastwards beyond the Iron Curtain. Like the man in the magic lantern show but in reverse, we were going to step into the movie screen and the narrow streets of Prague.

The beginning stages of the journey to the continent were by now familiar to me. First of all you had to get to London – things didn't really begin until you reached the capital. The three of us would tumble through the ticket gates at Lime Street, dishevelled, some of our clothes on backwards because we'd dressed in the dark, dragging our suitcases on their unsteady and unreliable wheels behind us. Sometimes we would get there before our train was even at the platform, but generally the *Red Rose Express* with its red and cream carriages stretching away up the platform would be waiting for us. At the head of the train, wreathed in a cloud of steam and quietly hissing to itself, would be a dark green Royal Scot-class locomotive, its smoke deflectors and chimneystack picked out in black.

Once we were on board, already hungry and tired even though we had only travelled two miles, there appeared a second reason for hysteria. Joe would get Molly and me seated in our compartment with all the luggage and here we would slump, breathless and sweaty, recovering from the trauma of the trip to the station. While my jumper would be askew and my shirt collar sticking up at an odd angle, and Molly's cotton summer dress would be wrinkled, her red hair in a mad tangle and her glasses steamed up, Joe invariably looked dapper and cool. With his thinning hair brushed back from his high, intelligent forehead, in his tweed jacket, high-waisted, pleated-front trousers and shiny brown brogues, he appeared calm and fresh as if he was a professor looking after a couple of refugees who had recently had a tough time at the hands of fascist insurgents. But Joe wouldn't sit down. He would stand between the seats, then look thoughtful for a second, turn and go out into the corridor with Molly shouting after him, 'Joe! Where are you going? Joe, where are you going? Lexi, where's Joe going?'

Making vague mumbling noises, my father would walk up the corridor to the door at the end of the carriage. From there he would step off the train and, once on the platform, make for the locomotive to see if he knew the driver of our express. Because he was a railway guard my father had a disturbingly casual attitude to the business of getting on and off trains. After he had left us in the compartment Joe would sometimes wait until the train was actually moving, the guard having long blown his whistle and the last door having been slammed, before nonchalantly swinging himself on board the final carriage at the last possible second. We often didn't know whether he had actually managed to get aboard the train because he wouldn't join us in our compartment until well after we had left the station and were huffing through the sandstone tunnels that ran under Crown Street. This gave rise to a good deal more screaming. 'Joe! Where's Joe? Where's your father? Joe! Joe! Lexi, your father's been left behind! He's been left behind! Lexi, we've left your father behind!' Sometimes, as the train was moving out of the station, we would look through the window to see Joe wandering along the platform back towards the ticket barrier as if he had decided at the last minute to go home, taking our tickets, passports and spending money with him. But he always managed to come smiling up the corridor a few minutes later.

The journey to London took four hours, and by the age of seven I took pride in the fact that I was familiar with all the landmarks on the line to Euston. There wasn't another kid in school who knew this route like I did. Edge Lane Station, where a government minister named William Huskisson, the first victim of a rail accident, had died was where we came out into the daylight. Next we rushed up on to an embankment from which we could see below us the terraced streets of South Liverpool, slate roofs and red brick. These quickly gave way to suburban homes, semis with curved metal windows and big back gardens. Soon after we would be thundering over Runcorn bridge that spanned the Mersey and the Manchester Ship Canal.

If the crew on the train was a Liverpool one then we probably knew the dining car staff, and if it was lunchtime, once we had left Runcorn behind we would rise from our seats to go and get a free meal in the restaurant car. By this time the three of us would be extemely hungry as we had been awake since 4.30 a.m. and had only eaten a bit of a boiled egg. I learned to measure out the journey by that meal. After Crewe there were lush green fields and soup. Roast beef, peas and gravy were served at the same time as the Universal Grinding Wheel Company at Stafford went by. And you could eat a whole sherry trifle and still be passing the sprawling GEC factory outside Rugby.

After lunch we would return to the compartment while the south Midlands reeled past. When the Arts and Crafts hen sheds of the Ovaltine Farm came into view you knew it was time to start getting your stuff together because London was only half an hour away. These hen sheds, with their giant painted tableaux of rosy-cheeked maidens clutching bundles of malt, had been constructed in fields outside Abbot's Langley in the 1930s. I always tried to see if there were any buxom maids emerging with baskets of eggs, or indeed any sign of hen occupation in the sheds, but eventually came to the conclusion that they were empty and had been built there just to give Ovaltine the impression of rustic healthiness to passing railway passengers. I decided the drink was probably manufactured in some giant sprawling factory on a shabby industrial estate next to a disused canal.

At Euston Station we would say goodbye to the guard, the driver, the fireman and the dining car crew, the last people who knew who we were. Then, passing through the stone arch, we were alone in London. A red-haired woman, a smiling man and a little olive-skinned boy.

From time to time, depending on the connections we needed to make with ferries or trains, we might spend the night in London, staying in a small hotel in Pimlico that sometimes advertised in the *Daily Worker*. But this time we were trying to get to Paris by nightfall as we had to catch a train early the next morning. Consequently we took another taxi from Euston, racing across London to Victoria Station. Molly had no sense of direction but that never stopped her from having vehement opinions on what route a cab should take, so our cross-town journeys could often be made more fraught by my mother having a violent row with the driver. On this occasion we didn't have much time to make the boat train to Dover so she kept uncharacteristically quiet.

The taxi took us down a long tree-lined avenue of deep red tarmac at the end of which there was a huge, squat, stone-faced building, hiding its ugliness behind gilded railings. 'That's Buckingham Palace, that is!' the driver said with pride in his voice. He seemed shocked when, rather than the expressions of delight or interest that he was used to from out-of-town-ers, there were scowls, a look of pure hatred and mutterings of 'Parasites' and 'Thieves' directed towards the home of the royal family from the trio in the back of his taxi. Soon we were back in busy, traffic-choked streets and edging our way under the fretwork canopy of Victoria Station.

The terminus had two distinct sides, possessing wildly different characteristics. One part dealt with the dull, suburban halts of the home counties – Maidstone, Brockley, Whitstable and Sevenoaks. It was neat and subdued, thronged with bowler-hatted city clerks and demure female typists. The other half had platforms dedicated solely to trains that connected with the Channel ferries and thus with the continent of Europe. On these platforms, segregated from the rest, the English Channel seemed an almost tangible presence, as if there was a tang of the sea in the air and seagulls weaving amongst the iron rafters of the high station roof. There were money changing booths and a feeling of decadence. Men wearing raincoats of an alien cut lurked in the entrance of the news cinema, as did women with bright red lips, brittle blonde hair and tight skirts who seemed far too friendly.

In the raffish half of Victoria Station, towards evening I would always see waiting on Platform 2 the blue and gold carriages of the Night Ferry Service run by the Compagnie Internationale des Wagons-Lits. Looking impossibly luxurious, this sumptuous train travelled overnight to Paris Gare du Nord, the carriages being loaded and unloaded on to a special ferry while the passengers slept in their own private compartments on crisp cotton sheets. No other train was allowed to use Platform 2, so during the day it remained empty, but on others there slid in and out the brown and cream Pullman coaches of the Golden Arrow, a luxury first-class service complete with its own special bar car called Le Trianon that ran to Dover Marine, where it connected with a first-class-only ferry.

Our free passes did not allow us to take any of these fabulous trains. We had to haul our suitcases past them, skulking like displaced persons to platforms so distant and insignificant that they had letters attached to their numbers. There we would cram ourselves on to the ordinary boat trains that rattled through the South London suburbs and into the green fields of Kent, passing hop poles and oast houses before pulling first into Dover Town, then backing out again to rattle and sway into Dover Marine right alongside the ferry that was going to take us to France.

Although it was happening on the edge of England, this going into a station one way and then reversing out seemed to be the beginning of continental Europe. In plain old Britain you always entered a station and then left it in the same direction. But abroad, in mysterious and mystifying Europe, your direction of travel and who you travelled with were a much more complicated and ever-changing affair. On a foreign train you would often enter a station one way, then exit it from the direction in which you had come, travelling backwards as if you were being sent back home having failed some test or, more worryingly, as if you were now, without leaving your seat, somehow on the wrong train. Even when you were going in a straight line there would be long, mysterious waits accompanied by enigmatic clankings, violent shuntings and inexplicable bangings.

Sometimes you would walk down the train to find that the carriages that had been there were now gone. Looking for food, you might discover that the buffet coach had vanished, to be replaced by two wagons crammed full of soldiers in battledress carrying rifles who said nasty, confusing things to you in strange languages and then laughed in an unfriendly manner. Or, wandering towards the front of the train, you might encounter a car in which all the blinds to the compartments were drawn, suggesting that every kind of unfathomable depravity or cruelty was taking place within. Once in a while you realised that, at some point during the journey, the entire rest of the train had been removed and we were now in what had become the last coach of a considerably shorter train. If you walked down the corridor you were able to see through a long narrow rear window, beside the shuttered connecting door, the track receding and home reeling away into the falling night.

** **14** **

A Night in Montmartre

The crossing to France took an hour and a half. When the boat docked at Calais, porters dressed in overalls of a particular shade of blue that you never ever saw in Britain, a blue that the French had even given a special class-war name to – *bleu de travail* or worker's blue – swarmed aboard yelling, '*Porteur! Porteur!*' Each wore a peaked cap adorned with a brass badge with a number engraved on it. They took your luggage and gave you a matching brass tag which you exchanged for a fee once you were through customs and passport control. The next time you saw your luggage it was in your train compartment with the chalk cross of the customs inscribed on it, like the home of a plague victim.

We had no sooner settled on to the deep green seats of the SNCF train to Paris than Joe said he was going to get off to find us a snack, as we hadn't eaten since lunch on the *Red Rose Express*. This time the train did actually leave the station, accompanied by much screaming from my mother, with Joe still clearly chatting away to the man in the platform kiosk. We steamed a few metres up the line and waited for a minute or two next to a white-painted concrete fence on the other side of which was France: a cobbled street lined with bars and tiny shops and vans driving up and down, vans that looked like little Nissen huts bouncing up and down on their soft springs.

The train then returned to a different platform at Calais Maritime and Joe climbed aboard clutching three baguettes containing salami that smelt of abroad. We all knew that the Paris boat train left the station and returned to a different platform, but me and Molly always worried that this time might be the time when it decided not to do that, that this time it would head straight for Paris without stopping at Calais Maritime. Joe, on the other hand, always believed that it would come back.

I had inherited neither Molly's nor Joe's attitude to foreign travel. My father's approach was to expect that everything would turn out well in the end, and if there was a problem he would rely on the affability of others to correct it. My mother's response was to go insane, often without provocation, and then in between to exist in a state of unsettling serenity. I inhabited an uneasy middle ground between these two extremities, suspecting that at any moment people might start either disappearing or screaming.

By now I understood that the notion that the Sayle family was a family that went abroad was very important to us. In some ways it defined who we were. We thought of ourselves as not being like the rest of the population of Anfield, ignorant and gullible people who believed what they were told by the TV news and went on holiday for two weeks in a caravan in Morecambe. And now we were going to Czechoslovakia, a place so foreign it had a 'z' in its name! I understood all this and tried to embrace it, but I did feel sometimes that it was hard enough to understand what was going on in Anfield – why was that boy saying this? What reason did that girl have for showing me that? What did all the teachers want? Why was everybody shouting? – without us travelling a thousand miles to the east. It was dawning on me that life could be baffling and scary even when most things were familiar and I spoke the language, but our family persisted in going to places where just about everything was alien. The smells were different – Gauloises cigarettes, coffee, sewers and onions. The cars were different – in Britain most of the cars were modelled on the British Museum (a large classical portico and a substantial building to the rear, with wood panelling and leather seating) but these French cars were bizarre things with flimsy doors, corrugated sides and seats of canvas. In France there seemed to be about nine different kinds of policemen. When British police cars drove along they rang a little bell as if everybody was being told dinner was ready in a boarding house, whereas these French police cars had sirens that sounded like a goat being slaughtered and you heard them all the time – 'nee naw, nee naw, nee naw!' And abroad just about everybody seemed to be carrying a gun – not just the police and *gendarmes*, but there were soldiers everywhere. And of course all these armed men spoke a different language, so incomprehension here, across the English Channel, was likely to get you shot.

We crawled across the flat fields of the Pas de Calais until small silver suburban trains began to swarm around us like pilot fish and we were suddenly on the edge of Paris. Around a curve in the track I suddenly saw the Eiffel Tower. It was gigantic and looked just like the photos of itself, but I didn't know what to feel about the Eiffel Tower – as far as I knew, the party didn't have a line on it. At the Gare du Nord we disembarked from the boat train, and as all the English speakers scattered we were submerged in the evening crowds of hurrying French. The three of us descended into the Métro, bought tickets of green cardboard at a reduced price and rode a couple of stops on rattling wooden carriages with silvery chromed door handles to the district of Montmartre. Montmartre itself, with its steep streets flowing like frozen rivers of cobblestones away from the basilica of the Sacré Coeur, shining white and lustrous in the summer night, was a disappointment. It bore very little relation to the restaurant of the same name on the Tottenham Court Road.

The night was spent in a small hotel and the next morning we travelled on from the Gare de L'Est to Germany. We arrived in Nuremberg in the late afternoon with a couple of hours to kill.

To pass the time the three of us tried to visit what was probably a beer hall, but they wouldn't let a child in. Fortunately there was a charity for displaced persons in the station, and due to me and Molly's woebegone appearance they gave us a refugee's meal of black tea and rye bread. Then we caught a train ultimately bound for Belgrade in Yugoslavia.

I had by now grown used to foreign border crossings. They weren't quite as elaborate as the ones you got at Channel ports – those between European countries were a bit like a visit to a hospital for the results of some tests you probably didn't really need. Everybody sat in a row and a man came in with your documents, and there was always a tense moment before he told you everything was all right and one time out of a hundred it was bad news for somebody else. The frontier between the Federal Republic of Germany and Czechoslovakia must have been more tense than most, seeing as it was the border between two nuclear-armed, competing ideologies which were constantly threatening to destroy each other. But I don't honestly remember it being different from any of the other crossings we had made.

I do recall that once we were inside Czechoslovakia the German Railways locomotive was uncoupled and steamed away, heading westwards, returning to its homeland. Our train without its locomotive seemed suddenly decapitated and lifeless, and so in the quiet of a summer afternoon we climbed down on to the platform and waited. The carriages we were in had begun their journey the day before in some distant part of northern Germany as clean as you would expect from the railways of that freshly scrubbed country, but, even by the time it reached Nuremberg, like any transcontinental express it had turned into a clammy mess. Even if nobody in your compartment was eating biscuits, after a few hours biscuit crumbs would magically appear on your seat, crushed in little gritty piles on the floor or somehow down the back of your jumper.

We were happy to stretch our legs and get a breath of fresh air, strolling up and down the low platform. On all British stations the platforms were high, making the track itself a forbidden and dangerous thing, but abroad, particularly the further east you got, they were often no higher than the kerb at the side of the road, as if it was no big thing to step on to the silver rails.

After a few minutes of waiting an apparition steamed into view. Over the coming years I was to become familiar with the steam engines of the East in all their forms, whether it was sticking my head out of the window into the cold snowy air and seeing the squat engine curving away around the track as it pulled us up into the High Tatra mountains and smoke blew into my face, or watching them huffing past the window of hotel rooms, or being conducted around the plants where they were made. But this was my first sight of a locomotive from the Soviet Bloc, and it was magnificent and alien. Sticky and black like a hot summer night, with massive air deflectors attached to the side of the boiler, an enormous single headlight just below the chimney and a large red star in the centre of the smokebox. I think it might even have been flying red flags from the front bogie as it snorted towards us, inky smoke pouring into the sky, seeming to embody all the industrial might and threat of rampant socialism.

＊　　＊　　＊

From the border we travelled through countryside not much different from that which we had seen ouside the windows in Germany – the same onion dome churches, the same ornate villas and the same haystacks. And finally, as evening descended, we reached journey's end: the town of Karlovy Vary, known to English travellers, for whom it had been a popular destination in the nineteenth century, as Carlsbad.

Though we were travelling independently Joe had had to make all the bookings for our trip, instigate the various permits, accommodation requests and visa applications, via an organisation called Progressive Tours, a travel agency set up and staffed by the British Communist Party in London. Maybe somebody at Progressive Tours was annoyed that an upstart railwayman from Liverpool, certainly not a person who was high up in the CP hierarchy, was trying to see the Soviet Bloc without taking one of their highly regulated official tours. Or maybe some bureaucrat in Czechoslovakia didn't understand why a minor trade union official and his family from an obscure town in the north of England wanted to come to his country. Whatever the reason, it became clear to us over the next few hours that, rather than a holiday spent wandering around the medieval town of Bratislava, marvelling at the baroque splendour of Prague or hiking in the forests and mountains of Bohemia, perhaps spending our nights in ancient castles and smart hotels, we had instead been given permission to spend two weeks in an out-of-season spa town, sleeping in a tent.

It was very late by the time we had walked to the place where we were supposed to be staying, and it was only then that it dawned on us that it was a deserted campsite. When we finally managed to rouse somebody from a nearby administrative block, the people who ran the place said they had received no notification of our arrival and had no idea what to do with us. Indeed, they were a bit nervous as to how to cope with these foreign people who had suddenly landed on them. Molly's response was to start screaming and crying.

Saved by the Party

The tent they eventually showed us to was in a row of identical structures. It was semi-permanent, with dull red canvas stretched over a metal frame, and inside there were six bunk beds with thin sheets and emaciated mattresses. We were not the sort of family that was emotionally suited to sleeping in a tent at the best of times, so we passed an unhappy night.

The next morning, maybe looking for something better, perhaps just trying to get away from our misery, Joe went for a walk. After a short while, he noticed on the other side of a meadow a large square building with the look of a clinic. Above the portico of this establishment were three large letters emblazoned in red: ROH. Joe knew that the ROH was the Czechoslovak trades union organisation, similar to the British TUC but controlled entirely by the government and the Czechoslovak Communist Party. In fact, back in England he had written several letters to their headquarters saying he was a British trade unionist eager to see their country, but had received no reply. Joe strode into the ROH building and began being genial. Almost immediately he encountered a man who had spent the Second World War as a fighter pilot, stationed in Oldham in Lancashire. Throughout our time in Czechoslovakia we constantly came across people eager to reminisce about the happy war years they had spent in Warrington, Stockport and St Helens – half the Czech population seemed to have been based in Lancashire during the conflict. When Joe told this man where we were staying he was so appalled that he went and found a woman who had been garrisoned in Burnley from 1939 to 1945, and she too couldn't understand what we were doing at the campsite. In the end they arranged for us to spend the weekend at a trade union-owned miners' sanatorium nearby.

Possibly because we were all in a heightened state of emotion, our first weekend in Karlovy Vary seemed extremely vivid. The sanatorium rooms were fairly austere, but the beds were soft and laid with snowy white sheets and at least the walls didn't flap. We walked into town along a river path. Karlovy Vary is a spa famous for its hot springs, and in a spirit of delirium brought on by our escape from the campsite I was persuaded to drink some of the waters, which tasted like a frying pan cordial.

The Karlovy Vary International Film Festival had just ended, marking the end of the season. Though all the filmgoers had departed, international flags and banners still flew and posters for films in ten different languages were gently peeling from the walls. Right in the centre of town stood the epitome of the European grand hotel de luxe, built in a florid, high-baroque style unseen in Liverpool. It was named the Grandhotel Moskva, and I probably remember it so clearly because I wished we were staying there.

Sadly, on the Monday, because the sanatorium was expecting an intake of tubercular Slovakian strip miners we had to return to our tent. When we got through the flap there was an odd stale odour, which soon revealed itself as the smell of the mice which had been eating our clothes. Extremely depressed, we went to a café to get some breakfast. Communism was turning out to be not all puppets and pastel-coloured, geometrically shaped coffee pots. While we were picking at our breakfast of bread and jam one of the officials from the campsite, who up to that point had been quite rude and dismissive, came running up and made it clear that we had to come back with him immediately to the office.

As we walked back down the path from the café, harried by the visibly nervous functionary, my gaze was drawn to the parking area in front of the rustic wooden administrative buildings. My eyes widened in astonishment, because parked on the semi-circle of gravel was a convoy of the most extraordinary vehicles I had ever seen. They were cars, all identical, all black and all shined to a high polish. Each had a large front windscreen, six big windows on either side of the passenger compartment and a back window split at the centre and curving around to the rear pillar. Large air scoops flared out from the wings, the rear wheels were concealed by spats and across the curved front, enclosed under a continuous one-piece glass panel, was a row of three enormous circular headlights. These cars were nothing less than the future rendered in metal and glass, and if they had

75

been hovering three feet from the ground as the vehicles did in 'Dan Dare Pilot of the Future' in the *Eagle* comic I wouldn't have been at all surprised. Beside these amazing automobiles stood a group of men in suits and hats. The campsite manager, now sweating and very on edge, urged us onwards. Though at the time we chose not to be aware of any of this, a fleet of three black Tatra limousines, a car reserved solely for the use of state officials, pulling up outside your campsite didn't usually mean anything good was going to happen.

As we approached, a round-faced man in a dapper grey tweed suit detached himself from the waiting group and came towards us. In perfect English he introduced himself, saying that his name was Ladislav and he had been sent by his boss, a man called Prukha, the Minister for Trade Union Affairs. Over the weekend he said they had uncovered all of Joe's letters to the ROH and, while obviously the tents were a fine place to spend a vacation, perhaps the comrades from England would like to come immediately to Prague, to stay in one of the best hotels at the government's expense and to accept a refund for the money they had paid to stay at this no doubt excellent campsite. Within seconds our mouse-nibbled luggage was brought and placed in the boot, which is to say the front portion of the lead Tatra, while we climbed on to the leather bench seat of the passenger compartment. The ministry driver climbed aboard, the man called Ladislav took the passenger seat, the driver pressed a button and the Tatra's rear-mounted V8 engine rumbled into life. Looking around, I noticed that all the switches and the steering wheel were in an elegant ivory plastic unlike anything I had ever seen in Britain – though, to be fair, as I had only ever been on the bus and in a taxi there wasn't much to compare them with.

Our fleet of limousines gathered speed, crunched across the gravel, turned into the road and took us away from the rows of red tents and towards Prague, the city known throughout Europe as 'The Golden City of Spires'.

Emil the Terrible

My parents' faith in Communism and the Communist Party had been vindicated in the most spectacular fashion. When we had been at our lowest ebb, Communism had seen that we were distressed and had sent Ladislav with his fleet of Marxist limousines to rescue us and carry us off to a city of almost indescribable magic and mystery.

Of all the heroes of that country and that city I don't think they once mentioned Franz Kafka to us. It's not really likely that they would, but he wrote, 'Prague never lets you go . . . this dear little mother has sharp claws.' He was right – the city held us enthralled. It seemed like there really were a million golden spires. There was an ancient castle, narrow medieval streets crammed with taverns and coffee shops, and right by our hotel there was a famous cobbled bridge, its balustrade lined with the life-sized statues of venerable saints, all look-ing in the early morning mist like a row of eighteenth-century ecclesiastical suicides.

A decision had been made within the highest levels of the bureaucracy of the government of Czechoslovakia that the Sayle family couldn't be allowed to languish in a tent. Like Kafka's *Metamorphosis* but in reverse, we had gone to sleep as insects and woken, in the very city where he had written that story, as people. And not just ordinary people, but people of the highest importance. Right to the end of our fortnight's stay we had Ladislav, a Tatra and a driver at our disposal night and day. Every morning, dressed in a different natty suit, Ladislav would be waiting for us and would then take us around the sites of Prague and the surrounding countryside, pointing out astonishing things in his punctilious English. In the evening there were formal dinners hosted by Ladislav's boss Prukha, a thinner, more watchful man, at which we were constantly toasted as visiting comrades from Britain. And wherever we went we were given gifts, vases of Bohemian glass, coffee sets and folklorique woven things whose exact purpose we could never quite figure out. You only had to look at something and people would give it to you.

After their success in Brussels at Expo '58 the Magic Lantern Theatre had been given their own purpose-built theatre right in the centre of Prague. We took in a performance, now sitting in the best seats, and it felt like we were visiting old friends.

Molly, Joe and Ladislav got on really well together. I had never seen my parents make a new friend before, so I found it compelling to watch. Ladislav had the same fascination with terrible puns as Joe and he found Molly's behaviour charming – I suppose that, as there had been Jews in Prague for over a thousand years they were used to her kind of carrying-on. But more than anybody else it was me who was the centre of attention. Everywhere we went I was spoilt and flattered; I suppose I was some sort of novelty, but whatever the reason I loved it.

The most famous, indeed the only famous Czech at the time was the athlete Emil Zátopek, also known as the 'Flying Czech' because he was so fast or 'Emil the Terrible' due to his ugly running style. Zátopek first came to the world's attention at the 1948 Olympics in London, from out of nowhere winning the ten thousand metres and finishing second in the five thousand. At the 1952 Olympics in Helsinki he amazingly won gold in both the five thousand and ten thousand metre races. We were already aware of Zátopek, who was particularly admired in our house because in the five thousand metres at Helsinki he had beaten a great British hero, Christopher Chataway. Chataway, an ex-public schoolboy and a bit of a Young Tory, was second, but after being overtaken by Zátopek he tripped and fell. We especially liked that.

Though not universal, it was instinctual amongst a great many British Communists to be noisily unpatriotic. It was not a matter of party policy but a way of thinking that had grown up, a prejudice that had formed like barnacles beneath the waterline of a ship. They assumed that taking pride in any kind of British achievement, in science or the arts or particularly sporting achievement, meant you were somehow taking pride in the excesses of the British Empire. To my parents and their friends it was as if by cheering on the English football team, the cricket team or Britain's runners you were somehow revelling in slavery, the Amritsar Massacre, the suppression of the Irish or the Opium Wars.

Very early on I sensed that this anti-nationalism was not a good thing to flaunt in front of other children. It might be all right to make fun of the Milk Marketing Board or go on and on about the many achievements of the Soviet Union, but it was not okay to deride the England football team for being beaten 6–3 by Communist Hungary in 1953. If I felt any of this unpatriotism I didn't voice it, and in fact slowly I came to question this attitude in my parents. At the very least, as well as risking getting hit in the playground it seemed ungrateful and ungracious to deride this country that gave us free milk and rail travel. But I kept all these thoughts to myself and it was perhaps the beginning of a certain secretiveness, an internal, critical but unexpressed mulling-over of what was said to me.

At any rate, Emil Zátopek, unlike his British rival on the running track, was considered impeccably proletarian because of his background and because he would train in any weather, including snow, and would often do so while wearing heavy work boots as opposed to special running shoes. I don't know if they thought I was good at running or were just flattering me, but Ladislav and the driver and then everybody else took to calling me 'Little Zátopek', saying that one day I too would be a great runner and compete in the Olympics. I loved this attention and did not see any reason to develop a critical attitude to the idea, which sounded perfectly plausible. I already had the feeling that there was something special about me, so why shouldn't I win gold at the Olympics, possibly as early as 1966?

Little Zátopek Wins the Big Race

The return trip from Czechoslovakia was a very sad experience. Ladislav and the driver waved us off from Prague Station,
and suddenly as the train headed west we became just ordinary people again – though admittedly ordinary people who
were loaded down with Bohemian glass, dolls and folklorique
woven things. One way to try and keep the special feeling alive
was to tell all the kids in the street and all the kids at school
about my adventures, and initially it seemed to work. I would
talk about Prague and become the centre of attention as my
classmates listened in rapt, enchanted silence. But then some
other kid would tell a story about how their cat could drive
and the same children would listen to that in fascinated silence.
My classmates accepted that everything I said was true, but
then they were at an age where they accepted that everything
was true. I wanted to shout at them, 'Look, this isn't like your
imaginary friend Gerald who wets the bed! I really have been in
a car that looks like a spaceship. I really did meet the Minister
for Trade Union Affairs. I really did walk across a bridge lined
with statues.' But it wouldn't have made any difference. Truth
was trumped by a good story any day.

In the early autumn of the year that we returned from our first
visit to the East, Joe attended a weekend conference of the
National Union of Railwaymen at a place called Earlstown in

Cheshire, an important railway town possessing a huge wagon works. Me and Molly came along too. The days were bright and sunny and to entertain the families the union put on a sports day. It was mostly for the older children, but there was a very informal hundred yards dash organised for the seven-, eight- and nine-year-olds such as me. On the starting line, poised in an anticipatory crouch, my heart was bursting with confidence, eager to fulfil my destiny because I was Little Zátopek.

Of course I won! My prize was a magnificent clockwork motor yacht presented to me by a senior union official. Made of polished wood and metal, the fitments meticulously rendered in minute detail, it was the most elegant toy I had ever owned, the sort of thing that the son of a press baron or a property developer might have. But the yacht was only the physical symbol of other things. Firstly, it seemed to prove the ideological superiority of Communism. Some people in Prague had said I was going to be a great runner, and it turned out to be true. But, more than that, it was my first experience of winning something and I found it sublime. The attention, the feeling of being special, the sensation of beating other kids, proving yourself better than them, was all brilliant with no apparent downside. Back at school on the Monday I told all the kids over and over again that I was now the NUR Under Ten National Hundred Yards Dash Champion.

The following spring, in another railway town in the south of England, possibly Swindon, there was another week-end conference and another sports day. I felt slightly queasy competing away from the north, my home ground. This place seemed alien and different, but I was quietly confident of being able to defend my title. After all, Marxist determinism seemed to state that it was inevitable that I should win.

Shockingly, I came last. Last by quite some way. I can still see the other kids disappearing into the distance, their shapes getting smaller and smaller, and I can still recall the horror of my mind telling my legs to move faster but them refusing to respond. After the race I was so clearly distressed at losing my title that the organisers, perhaps at the prompting of my parents, scraped around until they found a consolation prize for me – a toy gun with a broken handle.

This was my first experience of losing and it felt really, really bad. The pity of the organisers and the crappiness of my prize were hard to take, but more than that I couldn't figure out what had gone wrong. Was the first win an illusion, or was this loss some sort of abnormality? Either way, here was a new and unsettling realisation, that the pain of failure, sharp and nagging, was much greater than the warm but easily dissipated pleasure of winning. I thought about it over and over. I had lost by quite a margin, but in the end found it impossible to accept that Little Zátopek wasn't a good runner.

My parents' faith that I was special remained unshaken, but perhaps this was also a modern thing and not of their class. Most children in Anfield were brought up to think of themselves as being profoundly ordinary – if you had called them 'special' they would have been insulted. In our neighbourhood you believed the same things as everybody else, you wore the same clothes as everybody else and you planned to go into the same job as your father. I loved the idea that my mum and dad thought of me as some sort of Chosen One, but it also seemed like quite hard work. It was decided that perhaps a lack of training and preparation had led to me losing my title as the hundred yards dash champion, so when we got back to Liverpool I joined a running club, as its only junior member. They were called the Walton Harriers and they practised at a sports ground directly opposite the long brick wall and lowering grey blocks of Walton Prison. Over the next year or so I attended running practice at least once or twice a week.

My memory is mostly of me slogging round the running track, alone and in the dark. I refused to shower alongside all the big hairy men, so I went home on the bus smelling like a Victorian urchin. What I remember most is my enjoyment of the hot Ribena cordial you could buy from a little wooden shed after finishing training and the amazing taste of the flavoured crisps which were just then beginning to appear on the market. None of this told me or Molly that I wasn't destined to be a great athlete.

The Rivals

Having said that the most exotic thing about Anfield was us, there was this one other entity which, while it wasn't exactly exotic, certainly made the area different from a thousand other northern streetscapes of terraced houses. It was the stadium of Liverpool FC. Indeed, our neighbourhood was like some holy city such as Karbala or Lourdes because there were a number of holy shrines close to each other. Only half a mile away on the other side of our local park was Goodison, the blue and white home of Everton Football Club. Throughout my early childhood Liverpool Football Club had been in the Second Division, overshadowed by Everton, their richer and more successful neighbour. Yet despite playing in the lower division and their ground being a ramshackle mess, the Reds still regularly attracted crowds of forty-five thousand or more.

Liverpool's stadium was little more than half a mile from our house. As soon as you turned into Oakfield Road you were aware of its bulk, the red roof of the Kemlyn Road Stand rising high above the chimney pots of the surrounding houses. On match days the extra double-decker buses required to take the crowds to and from their homes were parked in our road. The front room would go dark as these enormous things were lined up on the other side of the street, shuddering and jerking forward with diesel smoke coughing from their exhausts. The more enterprising families in our neighbourhood rented out their back yards so men could park their bicycles for a shilling a go, while some of the local children would approach the few drivers who parked their cars in Valley Road to ask, 'Mind your car, mister?' in return for a tip of a few pennies. We eschewed such kulak-like behaviour.

During the match the roars from the crowd, jubilant for a goal, anguished for a near miss, angry for a foul, would boom into our kitchen. Then once the game finished thousands of men in fawn raincoats, with slouch hats or flat caps, red and white scarves around their necks, would rush to get on the special buses, squeezing on to the narrow platforms, elbowing and kicking each other while miraculously continuing to smoke.

Somehow for me, supporting one particular football team never took hold. Having both grounds so close meant that there was no particular geographical imperative to choose one club over another – no religious imperative either. Though it never truly resembled sectarian Glasgow, in the 1950s and early 1960s Everton tended to be the Catholic team and Liverpool attracted the Protestants, but neither side tried to reach out to the atheist Communist Jew community. I also came to associate going to football matches with a certain kind of disappointment, betrayal even. One Saturday I was walking through Stanley Park alongside Joe – there were a crowd of us, men and boys streaming towards the Kemlyn Road, all going to see Liverpool FC play Stoke City. It was a big event that Joe was home and taking me to a game, so I was terribly excited. Stoke's most famous player, indeed the most famous footballer in England at the time, was Stanley Matthews. In 1961 at the age of forty-six he had rejoined his home town club and carried on playing for them till he was fifty, but because he wasn't always fit they kept quiet until the last minute whether he was going to take part in the game or not.

'Will he play, Dad?' I kept asking. 'Will he play?'

'I don't know, son.'

'I bet he will play.'

'I'm not sure, son. Maybe he'll play.'

'I'm sure he'll play.'

When we got to the game and were sitting in the stands, it

was only after I had asked Joe if every member of the Stoke team, then every member of the Liverpool team, then the referee, the two linesmen and the newspaper photographers behind each goal were Stanley Matthews, that I realised with a sinking feeling that he wasn't going to show – I wasn't going to see this famous man. An act of bad faith so early on gave me the idea that football clubs could, at times, be heartless and calculating and weren't to be relied on, unless you wanted your heart broken.

None the less I continued to go to football matches, hoping to discover what others found in the game. Later on I used to go with some of the other kids from the neighbourhood to stand in the Boys' Pen, a special section for under-twelves, at Everton. There was a woman there who came round before the game dressed as a seventeenth-century milkmaid and throwing toffees into the crowd, but I never managed to catch one. Another disappointment.

My main problem was that I had great difficulty sinking my personality into that of the crowd, of submerging myself into a mass of people who all felt exactly the same thing, the same joy, the same anguish, the same rage, the same uncritical belief in the rightness of their cause. I, by contrast, couldn't remain partisan for more than a few minutes. If the opposition team were losing I would begin to feel sorry for them and start wanting Liverpool or Everton to concede a goal, or for one of our players to get injured or sent off. But even at the age of six or seven I had the sense to keep these Corinthian ideals very much to myself. When I was ten Everton won the league championship and the crowd all ran on to the pitch and I ran with them. But once there, on that springy turf where I wasn't supposed to be, I felt foolish and didn't know what to do next. All these people were jumping about and shouting and I just thought, 'Why do you care about this? Why are you so worked up?' I knew that I was acting, that my feelings and my actions were fake, and I wondered how many others were acting too, how many others' joy wasn't real – that it was just something they felt they should do to fit in with the mob.

What I did take to was the theatricality of it all. At Liverpool there was something called 'three-quarter time' where they threw back the red-painted gates fifteen minutes before the game ended, presumably so people could leave early. But it also meant you could sneak in and watch the last bit of the match for free. Since I didn't care about the result and wasn't capable of appreciating the skill and artistry of the players, fifteen minutes was enough for me to take in the extraordinarily pure colours of the teams' uniforms, the vibrant unnatural green of the pitch and the attention of the crowd fixated to a fanatical degree on those twenty-two tiny men in shorts, scuttling about in the distance.

In my heart, though, I knew that watching a sixth of the game and liking the bright colours wasn't enough – I urgently required a more profound connection with football if I was going to be a proper Liverpool boy. In the end, living so close to Anfield, the notion subtly grew in me that I was involved in some nebulous and unfocused way in the operations of Liverpool FC itself. It was as if we lived backstage at the club, that our street and our house were an extension of the stadium and Bill Shankly might come round at any minute to borrow our front room, so that he could talk tactics with his forward line while serving them drinks from a giant mahogany cabinet. Thus with my help in the 1961–2 season the Reds won the Second Division championship and gained promotion to the top flight, while in 1964, again with me working quietly behind the scenes, they became First Division champions.

In the late summer of 1960 the new season had yet to start and, though it was a Saturday, Valley Road was quiet. I was sitting on the low wall that divided our house from next door, playing with a new Dinky toy I'd got – a Chevrolet Impala. Out of the corner of my eye I saw a young vicar approaching. He had an eager manner and was sweating gently in his heavy black serge suit.

'Hello, young man,' he said.

'Hello,' I replied. Religious officials were used to deference back then.

'Can I ask you,' he enquired, 'if you are in any sort of youth organisation?'

'Yes, I am,' I said, smiling at him, seemingly eager to please. 'I am in a youth group. Yes, I am.'

'Is it the Scouts?' he asked.

'No,' I replied. Then there was a pause while we stared at each other.

'Are you in the Boys' Brigade?' he finally queried.

'No.' Then another pause.

'The Sea Scouts?'

'No.'

'The Orange Lodge Marching Band?'

'No.'

'The Army Cadets?'

'Err . . . hang on . . . no.'

Perhaps noticing my olive skin and my black hair he enquired, 'The Jewish Lads' Brigade?'

'No.'

'The Catholic Boys' Brigade?'

'No.'

'Well, what is it, then?' he shouted, peevish at being held up on his recruiting drive by an enigmatic eight-year-old.

'I am,' I said, standing and saluting with a clenched right fist held to the side of my temple, 'a Comrade Cadet, Grade One, Young Pioneers, fourth battalion, based at Locomotive Factory Number One, town of Trutnov, People's Republic of Czechoslovakia!'

I was, too. I wasn't lying. Certainly I'd said it to annoy and confuse the vicar, but I hadn't made it up. Exasperated, he went off in search of less smart-arse young boys.

The First Delegation of Comrades

A few weeks before my encounter with the vicar I had been inducted as an honorary Young Pioneer during our second trip to Czechoslovakia. I never went to another meeting, though I did from to time put on the uniform for a laugh. But if I had wanted to I could have attended any gathering of the Young Pioneers right across eastern Europe, in the Soviet Union and China too, just like Alcoholics Anonymous, an organisation that has branches in every town and city in the Western world. The role of the Young Pioneers in a Communist society was to take part in mass rallies, to be indoctrinated as a good party cadre, to spy on your parents and to undermine religion. In East Germany they used to schedule meetings to overlap with Catholic church services. The uniform, in a perhaps not-so-unconscious act of homage, was very close to that of the Hitler Youth, comprising a white short-sleeved shirt, black short trousers and a small scarf worn round the neck, the only difference between the Nazis and the Communists being that the Communist kerchief was red rather than black. In Hungary the Young Pioneers ran their own narrow-gauge railway, which travelled through the forest of the Buda hills in the western part of Budapest.

In fact there was a socialist youth group in the UK that I could have joined. They were called the Woodcraft Folk, and they formed the paramilitary wing of the Co-operative movement. But even at the age of eight I had an idea of how I wanted other kids to see me, and that didn't include being in something called the Woodcraft Folk. In Manchester I met a kid who was one of them at a Communist Party 'social'. A 'social' was what left-wingers called a party; everything had to be something else for them – they couldn't just hold a party, it had to have a higher purpose and a different name. There was also something 1930s' about the word 'social' – it had the whiff of socialist cycling clubs and mass rambles. Anyway, this kid talked about nothing but dolphins for half an hour in a weird voice. I found I much preferred telling people I was the only UK member of the Czechoslovak Young Pioneers to camping in the woods with the children of other lefties, cooking tinned stew over an open fire and singing folk songs.

Between our first and second trips to Czechoslovakia Joe had been extremely busy. While me and Molly were off being shown the sights Joe was having discussions with Ladislav and Prukha, who were very keen to be invited to visit Britain. So my father had, in a remarkably short time, organised for the Czechs to come to the UK in the spring of 1960, a few months before our second visit.

In 1960 the cold war between the East and the West was two years away from its most incendiary point, the Cuban Missile Crisis, but in fourteen months construction would begin on the Berlin Wall and in a year US forces in Vietnam would be tripled, dragging them further into that colonial war. Every interaction between the Soviet Bloc and the capitalist sphere of influence seemed fraught with tension, and there were constant attempts at espionage, infiltration and subversion. A pair of Czechs coming to the UK must have had approval from the highest level in Prague, if not Moscow, and yet it's hard to see what the Czech Security Service, the StB, got out of two of their nationals staying at the Seaforth Ferry Hotel, with a nice view of the River Mersey, as guests of the Merseyside Trades Council. There were no national secrets to be had in them taking trips to the Lake District or visiting the NUR's social club in Dean Road, Liverpool. Not much advantage for Communism could be gained by them sitting through interminable speeches, dinners and expressions of fraternity between the workers of the East and the West. Somewhat suspiciously, Ladislav did win first prize in the raffle at Dean Road Social Club, but it's difficult to understand what purpose a bottle of whisky served in this titanic clash of ideologies.

In return for all Joe's work it was suggested that, if he could get a group of railwaymen and their families together, then the Czech government would pay for hotels and entertainment once they were in the country. So Joe placed adverts in the union paper, the *Railway Review*, asking people if they wanted to take part that summer in something called a 'delegation' to the Socialist Republic of Czechoslovakia. Again, everybody seemed very unselfconscious about all this to-ing and fro-ing to the Soviet Bloc at almost the hottest point of the cold war.

The group for the first delegation comprised two married couples from Scotland and two from Manchester, all more or less my parents' age, plus two young men from Lancashire, Alf and Reg, who, though both married with children, had left their families behind. And finally there was a slightly older couple – a man called Prendergast and the woman he lived with, named Molly like my mother. I took to Alf right away. In the world in which I had lived, up until that point, there had only been kids my own age, grown-ups my parents' age and Uncle Willy. I had known nobody in their early twenties, someone who was an adult yet close enough to childhood to carry a little of that innocence and playfulness with them. Alf was tall, dressed in smart suits of a slimmer, more American cut than the baggy pre-war style of my parents' generation, and wore his black hair styled in a luxuriant quiff. He seemed funnier and more energetic than anybody I had met before, and I took to following him around and staring at him in mute admiration.

We all came together in London like a gang in a western movie and spent the night there, then the next morning we crossed the Channel and were in Paris by the afternoon. Because all the males in our party were railwaymen the jumping on and off the trains soon reached epidemic proportions – there were occasions on our journey when the train would leave the platform and half the group would still be in the street outside the station, buying melons.

By the time we reached Paris it had become clear that Prendergast was the comedy drunk in our western. He first went missing near the Gare du Nord, and by the time he was found we had missed our lunch. With a fractious and hungry group on his hands Joe immediately did what he always did in an emergency, which was to go looking for Communists. It only took a few minutes of searching before we were sitting down to eat a late lunch in the railway workers' canteen of the very station where we had arrived from the coast. All of us were astonished at the quality of the cooking and the simple stylishness of the surroundings. In British factories and workplaces the canteens were often vile places serving disgusting food, but here there were long wooden tables set with paper tablecloths. On the tables were Duralex glasses, sturdy and elegant, carafes of water and a rough but drinkable *vin de table*. The food, simple *cuisine de terroir* – fresh bread, coq au vin, fragrant salad – was of a quality you couldn't even approach in a top hotel in Liverpool.

From Paris to Prague we were travelling by night train, using a type of sleeping car called a couchette. I have no memory of the many hotel rooms I must have stayed in during those early years, but the couchettes are clear and distinct. If you were rich you slept in a wagon-lit, snug in your own compartment with a jug of water and two glasses on a tray and an attached bathroom; and if you were poor you slept upright in your seat jammed against the person next to you. If you were in the middle, like us, you slept in a couchette. 'Couchette' was a word like 'Secatrol' that seemed to crop up in conversation between me, my mother and father with great frequency and was used by nobody else in Anfield. I would say to some other kid, 'It's like a couchette in here!' and be met with complete incomprehension.

During the daytime the couchette compartment had a normal configuration of six seats facing each other in two rows of three, but some time in the late evening it underwent a transformation into something that resembled a Libyan prison cell. The attendant, who travelled in a cosy little compartment of his own at the end of the carriage, came around with a sheet, a pillow and a rough, scratchy blanket, each with the SNCF or Deutsche Bundesbahn logo on them, one per passenger. Then, wielding a special key, he converted the compartment into its night-time configuration, with three bunks on each side of the compartment. The seat you sat on became the lowest bunk, the back of the seat flipped up and became the middle bunk, and a padded panel above your head turned into the top bunk. You had to stand in the corridor while the attendant transformed the compartment and made up the beds, which always felt a bit like when you stood about all dozy while your mum changed the sheets in your bed because you had had an accident. A ladder also appeared from somewhere. I never knew where it was during the day – it just magically materialised at night so you could use it to climb into the top two bunks.

It was possible to join these long-distance overnight trains at many places – Calais, Boulogne, Ostend or the Hook of Holland after crossing by ferry, or somewhere on the continent, Paris or Vienna, and if you wished they would take you as far as Budapest, Sofia, Moscow, Istanbul or Tehran in great discomfort. Over the years we took night trains from all these departure points – to amuse my classmates I could say 'Do not lean out of the window' in three foreign languages with appropriate accents: '*Ne pas se pencher dehors!*' I would shout. '*Nicht hinauslehnen!*' and '*Pericoloso sporgersi!*'

To me there was always something unsettling about travelling by couchette. Superficially you were tucked up safe in your bed, but what was outside the bedroom window kept changing as if one were sleeping in a haunted house. You would drift off amongst fields and farms and wake in the middle of the night, lift the blinds of the condensation-streaked windows and, clearing a gap with your hand, see snow-covered mountains looming towards you at great speed – or you might fall asleep in a marshalling yard and wake hours later still in the same marshalling yard. Foreign railway coaches seemed foreign and unfriendly – they were much more streamlined, all steel and hard plastic, than the Edwardian club-on-wheels of British

Railways. The windows on a British train were tiny, fussy little glass panels with complicated catches that you could just about get your hand through, whereas continental ones dropped in two so you could stick half your body out of the carriage, if you wanted, in a way that required warning notices in four different languages. And instead of heraldic imagery – the British Railways emblem was a lion rampant on a wheel – they just had letters for their emblems, like SNCF or DBB.

In the morning the attendant brought you coffee and a continental breakfast. In western Europe this official would also take charge of passengers' tickets and passports at the start of the journey, returning them before arrival at the destination, to ensure that we were not disturbed by ticket and passport inspections. In the Eastern Bloc countries this was not done, and it was a part of night travel in the East to be woken before and after every border by each country's frontier police and rail inspectors.

Unlike in sleeping cars, couchette compartments were not segregated by sex, so you slept in your grubby clothes and often found yourself sharing your sleep with strangers. It was a lottery who was going to be in your compartment at nightfall. I would find myself frantically wishing, 'Please make the fat man with the breath that smells of garlic get off the train at Frankfurt during the evening.' For some, fellow travellers who shared your compartment for a few hours were a source of mystery and adventure, conversation and fleeting intimacy, but for me strangers were just somebody who was likely to wake you in the middle of the night with their screaming.

☆20★

Known Problems with the Sten Gun

We arrived at Prague Central Station late at night two days after leaving Liverpool, but still Ladislav and a whole fleet of Tatras were waiting for us, their engines clattering into life, their triple headlights flaring as we emerged tired and grimy dragging our suitcases on to the cobbled forecourt. Ordinary Czechs must have wondered who these foreign guests were – perhaps relations of the president of some foreign country that the Eastern Bloc was courting for its minerals. I think we must all have been excited to reach our destination, but some were elated even before we got to Prague. A little while after crossing the border from Germany the train had stopped at a station and I was dozing when Prendergast came into the compartment. He raised the blind and, pointing out of the window, said in a reverential, trembling voice, 'Look . . . look. That's where the beer comes from!' I blearily roused myself and, looking through the smeared glass, saw that the station sign read 'Pilsen'.

I don't know what we thought would happen on this trip but Ladislav, Prukha and presumably the Communist Party authorities at the highest level had decided that what the first delegation of British railwaymen to Czechoslovakia would like to see more than anything else were sights, locations and exhibits connected with the wartime assassination of Reinhard

Heydrich, the Butcher of Prague. The next morning the fleet of Tatras was waiting for us outside our hotel, and after we had climbed aboard it proceeded in a long line to the quiet suburb of Kobylisy. There the cars parked and we clambered out, looking around us and not knowing what to expect. We found that we were standing on a bend in a wide road, across from us there was a tram track that curved around and out of sight, and in the centre of the road was a tram stop with a little wooden shelter. Beyond the shelter there was a long brick wall behind which tall, green-leaved trees nodded and rustled in the breeze.

Before leaving the hotel we had been introduced to our new translator, a pretty blonde woman in her twenties named Nadia. Now that we were an official delegation Ladislav couldn't be with us all the time because he had to attend to his other duties as a senior ministry translator, but he assured Joe that he would join us as often as possible and in the meantime Nadia would look after our party. So there we were, standing at the side of the road in a tranquil suburb, when our pretty little translator began her tale of awful murder and terrible retribution.

Pointing to the bend where the tram track disappeared, she told us that on 27 May 1942 at 10.30 a.m. Heydrich, the Nazi Deputy Protector of Bohemia and Moravia, set off on his daily journey in an open-topped Mercedes from his home to Prague Castle. Heydrich was such a monster that even other leading Nazis like Himmler were afraid of him, and Hitler admired his cruelty to such an extent that he was considering Heydrich as a possible successor. Two Czechs, Gabcik and Kubis, who had been trained and flown in from Britain, were waiting at the very tram stop we were staring at. As Heydrich's car approached,

Gabcik stepped in front of the vehicle and tried to open fire, but his Sten gun jammed.

I thought of speaking up at this point, since I was pretty certain that I knew what had caused this particular problem. My parents' hope that I would grow up to be this kind, sensitive pacifist, possibly one who wore sandals over grey socks, backfired badly. Due to the ownership limits they'd placed on pretend guns, I'd developed an obsession with real firearms, military aircraft and armoured fighting vehicles of all kinds. If there was a war film on the TV I was more fascinated by the weapons than by the plot or storyline. There was a Graham Greene-scripted film that had recently been shown on TV called *Went the Day Well?*, in which at one point a British sailor opens up on the Nazi paratroopers trying to take over his village. His weapon is a .45 calibre Thompson equipped with the fifty-round drum magazine that I was particularly fond of. And when sometimes there was an exploded drawing of the internal workings of a rifle or machine gun in one of my comics I devoured every detail, noting the differences in ammunition, feed mechanism and recoil characteristics. This was how I knew that, though it was a serviceable and inexpensive sub-machine gun, there was a drawback with the magazine of the Sten in that it had two columns of 9mm cartridges arranged side-by-side in an alternating pattern, merging at the top to form a single column. As a consequence, any dirt in this taper area was liable to cause feed malfunctions. Rough handling could also result in deformation of the magazine lips, which required a precise eight-degree angle to operate. But I decided not to interrupt the story at such a tense moment by sharing this information with my fellow delegates.

The other Czech commando, Kubis, threw a modified anti-tank grenade at the vehicle and its fragments ripped through the car, embedding shrapnel and fibres from the upholstery in Heydrich's body. The assassins were initially convinced that the attack had failed, but Heydrich died eight days later from blood poisoning caused either by shrapnel from the bomb or by fragments of upholstery which had entered his spleen.

Next, feeling slightly sick, we got back into our fleet of black limousines and moved to the church of Saints Cyril and Methodius in the centre of Prague. This was where Heydrich's killers had been trapped and put to death after they were betrayed by a fellow partisan. As our guide talked I looked around and saw that the inside of the church was still riddled with bullet holes from the firefight. She told us that the Nazi retribution for the killing of Heydrich was savage. Ultimately more than thirteen thousand people were arrested, including Kubis's girlfriend who died in the Mauthausen concentration camp. In an attempt to minimise the reprisals among his flock, the bishop to whose diocese the church belonged took the blame for the actions in the church on himself, even writing letters to the Nazi authorities. He was arrested and tortured. On 4 September 1942 he, the church priests and senior lay leaders were executed by firing squad. Then we had lunch, and afterwards went to a museum to look at Heydrich's damaged car.

Towards the weekend, again in our fleet of government limousines, we went to the village of Lidice. As a punishment for the assassination of Heydrich, the Nazis, who suspected there may have been a connection between the perpetrators and a family who lived in Lidice, killed all the men of this village and deported the women and children to concentration camps. The buildings were burned to the ground and the stream that ran through it was diverted to another course. Grain was then planted over the site of the village in an attempt to eradicate any sign that the place had ever existed. What we were being shown here was the oddest thing, an absence, not something that was there but something that had been taken away. All the way back from Lidice in the lead car I sang 'One Man Went to Mow' at the top of my voice, while everybody else sat in hollow-eyed silence. Our holidays had never been conventional, but this one was in another league of strangeness. In the second week, between the visits to locomotive works and folk concerts we were given a private screening at the Ministry of Information of the 1943 film *Hangmen Also Die!*, a dramatic re-enactment of the events leading up to the assassination of Heydrich and the shoot-out in the church of Saints Cyril and Methodius; made in Hollywood by refugees from the Nazis, it was directed by Fritz Lang, scripted by Bertolt Brecht amongst others with music by Hans Eisler.

I don't know what the Czechs were trying to show us, if anything. In Britain there were many memorials to the Second World War, big stone things, unmoving and civic and dedicated almost entirely to the armed forces. My parents never paid any of them the slightest bit of attention, but as soon as we were on the continent their attitude changed. They would be constantly pointing out the plaques and the bundles of wilted flowers tied with red, white and blue ribbons that commemorated the spots where hostages had been executed for acts of resistance, and endlessly drawing my attention to the walls of the many buildings which bore a tracery of craters – the trail of machine gun and rifle fire. 'Look!' my parents would gleefully say, pointing at some inscription, 'It says here, Lexi, that twenty hostage nuns were massacred on this very spot,' or 'Over there, Lexi, that was where they hanged the entire football team.'

Lacking religion as we did, perhaps these were our places of worship. Communists believed in partisans in the same way that more ethereally inclined families believed in fairies; they were both mythical woodland creatures possessed of wisdom and nobility who ran around the forest making mischief. The spiritual families would seek out spooky caves or magical trees or the places where miracles happened, and for Communists the sights of Nazi reprisals were our Wooky Hollow.

Though it never seemed to be of concern to my parents, mention of the war sometimes caused in me a scintilla of unease because of the fact that my father had not fought. Railway guard had been what was known as a 'reserved occupation', a job considered so necessary to the war effort that even if he had wanted to volunteer Joe would not have been allowed to join up. Still, it bothered me just a tiny bit, even though Joe's was actually an extremely dangerous job because freight trains and marshalling yards were often the target of German bombers. Most of the others boys' fathers had been in the army, navy or air force but mine hadn't – and he hadn't volunteered to fight in Spain either. There was something in me that would have liked him to have been some kind of soldier or military hero, something spikier than just being a very nice man.

On another evening we went as a party to a performance at the Magic Lantern Theatre. The rest of the group were seeing it for the first time and were astounded by the show, but I was surprised to find myself a little bored by it all. I supposed there was a limit to how many times you could be impressed by teapots flying through the air.

Where's Alf?

As a bit of light relief from visits to locomotive factories and the horrors of the Second World War, one evening we were taken to the Good Soldier Schweik pub in the old town of Prague – the first pub I had ever been in. When I got back to Britain my parents bought me a Penguin edition of *The Good Soldier Schweik*, a hefty paperback with a grey cover. I do think they often forgot I was only eight years old. I didn't read the book for many years but I liked looking at the illustrations at the head of each chapter – a tubby, unshaven man in a shabby uniform, cavorting with dancing girls or mysteriously stuffing dogs down his tunic. When I did finally get around to reading the book, at twelve or thirteen, my holiday souvenir turned out to contain a message that seemed very much at odds with the socialistic seriousness we were usually presented with. It was as if a stick of Blackpool rock you had bought as a memento of a day out contained an offensive message running right through the middle of it.

The Schweik pub was 'themed' around the Good Soldier. There were beer mats with his face on, pictures of the author, Jaroslav Hasek, and there was even a shop where my parents bought me a little cloth figure of the tubby soldier. When I read the book I wondered if the Czech authorities knew what they were doing promoting with Schweik, letting a pub be opened in his name and selling cuddly toys in his likeness, since the message of the book, while it might have been anti-authoritarian, is certainly not one supportive of the ideals of socialist conformity. The worrying notion niggled away for years at the back of my mind that the governments of Communist states might not always know what they were doing.

The Good Soldier Schweik is set at the time of the First World War and tells the story of a petty thief who makes his living stealing dogs. Schweik seems determined to volunteer to fight for the Austrian Emperor, but nobody is sure whether he is an idiot or an incredibly crafty anarchist intent on undermining the war effort. Though I was fascinated by the book, I sometimes found the character of Schweik unsettling. I was still enough of an ideologue to find his total rejection of doctrine, his selfishness, his lustfulness and his dishonesty disturbing, but also worryingly appealing. The figure I found more congenial, as well as a wonderful comic creation, was Volunteer Marek. In civilian life Marek had been a writer, one who got fired from his job at a natural history magazine after writing articles about imaginary animals because he couldn't be bothered learning about real ones and found them too dull anyway. Marek is appointed to the post of historian for Schweik's battalion and in that role he begins writing, in advance, descriptions of heroic and poignant deaths for his fellow soldiers.

I supposed that Czech officialdom assumed that the book only mocked the authorities of the Austro-Hungarian Empire because that was when it was set, whereas in fact it was a satire on the corruption and stupidity of all officialdom. In retrospect maybe *The Good Soldier Schweik* also opened a window into the sly and sardonic nature of the people who had been our hosts and went some way to explaining a few of the odd confusing things that had gone on.

After two weeks' holiday culminating in one final huge dinner, with speeches and the presentation of much globular Bohemian glassware, we set out on the return journey to Britain, with Nadia our translator travelling with us as far as the border. It was night and we were approaching West Germany when, realising that I hadn't seen Alf for some time, I went looking for him. I searched all over the train until finally I came to a compartment with the blinds drawn. Sliding open the door, I saw in the darkness the shape of two figures springing apart, Nadia and Alf, their clothes in disarray. 'It's dark in here,' I said, switching on the reading lights. In the sudden brightness Nadia looked like she had been crying. This didn't stop me sitting down next to them and beginning to chat happily about whatever was on my mind. Oddly, they didn't seem to want me around. I couldn't understand it: people, particularly Alf, usually acted as if they found my company delightful, but these two definitely wanted me gone. So after a while I got up and left and spent the next few years wondering what had been going on.

I evolved this elaborate theory that Nadia had been trying to recruit Alf as a spy (since she must have had StB clearance to mix with foreigners) so that she could pass on to the KGB details of the Sunday timetables on the West Coast Line or where the waiting rooms were at Runcorn station. When, after years of theorising, I eventually thought simply to ask Molly what had been occurring it turned out to be a less complicated story. Nadia and Alf had begun an affair while we had been in Czechoslovakia and she now wanted him to divorce his wife, marry her and take her out of the country.

Along with being treated like a little prince, it was odd for somebody my age to spend such long periods as the only child amongst so many adults. That these extended periods should take place on transcontinental trains, in foreign cities and in the backs of futuristic limousines only added to the weirdness. A lot of the time I was bored and at other times just confused, but the result was that I tended to spend great stretches of time inside my head telling myself stories or inventing complex explanations for the bizarre behaviour of grown-ups.

•••••••: **22** :••••••••
Deadman's Hill

Throughout a large part of the 1950s I was a David rather than an Alexei. For many years I was uncomfortable with my first name and in a period spanning primary and junior school insisted that I should be called David Sayle, employing my middle name. Many of my junior school reports are for this other kid called Sayle who appears to be a rather dull child, judging by what the teachers have written about him. Clearly my parents went along with me being David – they probably felt that it was good practice for me to have different aliases, just like Trotsky and Stalin.

I returned to being Alexei soon after the *Bambi* incident, another part of the realisation that I was never going to be like everybody else and I might as well work on being unique. And there was one particular event which made me aware that having a distinctive name might not always be a disadvantage. There was a kid in my class named, with a spectacular lack of imagination, Fred Smith. I saw him one day by the entrance to Stanley Park where he had been grabbed by the park police-man for some misdemeanour. This huge man in a dark blue uniform was demanding to know my classmate's real name and wouldn't believe that he was truly called Fred Smith. In fact the more Fred Smith insisted that he was honestly called Fred Smith the more the policeman became enraged at having his intelligence insulted in this fashion.

My nickname at that point amongst my school friends, as a play on Sayle, was 'Wayley'. Seeing me, Fred Smith called out in desperation, 'Wayley! Wayley! Tell him, tell him my name's Fred Smith!' But the policeman wasn't interested in my intervention. 'Don't be calling to Wayley!' the man said and gave poor Fred a vicious clip round the ear for a crime he probably didn't commit and really for the crime of being called Fred Smith.

When the doorbell rang I must have been in the hall or on the stairs playing with my cars or drawing, because otherwise I don't know why it was me who answered the door. I wasn't exactly a door-answering type of child.

As soon as I saw who was on the step I knew them for what they were. Two gigantic men, so big that they blocked the light of the winter sun, dressed identically in belted raincoats and trilby hats. Coppers! Bobbies! Detectives! All of a sudden I felt weak. My family had talked about this day for so long, and now it was finally here. We had assumed it was inevitable that eventually they would come for us, just as they had come for the Rosenbergs or Pastor Niemöller. After all, we came both first and second in the famous poem:

First they came for the Communists [that was us!] and I
    didn't speak up, because I wasn't a Communist.
Then they came for the Jews, and I didn't speak up, because
    I wasn't a Jew. [That was us too!]
Then they came for the Catholics, and I didn't speak up,
    because I was a Protestant. [Not us.]

Then they came for me, and by that time there was no one
left to speak up for me. [Obviously not us, because we're
all dead.]

I racked my brains but couldn't think what crime we had
committed. Then came the terrifying realisation that of course
they didn't need you to do anything to arrest you. The authorities were perfectly capable of fabricating evidence against you
or punishing you even if you were innocent, just like they did
with Sacco and Vanzetti, Alger Hiss or poor Fred Smith. Then I
became conscious of the fact that, though we had talked about
it we hadn't actually ever made any plans for what to do when
the inevitable day came. There was no secret hiding-place in
the attic, no convincing cover story to tell, no Sten gun tucked
away under the couch to shoot our way out of trouble.

'Hello, son, Bedfordshire CID,' the bigger of the two men
said, flashing an unnecessary warrant card. 'Is your dad in?'

Not knowing what else to do, I showed them into the front
room – just, as I imagined, many victims of tyranny had done
in the past, politely letting the Gestapo, the FBI or the KGB
into the best room to sit on the couch – for want of any other
plan. Then I went to fetch my parents.

The adults closed the door on me, and I was left in the hall to
try and listen while we waited to discover our fate.

Up until that point our relationship with the police had actually been a rather good one. Molly said they were a tool of
repression for the capitalist state, but we seemed to call them
in more or less whenever we felt like it. If I ever went missing

when we were on the beach at New Brighton, Molly would jump up screaming, 'Lexi! Lexi! Where's our Lexi?' Then she would run off to find a policeman, even though I was only sitting three feet away.

When I was six we had accidentally acquired a dog. It happened one day when Molly and I were out shopping on Oakfield Road and we saw a small brown puppy running up and down the pavement in a distressed state, clearly lost or abandoned. We took it home and named it Bruno, which may or may not have been another *nom de guerre* of Maxim Gorky's. Bruno grew up into a very self-contained dog, which was probably the best way to survive in our house but it didn't make him particularly lovable. He had a sly sense of humour a lot like mine, and maybe that was why we never got on that well.

On a Sunday morning the only chore that was ever asked of me was to take Bruno for his walk in Stanley Park. At a newsagent's near the park I would buy two comics with my pocket money, the *Eagle* and a thing called a *Commando Comic*, which was solely concerned with the adventures of British soldiers during the Second World War, trained killers such as I would have liked my father to be. This comic came in a distinctive pocket-sized format and, despite the unsophisticated stories and simple sketched black and white artwork, once through the gates of the park I would let Bruno off the lead and become absorbed in tales of the war, in which nobody ever indulged in a debate about whether it was an imperative to open a second front or if the conflict wasn't merely a squabble between competing capitalist ideologies.

By the time I looked up again Bruno would have vanished. Usually he would just run around for a bit and then make his way home by himself, and he would often be waiting for me when I returned to Valley Road. But occasionally he would go missing for a few hours which meant Molly would be straight down to the police station in Anfield Road demanding an all-out search be mounted immediately. We would stand in front of the desk sergeant as he pretended to take down the dog's details and my eyes would wander in embarrassment to the poster display pinned to the wall behind him. For years the only Wanted posters displayed in police stations were to do with the Colorado beetle, a small red insect which was at the time considered a big threat to the UK potato crop. If you saw one you were supposed to put it in a matchbox and take it to the police station. After a few years the Colorado beetle poster was replaced with one showing the ejector seat of a Harrier Jump Jet, as if even the beetle threat had disappeared and there was now absolutely no crime occurring in Britain anywhere.

In our use of the police we were out of step with many others, since Liverpool was not a city in which the force were held in universally high regard. In 1919 the National Union of Police and Prison Officers had called for a nationwide strike over pay and conditions which typically, of all the authorities in the country, only achieved full support amongst officers on Merseyside, where the entire force abruptly abandoned their posts. In Liverpool even the coppers were militant. This sudden vacuum, a complete absence of law and order, resulted in what Liverpool people came to call 'The Loot'. In poor districts such as Scotland Road and Bootle people ran riot, shops were smashed open and their contents plundered. The government's response was to put Liverpool under military occupation with orders for peace to be brutally restored. During the police strike tanks patrolled the streets of our city and three thousand soldiers, less than a year after they had left the stinking trenches of the Somme, were used to seize key buildings. Then, once control was re-established, these soldiers and a few scab policemen were sent to roam through impoverished neighbourhoods, smashing down doors and seizing back looted furniture and goods, a lot of which had been paid for and wasn't stolen in the first place. Many working-class people were badly beaten, and at least one was shot dead.

In the Boys' Pen at Goodison Park when I went to Everton matches all the bigger boys would sing,

> Who's that twat in the big black hat?
> Copp-er! Copp-er!
> Who's that twat in the big black hat?
> Copper is his name!

The Bedfordshire CID had come to our house to interview my father about the murder of Michael Gregsten at Deadman's Hill on the A6 in Bedfordshire, on 22 August 1961, along with the rape and shooting of his lover, Valerie Storie. James Hanratty, a professional car thief, had been charged with the crimes. Hanratty's alibi was that at the time of the murder he had been in the Welsh seaside town of Rhyl, staying in a boarding house named Ingledene run by a woman called Mrs Jones, in the attic room, which had a green bath.

The police had discovered that Joe had stayed at Ingledene between 21 and 24 August, in the small front room on the first floor. He was there on behalf of the NUR, taking part in a recruitment drive. In his book *Who Killed Hanratty?* Paul Foot describes Joe as 'the most important witness from the prosecution point of view'. He says that Joe saw no sign of Hanratty, although he admits 'he was out on union business from dawn to dusk'. Which sounds typical enough.

Hanratty's trial began at Bedfordshire Assizes on 22 January 1962. On 17 February he was convicted of murder and sentenced to death. Hanratty's appeal was dismissed on 9 March, and despite a petition signed by more than ninety thousand people he was hanged at Bedford on 4 April 1962, still protesting his innocence.

Joe was away for a week attending the trial in Bedford. One night Molly spoke to him on the phone, and when I asked how he was she replied that he had told her he was frightened. I asked her what my father was frightened of, and she said he was worried that Hanratty might have criminal friends who could harm him in some way.

When he returned from the trial Joe told us that what had upset him the most was that he had been the final witness called in the trial. He realised that the last person Hanratty had heard testifying against him, the last person he had seen on the stand, the final person confirming his fate, was Joe Sayle. After that he was taken down, sentenced and hanged two months later. The last witness to testify against the last person executed in Britain was my father. Though he never talked about it, since he was such a good-natured man that must have been a heavy burden for him to bear.

Over the next few years the case did not go away: prosecution witnesses attempted or committed suicide and several books were written about the case, including one by Lord Russell of Liverpool. There were newspaper articles, radio and TV programmes, all of them contesting the soundness of Hanratty's conviction and reminding Joe that he might have taken part in the execution of an innocent man. When one of those programmes came on we did not shout at the TV as we usually did but simply changed the channel and said nothing. In 2002, the murder conviction of James Hanratty was upheld by the Court of Appeal which ruled that new DNA evidence established his guilt 'beyond doubt'. So the coppers got it right.

⇥ 23 ⇤

A Communist Christmas on Merseyside

Considering we were two-thirds Jewish atheist Communists, Christmas was a surprisingly important occasion in our house. Molly would say that for her, as a child in an Orthodox house, Christmas had been strictly forbidden, but her mother would still secretly slip the children oranges and simple stuff so they wouldn't feel left out amongst the Christian kids. On British television, during the 1950s and 1960s, the holiday period was also a time when presentations from the Soviet Union were prominently featured. It was as if there was considered to be something seasonal about performances originating from a godless, authoritarian dictatorship. The Moscow State Circus, with its spectacularly unfunny clowns, disturbingly dangerous high-wire acts and animal cruelty, would be transmitted live and at interminable length from a tent in Manchester. 'Best horsemen in the world,' Molly would say with a tremble of pride in her voice, referring to the Cossack horsemen who leapt on and off the backs of their stocky ponies as they hurtled round and round the circus ring. Presumably these men were the direct descendants of those Cossacks who had set fire to her grandmother's village. The Bolshoi Ballet, too, was a regular fixture of the holiday period, and I can vividly recall sitting on the couch jammed in between Molly and Joe. They fell asleep the moment the programme began, leaving me to watch three hours of *Swan Lake* to the accompaniment of stentorian snoring.

My parents were always remarkably keen to take me to see Santa in his grotto at Lewis's department store – I suppose they felt that Santa was a lot like Stalin. Their names were sort of similar and they were both kindly-looking, rotund gentlemen with facial hair and red uniforms whose headquarters were located in the northern snowy wastes and were based upon a system of slave labour. At first we would shop for my presents at something called 'the *Daily Worker* Bazaar' which was held at the Communist Party bookshop. On long trestle tables would be arrayed sickly pot plants, Marxist literature, Paul Robeson records and crudely carved wooden toys from East Germany and dolls from the Soviet Union, which when you unscrewed them sometimes contained scribbled notes from

Alexander Solzhenitsyn begging to be released from the gulag. After a while I refused to put up with this stuff and demanded to be given what everybody else was given. From then on Christmas was a happy event. I would wake up early and dive into what was known as a selection box. Molly very sensibly took an interest in healthy eating long before it was a general concern, so the only time I got my hands on the sugary confectionery that was beginning to swamp working-class areas was at Christmas. Then, after gorging on Smarties and Kit-Kats, I would open my other presents.

In the afternoon, after shouting at the Queen's speech on the TV ('Parasite! Liar! What's she got on her head? What about the Rosenbergs? Second front now!') we would have a lovely turkey dinner – just the three of us, just like everybody else. And on Boxing Day we would eat turkey sandwiches and then the table would be cleared and Molly and Joe would spread out their maps and Baedeker guides and continental railway timetables and plan where we would be going next summer.

One of my favourite Christmas gifts was something called a 'Give-a-show-projector'. This was a battery-operated slide projector accompanied by a number of strips with simple cartoon stories on them. You could throw these images on to the wall or the ceiling, wherever you wanted. Discovering a flair for entrepreneurship, over the holidays I held a series of shows in my bedroom, charging other kids for the experience. Growing bored with the official storylines that came with the cartoon strips, I started to make up my own.

This gave me a taste for performance and I began giving little impromptu shows for my parents, dressing up in clothes I had taken from the laundry cupboard. These shows were generally based on stories that were in the news or events taking place in the neighbourhood and were usually performed with a satirical bent, thus predating the satire boom on television by a good few years. If a neighbour or a visiting member of the Communist Party or the doctor was in our house when I suddenly decided to put on a show then they were trapped and would be forced to watch it too. Me and Molly couldn't see why they wouldn't want to be present at an improvised performance by a child prodigy such as me.

Another staple that appeared year in year out in my Christmas stocking along with the confectionery was a box of coloured pencils, some pens and drawing paper. Being an only child was a bit like taking an extraordinarily long train journey: you were always trying to find something to do to pass the time. At first I just told myself tales inside my head, but then I discovered that drawing was a great way to give the stories in my brain an external life. Initially I had employed water-colours and pencils along with the other children, but by the time of the first delegation to Czechoslovakia I was working mainly in the relatively new medium of the biro, illustrating, in a large series of drawings, the daily life of a country known as Saylovia.

Saylovia was a land where a number of visions of the present and the future came together. Clearly Saylovia was in many ways influenced by the Socialist Republic of Czechoslovakia. The flag of Saylovia was very similar to the Czech flag and all the cars looked like Tatras, with bold aerodynamic shapes, prominent air scoops and big fins.

But its primary model was more local in inspiration. At the beginning of the 1960s the reshaping of Britain had begun to gather pace. Those in charge of it, government officials, local councillors, town planners and architects, were determined that the rebuilding of the country would go far beyond a limited and sympathetic restoration of war damage and instead produce an entirely modern country in which inequality and social divisions would be designed out by the lavish use of ferro-concrete and central heating. The feeling amongst all these visionaries was that here was an opportunity for the wholesale reformation of society. Through road traffic management, hygienic plumbing, massive programmes of demolition, flyovers, underpasses and town planning the war-like and aggressive nature of human beings would be tamed. Never again would the ignorant masses want to take up arms against other nations, or indulge in racism or xenophobia, because instead they had a nice flat with a balcony and underfloor heating.

The public were not to be consulted on whether they wished to have their cities and towns torn down and rebuilt in an entirely original and untested style with no connection to what had gone before. But it was considered helpful if they could be convinced that this giant social experiment was what they had wanted all along. So articles began to appear in newspapers and magazines, accompanied by architects' drawings showing how fabulous Coventry or Cumbernauld was going to look once all the rotten old stuff had been swept away and the tower blocks, ring roads, tree-lined boulevards and shopping precincts replaced them. There was also a 'traffic expert' by the name of Professor Sir Colin Buchanan who proposed driving giant, multi-lane highways through the middle of every one of Britain's cities. His predictions, too, were accompanied by elaborate drawings. I was very taken with these images of utopia; the streetscape seemed so clean and uncomplicated compared with the cluttered and chaotic Liverpool town centre with its untidy jumble of buildings spanning the centuries. Everything would be so much better when the city was all pedestrian bridges and urban throughways.

So the capital of the People's Republic of Saylovia, Sayleville, came to possess a Palace of Congress built in the modernist style of Brasilia, with a bicameral legislature located in upper and lower houses. In truth, however, it remained, like Brazil and many of the newer states of Africa and the Middle East, a dictatorship, dominated by a capricious and vain despot who was capable of destroying whole neighbourhoods with a sweep of his biro.

Saylovia kept me going for years until in my early teens the drawings began to change. As a parting gift following the first delegation of comrades to Czechoslovakia, Ladislav had given me personally a lavishly illustrated book all about the assassination of Reinhard Heydrich, complete with a series of schematic drawings which showed from above, employing arrows and broken lines, how the shooting had unfolded. Here was the tram stop, here was the Mercedes limousine, here were Gucik and Kubis with their guns and bombs. In my drawings, in biro, I endlessly repeated these events, seen from a high vantage point so that the figures were tiny. The tram stop, the open car, the little men running and firing and falling down dead. Sometimes I would draw a parallel street where people were going about their normal business unaware that an assassination was taking place only metres away.

At This Moment in Time

Every Friday when he came home from work Joe would bring Molly a bunch of flowers, carnations or tulips wrapped in coloured paper. He did this every week of his working life and beyond. At the same time he would hand over his wages and from it Molly would manage to pay the mortgage, buy food and put a little money into a post office account for when I went to Oxford or the Sorbonne. Perhaps Joe would have liked to stay home but, after working such long hours as a guard, he would then go off to do union work. In order to spend time with him, me and Molly would often go along to union functions too.

In the early 1960s he became Liverpool and North Wales District Secretary of the NUR, which required a huge amount of time but paid very little money. At the weekend my father would often go for meetings at the edge of his empire, getting up early and leaving before I was awake. Later in the day my mother and I would travel to distant places such as Chester to meet him. We got the bus to James Street Station, then took an electric train under the River Mersey to Rock Ferry where we changed to one of the new diesels that carried us onward to Chester.

In some ways the rural landscape that surrounded Liverpool and the rolling farmland on the Wirral seemed more exotic and foreign to me than Karlovy Vary, Montmartre or Brussels. At least to get to those foreign places it took a lot of effort, days of travel and the constant handing over of your passport to men in strange uniforms – and when you got there everybody talked a different language and dressed differently and smoked cigarettes that smelt like an abattoir on fire.

Sometimes if the train driver at Rock Ferry knew my dad he would let me sit in the cab of the diesel with him, and so I was able to watch as neat farms with cows in the fields, woods and little villages made of sandstone came rattling towards us. I wondered how many of the people in those farms and villages were Communists or Jews. Was it like Liverpool, where it seemed that about one in ten of the population was a Communist or a Jew or both, or were an even higher proportion of these farmers on the Wirral members of the party?

As a District Secretary, Joe would often be a delegate to the union's annual general meeting which would be held at a different seaside resort every year. Other men might have seen it as an opportunity to get away from their families, but me and Molly always went with my father. After all, everything was paid for by the union, and it was a chance for us to get a little something back for all the time he was away.

The epicentre of the AGM would be the biggest ballroom in town. For seven days the grand Wurlitzer organ would cower in its oubliette beneath the stage while above it, in the dust-mote-spangled air, fat men dressed universally in scratchy grey droned on about 'resolutions back to congress', 'incremental payscale differentials' and 'clause nine arbitration agreements'. In its own way it was exciting. To be at the congress of a large trade union in the 1960s was a little like attending a rock festival where the stars up on the stage were balding alcoholics in ill-fitting suits talking gibberish. Trade union men like Vic Feather, Sid Weighell and Len Murray were constantly in the newspapers, on the TV and the radio during that era, in their ponderous, evasive and oxygen-sapping English uttering phrases like 'at this moment in time' and 'in the interests of the working man' and 'I'll have to refer that question back to my executive committee'. This language they had invented to hide their intentions and to repel the uninitiated.

Then in the evening a transformation would take place – the folding chairs were cleared away and there would be music and dancing. On the stage there appeared a dance band wearing matching outfits, their weary enthusiasm switching on as they stood to play. The most surprising delegates would reveal themselves to be proficient at the jitter-bug and the waltz, straightfaced, spinning and kicking their heels with their wives or women who they said were their wives, while others conspired against them in alcoves.

I remember at the age of five or six being forced to take a nap in a boarding house in the seaside town of Exmouth – I was supposed to get some sleep in the afternoon so that I could stay up late and attend the union's annual dinner dance. A window was open and the lace curtain fluttered in the breeze and in the distance a train whistle blew and I couldn't sleep because I was too excited. Though there were other dances thoughout the week the main social event, this annual dinner dance, was held on the Friday night after all work at the congress had been completed, wrapped up in resolutions and plans for strikes, and it was the climax of a week-long parade of functions. Before then, on the Monday after we were settled into our boarding houses and caravans, the mayor would host a reception at the town hall to welcome us to his seaside resort and there would be speeches of greeting and pork pies cut into four under an ornate crystal chandelier.

At the annual dinner dance the menu never varied – it would probably have taken a resolution back to congress to alter it. So there was brown Windsor soup, roast chicken, roast potatoes and peas, followed by ice cream. The only hint of exoticism would be supplied by fraternal delegates from foreign unions, men of the Deutsche Bundesbahn and the Italian Railways and French railway workers from the SNCF staring in horror at their brown Windsor soup and wondering if it wasn't in fact made out of the brown bits of Windsor.

While the men sat in sub-committees and steering groups ignoring the summer sun that streamed through the windows, the women and children had to be entertained. So during the day there were coach trips, visits to stately homes and castles and activities for the kids, especially sports days during which they had their hopes raised and then shattered. By and large

me and Molly turned our noses up at these trips. We didn't
like organised fun with people we didn't know and particularly
didn't wish to marvel at stately homes and castles, which we
viewed as the oppression of our class rendered in stone and
plaster. Why would we want to look at a Vanbrugh façade, a
ceiling by Rubens or a Palladian portico when we knew that
what had paid for it was slavery, exploitation and genocide?
When we looked at this beauty my family saw only ideology.

Me and Molly preferred exploring the resorts on our own,
ill-informed and pure in our class hatred, and in this we were
aided by a wonderful device. The AGMs of the big unions
lasted for weeks each summer and there was great competition
amongst resorts to be the host for hundreds of big-spending
trade unionists, their mistresses and their families. As a token
of gratitude the town council of whatever seaside town had
been chosen gave each family this magical piece of cardboard
– a pass. As the relative of a delegate, having a pass meant
that for a week you were entitled to enjoy all council facilities either free or at half price. Bus rides, swimming pools,
palm houses, model villages – we flashed that pass and were
ushered around like royalty. There was a little narrow-gauge
train that ran along the front at Scarborough and me, Molly
and Bruno our dog would, since it was free to us, ride it up
and down rather than walking. It was a terrible trauma to
come to the end of the week and to realise that your pass
didn't work any more, that you were cast back down with the
ordinary passless people. In Scarborough one of the events
we got into at half price was a re-enactment of the Second
World War sinking of the pocket battleship *Graf Spee*, held

three times a week on the boating lake of Peasholm Park, which for the afternoon became the Rio Plato. On our trips to Czechoslovakia and the rest of eastern Europe we were constantly being shown round the sites of concentration camps or the exact spots where hundreds of partisans had been machine-gunned by German storm troopers, and this was the British equivalent: model Spitfires on wires coming in over the laurel bushes, machine guns blazing, and quite small explosions going off in the water.

25
Flight Officer Sayle

In the summer of 1961, rather than return to Czechoslovakia we had decided on the previous Boxing Day to go to Hungary. We would not take a delegation, but while we were there it was arranged that we would meet senior members of the Communist Party and the trade unions with a view to bringing a group of railwaymen over the following year.

With the usual panic we had got to the Gare du Nord and were racing down the platform. Maybe because me, Molly and Joe were travelling further east than we had done before I was experiencing a particularly heightened sense of awareness. I remember dragging my suitcase along when on an adjoining track I caught sight of a train that presented such an image of glamour and speed that it scarcely seemed real. It was scarlet and silver with a cockpit for the driver like a bomber plane's, high above its long, aerodynamic nose and porthole windows down the flanks. In slanted metal letters along the side of the locomotive were written these magical words: 'TEE – Trans Europe Express'. This was the train I wished we were going to be riding on, racing swiftly across Europe in air-conditioned luxury, rather than the train that we were taking. I was afraid of the train we were taking.

The three of us were running to the Gare de l'Est, right next door, to ride the Orient Express from Paris to Vienna. This was as far as the famous express ran at that time, and from there we would be taking another train onward to Budapest. One of the films Unity Theatre endlessly showed was *The Red Balloon*, a 1956 short in which a young boy chases a red balloon, which seems as if it has a life of its own, all over Paris. I felt sometimes that boy was our family, though we were continually chasing trains rather than red balloons that symbolised an idealistic notion of hope.

When we got to the Orient Express we were reluctant to board. The passengers seemed very seedy and frightening, hanging out of the windows or snogging girls on the steps and refusing to move. Once aboard it was hard to get to our seats because the aisles were blocked by gypsies and their luggage – luggage which seemed to consist of large hessian sacks that appeared to be moving. Molly had been going on for months about how dangerous the Orient Express had become, hence my nervousness. Finally we settled into the ancient, dirty carriage, and a few minutes later the train jerked into life and slowly ground through the same Paris suburbs that we had come through a few hours before. However, somewhere between Strasbourg and Munich, in keeping with the train's reputation for mystery and intrigue, I did find ten Swiss francs in the toilet. The dining car of the Orient Express still hung on to a little of the glamour of the pre-war years. Lacy curtains fluttered in the breeze from the open windows and the staff's uniforms, stained with half a century of soup, even now evoked the bygone glory of the Austro-Hungarian Empire with their gold epaulettes and ornate silver buttons. They served these little tins of orange juice as a sort of hors d'oeuvre, and I will still occasionally taste orange juice from a can and be projected back like a time traveller to some foreign dining car, sunshine streaming through the window with consommé slopping from a bowl as the train rocks gently from side to side.

At least if we were in the dining car we were safe and moving in the right direction, but Joe had developed this terrifying new practice of making us all get off the train with him to eat in the station buffet, leaving all our belongings behind. He would force us to leave the security of the carriage, walk along the platform to a tiled, echoing underpass and cross under the tracks to emerge on the busy station concourse. It was an extraordinary sensation, terrifying but in its way also thrilling. We would traverse the marble floor of some German terminus, garish neon signs in blues, reds and yellows advertising hotel rooms by the hour and Teutonic singing reverberating from the station beer hall, with Joe insisting we had plenty of time because the train would leave from one platform in a few minutes but it would certainly return half an hour later to another. All the same, it took a great deal of confidence to sit still and eat a bratwurst while watching everything you owned clanking off up the line.

It was late evening when we got to Vienna, where we would spend the night in a small hotel near the station. The place where the three of us were staying didn't have a restaurant, so we went out into the streets to find a café. Eventually we located a large restaurant unlike anywhere I had been before. It had warped ancient wooden floorboards and in the centre of the room a huge ornate black iron stove with a fat pipe reaching up to the ceiling – waiters in long aprons pirouetted around this stove with massive trays of food held high above their shoulders. I ordered a Wiener Schnitzel, which came with a fried egg on top. It seemed such a brilliant idea to be eating something named after a city in the city it was named after.

On the way back from the café, in the window of an electrical shop I saw a radio in bright red plastic with four silvery antennae shaped like the Sputnik satellite. Here was another amazing thing. In Britain radios were shaped like radios and were dull and sober wooden boxes. It seemed like an act of extraordinary genius to conceive of manufacturing one that looked like something else, and in such vibrant materials. It seemed somehow very German, too. In the years to come, as German cars, machine tools and consumer products drove British goods from the shops I thought of that radio and wasn't surprised.

On the way back to the hotel we came across something else very German or Austrian – a group of young men on the other side of the road pushing people off the pavement, punching them and slapping them in the face. They passed us by, but it was an unsettling incident.

The next morning as the Hungarian Railways train headed east from Austria the weather gradually became hotter and the landscape outside the windows slowly changed. I noticed grain that was stacked in unfamiliar ways, I saw fields of sunflowers and peppers for the first time, white-washed houses with reed roofs and storks nesting in the chimney pots, horse-drawn carts on dirt tracks. At the border between Austria and Hungary we spotted a group of British miners who were so overcome to be leaving Hungary that they were in tears.

Once in Budapest we were put up in a grand baroque hotel, reserved solely for the use of foreigners, on the banks of the Danube. The imposing public rooms swarmed with citizens from all across the Soviet Empire mixed with people like us, Westerners who had come to marvel at a real-life workers' state. Though I was a child I was good on atmospheres: having no older brother or sister to ask what they thought might be going on meant I quickly became attuned to changes in the psychic weather in a room. I suppose I got a lot of practice, since having Molly for a mother was like living in the emotional equivalent of Darwin in northern Australia where there are fifteen lightning storms a day. So in that big hotel by the Danube with its sweeping staircase I began to notice that there was one group of comrades who, though they went un-noticed by the Westerners, seemed to send an uneasy *frisson* through the hotel's staff and some of the other guests from the East. These people were the Russians.

There must have been Russians around during our two trips to Czechoslovakia, but this was the first time I had been amongst them as a distinct group and it was only the slight apprehensiveness that followed them which drew my attention. In a bar at the top of the stairs there was one Russian who seemed especially fond of me. As my parents looked on, smiling, he sat me on his knee, and as the smell of vodka and onions cascaded over his metal teeth he pressed gift after gift on me. This Russian must have been in the Soviet air force, some sort of 'adviser' perhaps, because amongst the things he gave me were a pilot's wings, first class, and a huge golden cap badge with laurel leaves, a red star and a hammer and sickle at the centre.

After three trips to the East I now had a lot of stuff like this – stuff that I didn't really know what to do with. I did briefly wonder whether having pilot's wings might entitle me to take the controls of a Mig 17 fighter jet with no further training. I told the kids at school that it did, but never put it to the test.

It was hard to stop people in Communist countries giving you things. They were particularly keen on badges, the usual images of Marx and Lenin but also little metal sputniks and national flags. My parents already possessed Liverpool's largest collection of Bohemian glass, oddly shaped bowls in red glass shot through with little air bubbles and decanters and wine glasses tinted in shades of blue and yellow. What I seemed to have ended up with mostly were pennants. The walls of my bedroom were already covered with these triangular pieces of shiny silk celebrating youth conferences in East Germany that I hadn't attended and Brazilian football clubs I had previously been unaware of. Every day I was in Hungary I acquired more souvenirs that I didn't know what to do with. When I got home I put my pennants on the wall and then thought, 'Now what?'

By the age of ten or eleven I had, either with other boys or on my own, taken part in train-spotting, car-spotting, bird-watching and egg-gathering. In a rudimentary fashion I had tried to collect comics, rocks, toy cars and butterflies. But each time at some point I had been plagued with the twin thoughts 'Now what?' and 'Is that it?' At which point I always abandoned my latest hobby. I kept trying and trying, but perhaps I just didn't have that collector's impulse or maybe it was simply that my hobby and my family's hobby was the elimination of private property via the violent expropriation of landowners, industrialists, railroad magnates and shipowners, organisation of labour on publicly owned land, in factories and workshops, with competition among the workers being abolished and centralisation of money and credit in the hands of the state through a national bank and the suppression of all private banks and bankers. So writing down numbers in a book was likely to have a hard time competing with that.

For a while I tried to get into Airfix kits. With the occasional and sporadic help of my dad, at the table in the living room, I put together, very badly, a model of the battle cruiser *Warspite* and a Fairey Barracuda dive-bomber, painted them, put on the appropriate insignia and sat back with the usual sense of dissatisfaction. Then I had an idea: the next time I got my pocket money I hurried down to the toy shop and bought not one but two kits. One was for a Lancaster bomber and the other was of an SRN1 hovercraft. I then sat at the dining table and proceeded to combine them, so what I ended up with was a gluey lump which was basically a hovercraft with four Merlin engines, large wings and a number of swivelling turrets equipped with machine guns. I thought to myself, 'This is more like it.' Rather than just accruing things, arranging them and exulting in my possession of them I was making a new and original thing – a Bombercraft or a Hovercaster. I played with my Hovercaster for a while, then tired of it and set it alight in the back yard. Due to the massive amounts of glue employed in its construction the mongrel model caught fire very quickly and burned with great intensity.

The Shores of Lake Balaton

We spent a week in Budapest, then travelled sixty miles to Lake Balaton which we were proudly told was the largest body of water in central Europe, as if the slow accumulation of rainwater in a hole over thousands of years was in itself an achievement of socialism. We were to spend the second half of our holiday in a union-owned motel on the shores of the lake. The area round about had in the late 1950s become a sort of Malibu for revolutionaries. Fidel Castro, Mao Tse-tung, Leonid Brezhnev and cosmonaut Yuri Gagarin all had villas on the south-east shore, furnished in the latest 1950s'/1960s' modernist style.

Alexei Sayle

The place where we were staying was a white, modern, single-storey building with rooms clustered around a central courtyard and its own private beach. After the troubles of the 1950s Hungary had been given a degree of freedom not allowed in other states of the Soviet Empire, so food at our motel was plentiful, colourful and sumptuous. Back in Anfield we had thought with a certain amount of pride that on Sundays we had been eating salad, but really all we had been eating was lettuce and tomatoes in a bowl, sometimes with a hard-boiled egg on the top and no dressing except perhaps the industrial solvent known as 'salad cream'. Now I saw what a salad really could be under socialism. There were red, green and yellow peppers, corn on the cob, huge tomatoes stuffed with Russian salad, artichokes, celery, lentils, okra and fresh herbs, all of them covered in rich oils or mayonnaise.

Until our holiday in Hungary all my summers had been spent in Northern countries, and this was the first time I had encountered the true sensuous heat of the South. My skin was toasted brown by the hot sun and occasionally my parents let me sip the warm red Hungarian wine known as Bull's Blood. Meals were always accompanied by gypsies playing violins whether you wanted them to or not. In Lake Balaton I learned to swim. It seemed that Communism could do amazing things for a person, just as it could for salad. I had spent hours in the swimming baths at junior school splashily drowning, but the waters of the lake were so buoyant that I could float with only a finger holding me up and from there I simply lifted my arm and drifted free. This gave me a great sense of achievement. I had started to worry that I wasn't the sort of kid who could swim, that I was teetering on the edge of being some sort of pallid, inactive mummy's boy who stayed in the house and collected things and possibly played with dolls – but here I was swimming. I would dive down beneath the surface and cruise just above the sandy bottom of the lake, holding my breath for what seemed like minutes on end. Then I would kick upwards to emerge like an arrow into the bright sunlight, wondering if Mao Tse-tung wasn't watching me from the shore with frank admiration.

Behind our motel in the pine woods there was a campsite, with tents scattered under the trees on the spongy ground. The people who stayed in these tents were only allowed access to a scrubby bit of public sand and were forbidden from using our stretch of perfect beach. Our family's only experience of campsites had been those unfortunate first days in Czechoslovakia, so we didn't consider it a practice that anybody would actually choose to indulge in. But one day while walking through the woods I came upon a brand-new, dark red Vauxhall Victor, bearing British number plates, parked next to a large tent. A Western automobile was a very rare sight on the roads of a Communist country, where even Soviet Bloc cars such as Skodas and Trabants were extremely scarce. As I passed there was a small crowd of young Hungarian men trying to see into the interior of the car.

A little while later my parents met the people who owned this Vauxhall – they were a family from London, husband, wife and their two sons who were about the same age as me. I knew right away that these people were what I had heard my parents frequently refer to as 'progressives'. Calling them 'progressives' meant that, while definitely not Communists, they were people who were generally sympathetic to ideas of social progress and liberalism. In the world of my parents there was a whole taxonomy, with 'party member' at its centre and radiating outwards, classifying the political allegiance of people you met or saw on the television. Closest to party member was 'fellow traveller', indicating people who, without being party members, had distinct Communist sympathies – they came to big meetings, read the *Daily Worker*, and you could trust them to mind the shop while you were out. Next came 'fellow revolutionaries' – all manner of anarchists, nationalists and socialists who you might make a temporary alliance with and then when they ceased to be useful you would try to kill them and they would try to kill you. After fellow revolutionaries came 'reformists', which in Britain meant members of the Labour Party, people who thought you could round off the corners of capitalism without doing away with it. Then came 'progressives'. Lenin was said to have another term for those progressives of a liberal bent who came and wrote admiringly about the Soviet Union: he called them 'useful idiots'. Then there was a list of people and organisations who were completely unacceptable to us. These included fascists, Trotskyists, Conservatives, the Blundells at number 7 and the British Transport Police.

There didn't seem anything the least bit odd to me in classifying people according to their usefulness, sometimes just from their footwear. 'Ah, yes,' you'd say to yourself. 'Desert boots. This person is clearly a progressive with pacifist tendencies.'

* * *

The Vauxhall Victors were, with their brand-new car and nice accents, clearly a lot better off than us but also they appeared to be a lot more naïve. Our enthusiasm for the East, for Communism, was the zeal of the professional whereas they just seemed to be terribly enthusiastic, in a middle-class kind of a way, about everything they had seen in Hungary. What I couldn't understand was why they were staying in a tent and swimming from the public beach. Didn't they know anybody in the party?

That autumn, on a cold and misty November day we went to visit the Vauxhall Victors. They lived in a suburb of south-east London called Forest Hill. Because of the freedom of travel conferred by our passes me, Molly and Joe would sometimes decide to drop in on people who lived hundreds of miles away. Occasionally I suspected that these people were a little discomfited that we had come so far to see them at such short notice. On this trip I became conscious for the first time of the terrible vastness of London. As our local train stopped at yet another station, passed through yet another neighbourhood, ran alongside another park, overtook another town hall I thought what a daunting city it must be to live in and I imagined you would have to be a very confident person just to go down to the shops.

Mr Vauxhall Victor picked us up in the car from the nearest Southern Region station, then we drove past even more parades of shops and down more streets of suburban villas and large semis until finally, after about a week, we came to their enormous double-fronted Victorian house. This was the first middle-class property I had ever been in and it was a very different place from the austere homes of Valley Road. We were shown into a large living room with French windows leading to a garden that seemed as unending as the suburbs in the gathering twilight. There were paintings on the walls, books stuffed higgledy-piggledy on the shelves and brass music stands with sheet music on them in the middle of the floor.

My parents were chatting inconsequentially to the couple when I, who never thought that my interventions might be unwelcome, remarked on what a lot of coloured people we had passed on the way to their house. Immediately a look of panic passed over the faces of the couple. I reckon they knew as few of the proletariat as we did of the petit-bourgeois and they secretly suspected, as a lot of the liberal middle classes did, that all working-class people harboured racist views. Now, right here in their home, one of them was openly expressing these opinions. I took their silence to mean that they hadn't understood what I was saying, so I attempted to make it clearer. 'You know,' I said. 'Blacks, negroes, you've got loads of them round here.'

Then they gave us tea, and afterwards the two sons played classical music for us. I think one of them played the flute rocking backwards and forwards, eyes closed, lost to the world. It was late evening when the father gave us a lift back to the local station. As we waited on the foggy platform, without needing to say it out loud me, Molly and Joe agreed never to do that again.

(27)
This Might Be It, People

The reason I had noticed how many black people there were in south-east London, wasn't racism but rather extreme envy. My parents had gone to a lot of trouble to tell me about racial prejudice and what a bad thing it was, and so over the years I had become desperate to express my tolerance and solidarity to a black person at the earliest opportunity. Unfortunately Anfield was more or less a hundred per cent white, so there were no minorities for me to show my lack of racial prejudice to.

Then one happy day a black man started walking down Valley Road in the mornings – presumably on his way to work, or perhaps he was a student at the university. I took to sitting in the bay window of the sitting room waiting for him; then, when he appeared, I would rush out and stand in front of him so he had to stop. I would be wearing a big smile on my face, a smile that I thought radiated a beatific sense of liberality. Then I would say, 'Hello!' to him in as unprejudiced way as I could, so he would understand that here was one British person who didn't think he was inferior in any way. In fact this small British person thought he was probably superior, since his suffering had given him all kinds of insights which white people couldn't guess at and he was almost certainly good at dancing too. After a while he stopped walking down our street, presumably taking another route to work.

*   *   *

Towards the end of 1962 I came to test everybody's tolerance for me, when throughout that autumn the entire world was thrown into an enormous panic by the Cuban Missile Crisis. For a few months nuclear war between the Soviet Union and the United States seemed not just a possibility but almost a certainty. In October of that year reconnaissance photographs taken by an American U-2 spy plane revealed missile bases being built in Cuba, prompting a US blockade and an armed confrontation between the superpowers. Unlike the rest of the country number 5 Valley Road remained an oasis of calm. We knew the truth of the matter, and it wasn't what everybody else believed.

Me, Molly and Joe believed that the whole crisis was simply a pretext, part of a shrewd plan conceived by the Communist Premier Nikita Khrushchev. Rather than being caught out trying to militarise the Caribbean, the Soviet Union had deliberately created the emergency. It was in fact a brilliant strategy designed to force the USA into agreeing to never again invade Cuba (something they had tried the previous year at the Bay of Pigs) and to remove the nuclear missiles which they had recently installed in eastern Turkey along the Russian border. All this would be achieved in exchange for the Russians simply dismantling some rockets which they hadn't really wanted to put into Cuba in the first place.

Unfortunately, apart from members of the British Communist Party such as us nobody else in the UK was in on the ruse. So while I remained eerily calm all the other kids at school, their parents and the teachers were experiencing a great deal of stress. As far as they knew, the world was in very real danger of imminent extinction. During those two frantic weeks there were reports on the TV and radio and in the newspapers of demonstrations, candle-lit vigils, suicides and people building nuclear bunkers in their back gardens – everywhere you went there was a tense atmosphere. In the midst of this febrile mood I would sit in class with a knowing smile on my face giving everyone the thumbs-up sign, or I would walk along Oakfield Road whistling, grinning and saying to passers-by who I thought looked especially worried, 'No need to fret – it's all going exactly to plan. Mr Khrushchev's got it in hand. They don't want them missiles there anyway.' This made people feel even more disturbed and upset, since they now believed the situation had become so intense that an olive-skinned child in a knitted tank-top had been driven mad by world events.

The Undoing of Pemberton

In 1962 we took our third trip to Czechoslovakia. Again Joe had put together a delegation of railwaymen including Prendergast, Alf and his friend. But this time I too would be taking a companion, a boy from school who was my best friend. By the age of ten a clear distinction was already emerging in the way children behaved with each other. Some kids at school or in the street were popular types who had a big circle of mates, while others were loners who kept to themselves. And then there was me, who occupied some odd middle ground. I was a serial best-friender. I would become close to one other boy and spend all my time with him. I would invest all my emotions in him and visit his house constantly, dropping in at all times of the day and night whether I was invited or not. Eventually there would come a point where my best friend would let me down in some way – lie to me about where he was going, or leave me waiting for him at some agreed spot and never turn up. After that I would refuse ever to speak to him again and would have to embark on the whole tedious business of finding a replacement. So far I had had three best friends: a boy called Colin Noakes, another named 'Tubby' Dowling, and now I was on to my third, a boy from junior school named Peter Pemberton.

Peter lived in a big Victorian house off Breck Road, a busy shopping street about a quarter of a mile away from Valley Road. Naturally I spent a great deal of time at his house, which had a long, overgrown garden leading to a group of ramshackle workshops in a mews behind. We used to climb on to the roof of these sheds and pull off bits of lead which we tried unsuccessfully to fashion into coins for use in slot machines.

In terms of friendships I was very much self-taught, the Communist Party was no use in this department, since it viewed all human relationships as no more than tools for bringing about the proletarian revolution. My parents were both very popular in their own ways but I wanted to make friendships in my own distinctive fashion, radically different from theirs. So what I ended up with were relationships that were wonkity things very much like the model Airfix kits I made – badly constructed, eccentric in appearance and liable to burst into flames.

Me and Peter were such good friends that I decided it would be perfect if he came to Czechoslovakia with us. Despite already having had several friendships founder, I remained relentlessly optimistic that this one would be fine. I thought it would only make things better if we took Peter on holiday with us. Then I wouldn't be with my parents all the time and would have a best friend of my own age to play with. That's what I told myself, but I think the real reason I wanted Peter Pemberton with us was that I would have somebody to show off to. Given what went wrong, I think that what I was after was a passive and admiring audience, for him to sit in awe while I explained the wonders of eastern Europe, told him how incredible they were and how incredible I was for being so familiar with them.

Peter's parents can't have been rich and it must have been an effort for them to get the money together to pay for such a trip, yet as far as I can remember they did it willingly. I was convinced we were going to have the best time anybody had ever had ever. In fact, of course, I was far too worked up and expecting far too much from a holiday, so that once we got to Czechoslovakia and things weren't perfect in every respect I turned into an absolute monster.

The delegation spent the first week in Prague and the second in the countryside, on this occasion at a resort in the High Tatra mountains. Everywhere we went I tried to point things out to Peter. 'Look,' I would say when we were in the department store opposite our hotel. 'Isn't it fantastic? They've only got one kind of pen for sale here and on the box it just says "Pen" in Czech.' I was showing him this because I had become fascinated by the products on the shelves in the shops in Czechoslovakia and Hungary, their graphics and their packaging. Unlike a department store in Britain there was only one of everything – one style of pen, one brand of toothpaste, a single type of soap, and all very simply packaged. I found something attractive in this utilitarianism, the bold use of colour, the blocky shapes and the simple lettering.

Peter had no idea what I was going on about. 'What's so good about there being only one kind of pen?' he would ask. 'I've got two pens back home and they're both different.'

I wasn't able to articulate what it was that I felt about the pen and its box and why it was so important that he understood what I meant, even though I didn't really know what I meant either. And that would make me really angry with him.

And then we went to the mountains and my behaviour got much worse. We had been playing table tennis in the hotel's recreation room and suddenly I found I was attacking him with my bat. I was hitting him and hitting him and he didn't seem to be feeling the blows, and that made me even more angry with him so I hit him some more.

Then for a while I would calm down and we would be friends again, but my insane behaviour would inevitably reappear. I can't imagine what it was like for the poor boy, being trapped thousands of miles from home behind the Iron Curtain with a crazy person who kept attacking him. Maybe that's why he never seemed to react.

At the end of two unhappy weeks our homeward-bound train stopped on the border between Czechoslovakia and Austria.

We were forced to get down and hang about for an hour or so, wandering about on the low concrete platform. There was generally a long delay at the frontier when you were leaving a Communist country. People's papers had to be checked more assiduously than on the inbound journey, since while there weren't many people trying to get into the Soviet Bloc there were a lot trying to get out.

The border station was little more than a halt, really. Nobody ever got on here or got off unless they were being chased into the woods by the guards, but unlike most other railway stations in the world this one was equipped with a line of wooden machine gun towers, row after row of barbed wire, an actual minefield and a shop. The shop was the other reason why they held you at the border for over an hour. When you left Czechoslovakia or any other Communist country you weren't allowed to take any of their currency with you. The rulers didn't want to have to convert their money, which was worthless outside the Warsaw Pact countries, back to pounds, francs or dollars, losing some of their precious Western cash which they could use to buy luxury goods for themselves. So on the border there would always be a shop stocked with peculiar products offered at ludicrously high prices and staffed by the extremely unhelpful family members of the frontier guards. Here you were forced to spend any krona or zloty that you hadn't managed to get rid of while in their country.

These border railway stations, with their armed guards and barking dogs and sinister secret policemen watching everybody with cruel eyes, were always disturbing places, but the shops themselves possessed an even more depressing atmosphere.

They were like badly attended museums of failed products, their dusty shelves lined with crudely made folk items, kitchen implements of no conceivable use, jars of peas in vinegar and boxes of pre-war liqueur chocolates, filled with a cherry brandy that had long ago evaporated leaving nothing but a toxic sludge behind. It always took a long time to buy anything in these places, since your main thought was to try and figure out what would be the least inconvenient thing to carry right across Europe. But on that particular day I was in the shop till the train whistle blew for the final time, desperately searching the shelves, thinking I might find something to buy for Peter Pemberton, some wonderful product that would make up for the way I had treated him. But of course there was nothing.

An Inside Man

At the age of eleven I began attending Alsop Grammar School for Boys, and being born in August I was one of the youngest in my class. I had taken and passed the eleven-plus exam the previous spring. As soon as the results were announced – who was going to grammar school, who had failed the exam and was going to secondary modern or technical schools – a kind of poison spread through the street. There was a boy from the other end of Valley Road who I had been friendly with and who had failed the exam, and from that moment he never walked past our house but would circle round and go down the next street rather than risk bumping into me. At least that's what Molly told me – though maybe he just didn't like me and she was putting a socio-political gloss on it.

It was a scary thought going to big school, but the anxiety was made easier to bear in my case because of the fact that, as Communists usually did, we had made sure that we already had a man on the inside. In fact we had two men on the inside. One was on the staff, a maths teacher called Bill Abrahams who had been in the party for many years and was a long-time friend of Joe's. The other was a pupil, a boy a couple of years older than myself called Cliff Cocker whose parents, Maeve and Len, were also long-standing members of the CP from the southern end of the city.

On the first day, in my new school uniform of blazer, short trousers, cap, shirt, and black and green striped tie, I walked with a couple of other kids who were going to Alsop to the bus stop on Priory Road. There we caught the number 68 bus to ride the two miles or so to our new school.

Compared with the friendly and familiar scale of our neighbourhood junior school Alsop seemed huge and threatening. At the rear there was a long sandstone wall which backed on to Walton Village, an early Victorian hamlet of narrow terraced streets with a row of small shops and a church. Those of us who caught the 68 entered via the rear gate in the wall and the first building we saw, standing in front of a patch of dark and overgrown woodland, was a three-storey house built in the Gothic Revival style and known as the Rectory. To a troop of small boys already in a state of heightened emotion it appeared spooky and lowering, built as it was from blocks of blood-red, carved sandstone with an open porch of three broad pointed arches, a huge black painted wooden front door with studs in it and arched mullioned windows. I would have thought it was the sort of house a vampire lived in if I hadn't been aware that vampire stories were superstitious legends designed to subjugate the enslaved rural classes into unquestioning obedience of feudal autocracy.

In a tight little group we approached the main building, a stock school of the 1920s which faced on to Queen's Drive, Liverpool's inner ring road. After the Second World War further structures had been added in a haphazard fashion, each of them built in the dullest example of the architectural style of their period – a dining annexe, an assembly hall, a library and an art room, then later a new block with laboratories, a gym and the metalwork shop. All of it formed a rough square of buildings enclosing a sports field of springy green grass with a running track and a cricket field marked out in fresh white paint.

Somehow we were marshalled into the school's assembly hall where we were addressed by the headmaster, Mr L.W. Warren, who was known as Les or the Bazz. He had a thin moustache, Brylcreemed hair and, like most of the teachers, he always wore a flapping black gown. Mr Warren gave us his speech of welcome before we were sent off to find our classes. Right away I encountered a problem familiar to all those involved in espionage. My control, Molly, had given me inadequate information for identifying my fellow Communist agent amongst the schoolboy cadre. The only thing my mother had told me about Cliff Cocker was that he was a boy with black hair and glasses. The first morning at grammar school was unsettling. First we were given an incomprehensible chart telling us where all our lessons were – it came as a shock to me that you had to move around, rather than your teachers. The only thing that allowed me to remain calm was the thought that as soon as I located Cliff Cocker he would explain everything and assuage all my confusion.

My plan was that lunchtime would be the best time for me to hook up with my fellow comrade, to begin the vital work of bringing Marxist-Leninist thought to our school, or at least for him to let me know me where the dining hall was. So when the lunchtime bell rang and we were ejected into the playground I went up to the first bigger boy I saw with black hair and glasses and stood in front of him, smiling in much the same way as I had done with the black man who used to walk down Valley Road. 'Hello, Cliff!' I said. 'Long live Lenin! Long live the proletariat!' To his credit I don't think this bigger boy, whoever he was, actually hit me, but he made it very clear that he wasn't at all pleased at being addressed by some new kid and he told me very forcefully to get lost.

All morning, because I had been hanging on to the thought of Cliff Cocker as my saviour I hadn't bothered trying to get to know any of the other kids in my class, nor had I paid any attention to what was being said to me about school rules or where anything was. After losing that first vital morning it took me months to catch up, if I ever did, and it was several years before I got to know Cliff Cocker. I did meet

Mr Abrahams on that first day – indeed it was impossible to avoid him since he was teaching my class first-year maths. Mr Abrahams took an instant dislike to me. The Abe, as everybody called him, was a Jewish Communist who was mad about cricket, maths and Everton football club. I was useless at the first two and didn't much care about the third. He may also have found me annoying because he was a strict disciplinarian, while I might have got the idea from somewhere that since we were comrades in the proletarian struggle it was perfectly fine for me to address him as Bill in class. Which he didn't like at all.

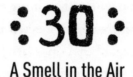

A Smell in the Air

A few weeks before I went to grammar school, in the summer of 1963, Joe led his first delegation of railwaymen to Hungary. I assumed I was really going to enjoy our second trip to the land of the Magyars. After all, there was no Pemberton to enrage me and this was a country where on our first visit several important and pleasurable things had happened – I had learned to swim and had come to understand the true meaning of salad. But the holiday unfortunately coincided with a change in the way I saw things. I suppose it was one of those cognitive shifts that everybody goes through as they grow up, but in me it always seemed to take a violent and abrupt form – the sudden opening of a trap door rather than something more gradual and easier to get used to. Up until that point, even if I was confused by events I sort of accepted them, assuming that somewhere out there was a single, simple explanation for what was going on. In Hungary I started for the first time to be aware of the shifting sands of human relations, to see that there was often no simple explanation for what was happening; rather, there were a thousand explanations and none at all.

Yet when we embarked on the journey I was still hoping that somehow I could rediscover my previous certainty, that I could find the equanimity that had deserted me. Sadly, if you are beginning to feel unsettled about people's motivation then visiting a country from which some six hundred thousand citizens were deported to Soviet labour camps after the Second World War, where they spoke a weird Finno-Ugric language completely unrelated to those around it, where there were great tensions between the various ethnic groupings, Hungarian, Romanian and gypsy, and where a revolution had been brutally suppressed only seven years before, probably wasn't a good idea.

As soon as we left the main railway station I noticed a distinctive smell in the air which I hadn't really noticed on our previous trip. A lot of the buses and trucks in Hungary used some sort of cheap diesel that had a strong aroma and formed clouds of black smoke that blew everywhere. And the trucks expelling these noxious clouds, though they were carrying commercial goods, were military or ex-military vehicles, with long bonnets and a hatch for a machine gun in the roof of the cab. And waiting for us outside the station, coughing out its own cloud of black smoke, wasn't the fleet of Tatras we were used to but a coach.

We drove to our hotel, which once more was on the banks of the Danube. From the window of my room I could see the famous Chain Bridge, the Széchenyi lánchíd that linked Buda and Pest and beyond it the Adam Clark Tunnel which ran under the hill beneath the Buda Castle. In front of the tunnel was a big traffic roundabout and on that roundabout the Russians had placed what was supposedly the first T34 tank to have liberated the city in 1945, its 75mm gun pointing directly at the window of my hotel room. As we travelled around the country I noticed that most towns seemed to possess their own T34. Certainly as a memorial it was a powerful reminder of the Second World War and the sacrifices that the Soviet Union had made to defeat the Nazis. But there was also a threat there – after all, it was only a few years ago that the sisters of these tanks had suppressed the Hungarian uprising, and it was as if the Russians were saying that it wouldn't take long for them to return.

In Budapest there was a trade union leader called Szabo who fulfilled the same role as Prukha in Czechoslovakia, but he never came to Britain and, though we spent a lot of time together, there was never quite the same affection between us; the Czechs were our first love and we wouldn't allow ourselves to get too close to anyone else. Our translator, another brittle blonde, became a major source of confusion for me. For some reason we were visiting a radio station when somebody in the group rather bravely asked our translator a question about the '56 uprising and the bullet marks all over the city. Her reply was that the revolt had been the work of 'bandits' whose only motivation was that they wanted to kill policemen. My parents and the rest of the delegation seemed to think this a reasonable explanation. Later, as we were travelling around the city's ring road on our bus and passed some bleak concrete apartment blocks, she made some dismissive remarks about gypsies, saying that the authorities had tried to house them in nice modern flats but they had used their front doors for firewood. Nobody else appeared to object to her remarks even though I had been told that Communism was supposed to have eradicated these types of attitudes. Yet here they still were.

A few months after we returned from Hungary our unpleasant translator managed to come to England. When she reached Liverpool she came to stay with us for a few days, but cut her visit short because she was appalled by our poverty. She had expected us to have a big house and a car to take her around in, but instead we found ourselves being pitied for being poor by somebody from a Communist country!

While we were in Budapest we also paid a visit to the railway run by my fellow comrades in the Hungarian Young Pioneers. Not only did they run it, in the early 1950s they had actually built the twelve kilometres of narrow-gauge line that ran through the Buda hills. The carriages were painted red and white and seemed to be about half the size of a standard coach, though with normal seats and luggage racks, so I felt a bit like I was riding through a forest in one of the passenger cars from my Hornby train set.

Nearly all the work was done by children, who bore a serious, pompous, self-important look as if the chess club at school had been given their own railway to run. The junior guards and adolescent signal operators were dressed in the normal Young Pioneer costumes of white shirt, shorts and red neckerchief but with the addition of a peaked cap, while for the more senior staff, such as the child stationmaster or juvenile ticket collector, there was a special dark blue uniform, a small-scale replica of what grown-up Hungarian railwaymen and railwaywomen wore. Clearly there were only a few of these uniforms to go round and they tended to be on the large side – the sleeves would dangle way beyond the boy or girl's hands and their caps covered most of their heads. Their ill-fitting suits gave you the feeling that your ticket was being punched by one of the chimps that advertised tea on the television.

At the start of our second week, on the way to Lake Balaton in our coach, beside a field of maize we came upon an ambulance blocking the road and a crowd of people gathered around the body of a teenager who had been knocked off his motorbike and killed. It was the first dead body I had ever seen. I thought things like that didn't happen in a socialist state – that young men got knocked off their motorbikes in the corrupt West but not here on this road in the workers' paradise.

The most enduring thing that came from our second trip to Hungary, apart from a nascent sense of unease about the Communist experiment, was the nickname applied to me throughout my early years at Alsop. During the first week we had a double games period and not showering wasn't an option, so I had to get changed in front of the other boys in my class. I had always bronzed easily and, because of our week on the sandy beaches of Lake Balaton under the hot Hungarian sun, apart from a white strip where my swimming trunks had been my skin was deeply tanned. Some other boy, noticing my dark complexion, decided to give me the nickname Sambo. And that was what I was called for the first couple of years – Sambo Sayle.

My nickname clearly wasn't meant kindly but I don't honestly remember being bothered by being known as Sambo, and in a time when you could still buy nigger brown paint in the hardware store such a racist epithet didn't quite have the force it would have today. But the truth was that I was such an oddly wired-together child that, while the most innocuous events could send me sideways, things that were intended to annoy, bother or intimidate me simply didn't. Plus as a last resort, like a sort of superpower, I had inherited a version of Molly's rage, so if a situation started to look like it was going bad I was able to turn from dreamy good humour to snarling, unhinged fury in a split second – which was enough to put most people off messing or indeed in some cases eating their lunch with me.

Anyway, after a couple of years my nickname was contracted to Sam.

At the age of eleven, when I had begun attending Alsop Grammar School, I was still quite a small boy. Once I was into my early teens, however, my body quickly began to grow, until by the third year I was above average height for my age, with thick black hair sprouting almost everywhere and short but extremely strong legs. The only parts of my body that weren't covered in hair and hadn't grown explosively were my arms, which remained as thin and slender as a consumptive girl's in a

Victorian novel. This was probably a blessing. If my arms had matched my stocky legs in strength I might have been sorely tempted to become a proper bully, because I would have been able to hit people very hard. As it was, I possessed the look of somebody who, as long as they didn't take their shirt off, could handle themselves, without actually having the ability to do so. As a result of my appearance, and since I couldn't be provoked, was funny and in an emergency could go completely nuts, I was able to be on good enough terms with the real hard cases, which meant that I didn't get bullied but on the other hand I was not tempted to be a hard case myself.

After attending Alsop for a couple of years the people I did end up bullying were the staff. Because he had never liked me I never missed a chance to annoy the Jewish Communist Mr Abrahams. I messed about in all science classes, seeing myself as more of an artistic type, and refused to pay any attention at all during religious education lessons, which in those days meant the Old and New Testaments, thus depriving myself of any understanding of the foundation of nearly all Western art and literature. However, it was a highly strung English teacher called Mr Johnson who I picked on the most. When discussing any work of literature I would argue with him vehemently for hours on end, using up entire lessons, taking as my viewpoint an unwavering but mostly misunderstood Marxism combined with an all-purpose half-baked radicalism. Just as academics were doing in all the new universities springing up across the country – cutting-edge institutions with concrete campuses, artificial lakes, meandering paths and clumps of vegetation ideal for lurking sex offenders to hide themselves in. Still, such behaviour was unusual in a thirteen-year-old schoolboy and a lot of the teachers didn't know how to deal with it. I wasn't being disruptive in a conventional sense, but on the other hand they could see I wasn't trying to help either.

In some ways I was the prototype of a new-type school student who would be arriving in larger numbers in later years – vain, argumentative and nebulously anti-authoritarian. And if I was a new type of pupil, Molly was definitely a model of parent they had never encountered before. At junior school she had occasionally interfered, getting me moved up a class because she felt my academic abilities weren't being recognised, but at Alsop my mother adopted the practice of coming down to the school unannounced if she felt I was being persecuted or my education was being adversely affected in some way. There was also an incident at a parent-teacher meeting, round about my third year. The usual drill at these things was that parents moved from teacher to teacher, sitting at a desk in the hall. The teacher told the parents their child was either stupid and would most likely become a fireman or clever and should consider carpet retailing as a career, and the parents gratefully accepted this information. Not Molly. One of the first teachers she approached told her they weren't going to let me do physics and chemistry any more because I was so incompetent. Rather I would be taking some lame hybrid, supposedly so I could spend more time studying O-Level art. This prompted my mother to stand and make a speech to the entire hall about how no false divisions should be made between the arts and the sciences, invoking the spirit of the Russian composer Shostakovich who she mistakenly thought had a science degree.

It was poor Mr Johnson who reacted most badly to being tag-teamed by the Sayles, mother and son. He was supposed to take our class for general studies as well as English, but after a while he refused to deal with two doses of me in a week and handed the class over to a more phlegmatic teacher, Mr Lucie, because he was afraid of what Molly would do to him if he taught me the wrong thing.

During my early grammar school years I hadn't given up on my ambitions to be an athlete and still occasionally trained with the Walton Harriers. As soon as I arrived at Alsop I signed up for the school's cross-country team. My thinking was that, despite my early success in the hundred yards dash, the sprint wasn't my discipline so maybe a longer distance would suit me better. Alsop's football and cricket squads did reasonably well in inter-city championships, but the cross-country team was not a premium outfit. In fact we were pretty useless, and I was far and away the worst member of the squad.

We would have training runs round Walton Hall Park, opposite the school, in the evenings. The teachers would be desperate to get the run over with so they could go to the pub, but they couldn't leave until I came huffing up a good twenty minutes after all the other boys. Maybe they suspected me of subversion, but I really wasn't trying to finish last. It was just that, despite putting all my effort into it, I would always come in way behind the rest. Even though I had cut the corners off a couple of fields, rowed across a boating lake and burrowed through a hedge in order to shorten my route.

The cross-country team generally competed on a Saturday

morning. I would travel to unfamiliar parts of the city on the bus, then meet up with my team-mates to run through parks, fields and ancient woodland. What I liked most about being in an athletics squad was that after the race we often got given a very nice spread provided by the other boys' mums, with homemade cakes, sandwiches containing unusual commercial fillings and unhealthy-looking drinks in a selection of vivid colours that I wouldn't be allowed to drink at home.

The only success we ever achieved, beating another team and me coming in third from last rather than last, was when we competed against a team from a Catholic school in the south end of the city who were already, by the age of twelve, heavy smokers. I was filled with a transcendent sense of triumph as I stumbled, covered in mud, past one white-faced adolescent after another as they sat gasping on tree stumps clutching their sides or sprawled vomiting in the claggy grass.

31

Making a Profit from Nuclear War

In November 1957 J.B. Priestley wrote an article for the *New Statesman* entitled 'Britain and the Nuclear Bombs', which proposed the idea of unilateral nuclear disarmament. The magazine received a great many letters of support for Priestley's article and it led to the founding of CND – the Campaign for Nuclear Disarmament.

The following Easter a march from London to the Atomic Weapons Research Establishment at Aldermaston was organised by a group called the Direct Action Committee, supported by CND after some initial reluctance. Thereafter, CND took over the organising of the annual Easter marches starting at Aldermaston and ending in London. Sixty thousand people participated in the 1959 march and a hundred and fifty thousand in the 1961 and 1962 marches.

The Communist Party had an ambivalent attitude to CND. They thought they should support it because it was popular and anti-government, and there were opportunities for recruitment to the party if they sent members on the marches. What they really wanted was for the West to give up its nuclear weapons while the USSR hung on to theirs, but they couldn't really say that – they had to pretend they were in favour of everybody giving up their bombs.

On the matter of the Aldermaston marches I took a different atittude from the party's. Glen Cocker, Cliff's older brother, had been on the very first demonstration and one night, somewhere between Berkshire and London, he had lost his virginity on the floor of a village hall to a female demonstrator. When I watched footage of the protests on the TV news, I always got an erotic *frisson* from seeing grainy film of people in duffel coats trudging through spring rain, accompanied by the music of a trad jazz band.

You couldn't say that the British left has produced many timeless classics of graphic design. In fact there is only one, the badge of the CND, a motif which has gone on to become the universal symbol of peace and the visual representation of a decade. It remains a masterpiece. Designed in 1958 by a man called Gerald Holtom, the badge is based on the semaphore symbols for N and D placed within a circle. Holtom later said that it also symbolised 'an individual in despair, with hands palm outstretched outwards and downwards in the manner of Goya's peasant before the firing squad'. The CND badge quickly became a fashion item, particularly because for young people it was something of a breakthrough. Previously if you had wanted to advertise your radical credentials you had to invest in a whole new wardrobe or even actually do something radical, but now you could attain the same effect simply by wearing a shiny metal badge – except that these badges quickly became almost completely unavailable, at least in Liverpool. It was an odd experience – something connected with what we did had become the height of fashion and I suddenly became the centre of attention, with kids at school showing a previously undisclosed interest in coming on marches and joining CND.

I knew that what they really wanted were the rare badges and I sensed an opportunity. Through my network of left-wing activists (Molly and Joe) I discovered that a woman called Pat Arrowsmith, a famous peace campaigner and founder member of CND who had once been force-fed while on hunger strike in prison, was living near us in a little house off Breck Road. One afternoon I walked round there and knocked on the door. It was answered by a woman with very short hair wearing a checked shirt of a very mannish cut. 'Excuse me, Pat,' I said, 'I'm a young schoolboy very interested in the peace movement, planning to start my own branch of CND, and I was wondering whether you had any badges . . . you know, for the kids at school? To get us started, like.'

She sighed, but after a few seconds went into the hall and came back with about twenty-five brand-new, black and silver enamel CND badges, which she poured into my outstretched hands.

'These aren't toys, you know,' she said to me.

'Oh, I know, Pat,' I replied. 'The struggle for nuclear disarmament is a serious business. The younger generation such as myself are only too painfully aware that we're only ever a few minutes away from nuclear extinction.'

The next day I took the badges into school and a crowd gathered round me wanting to see them. Several kids asked if they could have one. 'Sure,' I said, 'but maybe you should make a little donation to . . . you know . . . the cause.' So each of my schoolmates gave me a few shillings for a badge. At first I had thought I was taking a chance asking them for money, but to my amazement it was them who were grateful to me for having found this hard-to-get fashion item and they were also impressed that I had had the contacts to locate them. My fellow pupils started to see me in a new light – after all, none of them were mates with ex-jailbird lesbians.

The cash they gave me for the badges never found its way to CND, I don't know whether I ever intended that it should, but my feeling was that I considered the money as a small stipend, a trifling amount of compensation for all the travelling, all the trade union meetings my father went to, all the work I had put into the struggle for peace and justice, and all the effort involved in being the only child of Communist Party members Joe and Molly Sayle.

32 ⚡

Sticks and Stones and Sticks

It was only slowly that I became aware of the power of swear words. It was a gradual thing, a creeping realisation that blossomed into full comprehension round about my second or third year at grammar school. I heard bigger boys or ones from rough homes using these special, explosive, forbidden expressions, and once the realisation of their power dawned I knew that swearing was a thing I wanted to be intimately involved in.

Once I had got the most powerful obscenities straight in my head I came home from school determined to try out their effect on my mother. Full of excitement, I sat at the dining table in the living room. Molly put my evening meal in front of me, but instead of eating it I said, 'I . . . I . . . I don't want that. It's . . . it's . . . it's fucking shit!' Then I sat back, waiting to hear what kind of explosion it would prompt. After all, I conjectured, if the bathroom sponge going missing for a few seconds could prompt a screaming fit from my mother, a paroxysm of grief that might involve weeping and howling and crying out to the gods of justice, then me saying 'fuck' and 'shit' was bound to provoke a tremendous reaction that would be heard at the back of the Spion Kop.

For a short while nothing happened as Molly considered what I had said in a calm and reflective manner. Then finally she said, 'I don't care if you eat it or not . . . but it's not fucking shit and if you don't fucking eat it I'm not going to fucking make you anything fucking else so you can fucking go and get your own fucking food in some other shit-fucking place you fucking little bastard shit fuck.'

After that day Molly rarely spoke a sentence without an obscenity in it, and I was often too embarrassed to bring school friends home because I was worried about them being offended by my mother's foul language.

It was late in the afternoon. Joe must have been working nights and so had been upstairs sleeping. Suddenly I heard him calling out in a frightened voice, full of pain. 'Molly!' he called. 'Molly, call an ambulance! Molly! Molly! Call an ambulance! It hurts, it hurts.' An ambulance came quickly and took Joe to the big hospital in Stanley Road. Molly accompanied him while a neighbour looked after me.

There was a period of a few hours when there was no news from the hospital and in that time I experienced an enormous level of anxiety. I desperately wanted someone to tell me what was going on. My always active imagination was spinning endless scenarios of catastrophe. While I looked like I was watching telly, internally I was overwhelmed by fear.

By the time Molly returned from hospital where it turned out, after some confusion, that Joe had gallstones, the removal of which would require him to have an operation, I concluded that emotions were so painful that it might be a good idea, in the future, not to feel them.

While waiting for a consultation with the surgeon Joe got into conversation with a woman, the wife of another patient, who mentioned that she had had her varicose veins removed at the same time as she had been in for other surgery and what a relief it had been. Joe too suffered from varicose veins, so he asked the doctors if he could have them removed at the same time as he was anaesthetised for the gallstones operation.

It was on Guy Fawkes night, with rockets scrawling into the sky, bangers exploding in the street and a bonfire burning at the top of the road, when the hospital called to say something had gone wrong with the operation on Joe's leg. Instead of cutting a vein the surgeon had inadvertently severed a nerve in my father's right foot. The prognosis was that he would have no feeling in that foot and might have difficulty walking on it in the future.

When we went to see him for the first time Joe lay in a large ward of shrivelled men in new pyjamas whose steel-framed beds seemed to go on and on to the horizon, as surgeons in white coats stood over him trying to evade responsibility. Tall men, kindly and infinitely superior in their attitude, spent a few minutes trying to patronise Molly before they realised that they couldn't get away with it and, after a little bit of stalling, early in 1965 we were awarded the almost unheard of sum of one thousand pounds by the hospital in compensation.

Joe was in Stanley Road for quite some time recuperating, so Molly bought him a little transistor radio to listen to in bed on a single earpiece. Transistor radios were quite a new thing at that time – it seemed amazing that you didn't need to listen to the BBC via a set the size of a gas oven that employed giant valves. The radio, made by Pye, was in blue and white plastic with a carrying handle that slid out in an arc from a recess in the top. After he got back from Stanley Road I took that radio for myself.

From then on Joe had to have a bar put in all his shoes which gave some support to the arch of his dead foot, but for the rest of his life he would walk with a limp. Soon after he got out of hospital we were at the top of the street and Joe tried to race with me like we had done so many times in the past, but all he could manage was an unsteady stumble as I easily out-distanced him.

Still, we were in possession of one thousand pounds which was a great deal of money. It could have bought us all kinds of things: a luxury car, a cottage in North Wales, a small business importing dried fruit. Instead we bought a boat.

What a family of spectacularly unmechanical, two-thirds Jewish Communists thought they were doing buying a cabin cruiser moored on a canal bank just outside Chester is anybody's guess. Molly always blamed me for this unwise purchase. The guy who sold it to us was some kind of super-secondhand-car-salesman. Joe was keen but Molly equivocated and so the salesman turned his oily charm on me, saying, 'What do you think of it, son? Isn't she a lovely craft? A beautiful craft. All the girls love a boy with a craft such as this.' I was so unused to having my opinion solicited that I responded with enthusiasm, saying, 'Yes, a boat. Let's get a boat. This boat. I want this boat.' My parents folded and purchased a secondhand cabin cruiser for far too much money. No matter how much I pointed out, later on, that I was twelve and what were they doing anyway letting themselves be influenced by a child in such a crucial decision, Molly was implacable that what followed was all my fault.

Once again our distrust of the spiv, the self-employed, the smooth-talking, fur coat-wearing petit-bourgeois had been vindicated. This was a familiar story. I knew from listening in to the tales my parents' political comrades told that all of them were constantly being taken advantage of by plumbers, builders, hoteliers, driving instructors and every other kind of sole trader. There was some naïve quality in Communists which meant that they simply couldn't understand the mind of the self-employed, could never haggle for a bargain, do a deal or ensure their roof was repaired properly. Perhaps some of the motivation for them being Communists was the desire one day to have all the self-employed who had robbed them over the years either collectivised or shot.

There were many things wrong with our boat. In the best of circumstances a cabin cruiser is just a pointy caravan that floats and leaks, but ours was much, much less than that. Apart from anything else, our boat was quite small. There was a tiny cramped cabin at the front with thin foam seats which could be folded out into a double bed, while at the rear of the cabin on a cupboard was a little cooker and opposite it a cabinet the size of a coffin with a chemical toilet inside. At the stern part, where you steered the boat from, there was an open space with more seats. This area could be shielded from the weather with a folding canvas cover a bit like a giant pram's or a huge sports car's. At the prow it had a name in Welsh, *Ty Mawr*, inscribed in gold stick-on letters which we never bothered to have translated but probably meant 'Big Mistake'.

But it was at the very stern of the boat that the source of a lot of our problems resided. Although in most ways *Ty Mawr* was a quite substandard craft she had for some reason been fitted with a gigantic outboard motor, an American-made 75hp Evinrude which would have been more suited to a speedboat hurtling between the Florida Keys than to a cabin cruiser on the Chester Canal. Right from our first day of ownership we had great difficulty controlling the power of this enormous machine, particularly given the very imprecise, and, once we owned it, badly maintained throttle linkage that ran to the stern from a lever beside the steering wheel.

It was a warm summer Sunday when we had our first day out on the boat. Getting there involved us taking two trains to Chester, then a bus to the mooring on the outskirts of the city. Once we had arrived we stared at this thing we had bought and wondered what to do with it. Then after a pause we climbed gingerly aboard and I was given the job of steering. It took ages to start the engine, pumping a little rubber bladder to get fuel into the system and then pulling violently on a string to turn it over. Once the Evinrude was ticking smokily to itself we pushed off from the bank with a lot of screaming and shouting from Molly, 'Lexi! Lexi! Lexi! Mind that fucking swan!'

At first things went well enough as we puttered slowly between canal barges with their gaily painted sides and flowers planted in enamel pots. With the propeller turning slowly we passed fishermen sitting contemplatively on the banks, their lines dangling in the water, children in kayaks laughing and splashing each other and fellow cabin cruisers meandering gently along, their brass fittings polished to a high shine and the husband and wife seated in the cockpit, eating sandwiches and drinking Pimms.

Then I tried to speed up just the tiniest bit. I shifted the accelerator lever a millimetre and immediately the throttle jammed open and the peaceful bucolic scene was shattered. The noise of the Evinrude climbed to a tortured scream and the bow of *Ty Mawr* rose steeply out of the water like a German motor torpedo boat reaching the open sea. Now completely out of control, our little cabin cruiser sped up the canal weaving in and out of the other boats with all three of us yelling and screaming until we crashed into the bank, driving so far up the soft grass and mud on this remote stretch of the canal that we nearly ended up in an adjacent field.

This was how our days out usually went. There was one particularly shaming experience when the lines of a large number of fishermen became entangled in our propeller and I wasn't able to stop, so I ended up dragging them along the towpath, their faces red and sweating as they ran swearing and screaming at me at the top of their voices.

Its uncontrollable nature wasn't the only problem with our gigantic outboard motor. Where the cabin cruiser had been tied up near Chester the boatyard was secure because access could only be gained via a large metal gate. Unfortunately after a while, maybe because it was a bit nearer, we decided to move *Ty Mawr* to a mooring just outside Maghull in Lancashire on a stretch of the Leeds–Liverpool Canal. This was just an open expanse of towpath and wasn't at all secure, so we became afraid that somebody was going to steal the Evinrude and therefore we never left it on the boat. Since we didn't own a car, every time we wanted to go for a sail we had to take the giant outboard motor with us on the bus. It's hard to describe how stupid I felt sitting on a bus with a giant Evinrude outboard motor on the seat next to me. It was very heavy, too, and we had to carry it on and off two buses, a Ribble from Maghull to Scotland Road and then the number 27 to the stop in Oakfield Road near our house. Between visits to the Leeds–Liverpool Canal the Evinrude lived in our front sitting room.

Lurking in the Rectory

During our last trip to Czechoslovakia, with the unfortunate Peter Pemberton, our delegation had attended a comedy football match. The referee made outrageous decisions and at one point two men in white coats and curly blonde wigs came on with a stretcher to take away a man who was playing really well and pretended he didn't want to be taken off. I was unsettled by this blurring of genres – was it a football game or a comedy performance? On the other side of the field a man was painting a house and Alf said, 'That bloke looks familiar.' Later a party was held in our honour at the local community centre and the same man was there. Alf approached him, found he spoke good English, and after they had both racked their memories and drunk a lot of plum brandy they suddenly recalled that during the war they had shared a ham sandwich in Glasgow during an air raid.

That same night at the community centre we were entertained by a folk dance troupe wearing traditional dress. Several of the dancers were very pretty blonde girls who entranced me with their twirling, spinning and complicated hand movements. Joe and Molly, too, were very taken with this group and decided to try to bring them to Britain to show the human face of Communism. Once we returned to the UK they began planning a tour for the dance troupe, yet no matter how much hard work they put in it seemed to take ages for anything to happen. My early teenage years were overshadowed by the constant possibility that these girls might be coming, until finally the possibility turned into reality with the news that they would be arriving in a few months and appearances had been scheduled at Hope Hall in Liverpool and various other venues around the North-west.

As the date for their arrival came closer I thought more and more about these dancers. In my imaginings I was the sophisticated host showing them around my home city. In fact it was only the pretty blonde female ones who were in my daydreams – the boys had mysteriously vanished. Unfortunately, that was the limit of my powers. No matter how hard I tried, I couldn't seem to get the girls of my imagination out of their folk costumes and into something more attractive. Whatever I did they remained in their woven skirts, puffy white blouses and oddly shaped headdresses. After a while I formed a composite image of a single attractive girl dancer in my mind, and whatever I was doing or wherever I was I would show it to her. She was constantly in my head, a silent observer but somehow always fascinated by my amazing life. 'This is what we call a steak and kidney pie,' I would say to my lovely flaxen-haired dancer. 'We eat it with chips.' And her eyes would widen in astonishment. Or 'That's Mr Abrahams. He hates me.' Or 'Those two men are called Morecambe and Wise. Though they share a bed they are not homosexual lovers.'

It was only a few weeks before the tour was due to begin that we got a message from the authorities in Prague saying that the dance troupe would not after all be coming, though they offered no explanation. Perhaps it was an early sign of the internal upheavals within Czech society that they weren't being allowed out – it's impossible to say. But though she never arrived in person I continued to carry this idealised blonde dancer in my mind and in my imagination I continually showed off to her – until, that is, I got to an age when I began doing stuff that I was too ashamed to let her see.

I sometimes wonder why it is that I remember what it is that I remember. Did the things that stayed with me form who I became? Or was I already fixed by then, as the kind of child for whom all the endless visits to galleries, castles and historic monuments blurred into a few vague impressions while what really stuck in my mind was two men's memory of eating a ham sandwich and a folk dancer who never existed? I would have really liked to retain hundreds of clear and precise images of all the baroque ceilings and Renaissance architraves I stood in front of during our travels, but I had no matrix, no philosophical framework with which to retain them. So they became like pretty pictures hung on a wall with flimsy string that soon snapped.

During 1964, in my second year at Alsop, class 2B moved into the Rectory where we had our form room on the second floor. Some of the kids developed a fad for jumping out of the window, landing in the grassy land at the back and then running back into class. I didn't join in.

I loved the Gothic feel of the Rectory, the worn elegance of the stairs and doors, the creepy, High Church romanticism of the mullioned windows and sandstone arches being forbidden fruit to the son of Communists. The civic centre of Liverpool, clustered around St George's Hall and the Walker Art Gallery, favoured the classical style, supposedly radiating rationality and science, as if ancient Rome had somehow acquired double-decker buses and a railway station.

On the floor above 2B was a wood-panelled form room for the upper sixth Classics. In common with a lot of provincial grammars, Alsop attempted to ape British public schools. It did this, though, in an unconvincing fashion, like somebody who has learned a foreign language from a book. And fortunately, for whatever reason, it decided it could get along without the vicious bullying and the Byzantine cruelty of those supposedly superior establishments. The boys above us on the second floor attempted to give the impression, mainly to themselves, that they were at Winchester, Harrow or Eton. Through studying

Latin and Greek A-Level they were hoping to go to Oxford or Cambridge where, if they got in, they planned to lie about where they came from. When they weren't in class these boys would sit about in leather armchairs conjugating Virgil or editing the school magazine, while in the winter they actually went so far in their fake Billy Bunterism as to toast crumpets over an open fire.

That year we had a maths teacher called Mr Cornes who earned my respect by disdaining to teach us any maths at all, scuppering my already weak chances of ever understanding geometry. For the entire lesson Mr Cornes would just stare out of the window. On one occasion the only thing he said to us was, 'I've been watching those workmen out there for forty minutes and in all that time they've done nothing.' He dressed smartly in tweed suits with a flamboyant handkerchief in the top pocket and looked a little like a young Alfred Hitchcock. The most interesting thing to me about Mr Cornes was that he would come to school every day in a different smart car which he would park outside the Rectory, alongside the other teachers' much more shabby vehicles. One day it would be an MGB coupé, another day his transport might be an Aston Martin DB4 or a 4.2-litre Mark II Jaguar with wire wheels.

Though he was unaware of my existence, I really liked Mr Cornes and tried to imitate his enigmatic manner. I saw that if you say nothing, people find it unsettling because they don't know what to make of you. Another of our family hate figures was the Spanish fascist dictator Generalissimo Francisco Franco. Also a fan of being inscrutable, Franco once said, 'You are the slave of what you say and the master of what you don't say.' He might have added that that approach isn't always guaranteed to work. If you attempt, for example, to be sphinx-like, mysterious and enigmatic when you get to the front of a long queue at the chip shop, you do risk being punched quite hard in the back of the head.

Under the influence of Mr Cornes my artwork began to change. The futurist utopia of Saylovia, with its high-rise buildings, eight-lane highways and pedestrian walkways started to be of less interest to me. The new Britain that the architects' blueprints and the articles in the newpapers had been preparing us for had begun to appear, and it didn't look anything like they had told us it would. The optimistic line drawings in the magazines hadn't found a way to render the rain-streaked concrete of the new Kingsway Tunnel that had been built between Liverpool and Wallasey, destroying huge swathes of Scotland Road, obliterating thousands of homes and hundreds of small businesses in the process. They had somehow failed to include the litter that skittered about at waist height in the new shopping precincts, whipped up by the storm-force winds that were permanently channelled between the flimsy buildings. The people who had once occupied these neighbourhoods had been moved out to estates on the edge of the city, the only real difference between Stalin's forced migrations and those in Liverpool being that the Liverpudlians went willingly, believing the lie that they would have a better life in these purpose-built new towns, the promise of electric storage heaters and twin sinks taking the place of the bayonet and the forced march.

Instead of Saylovia I began to draw an elaborate and ever-changing fantasy in which a slightly older version of me drove to London in one of Mr Cornes's cars, an open-topped MGTF with wire wheels, my luggage strapped to the chromed rack on the boot lid behind the driver's seat. I was a bit vague about how you got to London by road as I had only ever travelled there by train, but I thought it might be somewhere up the A1 and I had an idea that Bedford was on the way. So I would often draw me in my MGTF in Bedford high street with a pretty girl giving me an admiring look as I stopped for her at a zebra crossing.

As an artist I was clearly part of no movement. I worked alone, unconnected to the cultural elite, like a teenage William Blake. Nevertheless the drawings I did, scribbled down the margins of my school books, filling lined foolscap pads and scrawled over the backs of envelopes, were expressing the spirit of the age. I wasn't aware of it, but Jack Kerouac's *On the Road* had been published eight years before and the idea that travel for its own sake could be a quasi-mystical experience was slowly crossing the Atlantic.

More influential for me than Kerouac's beatnik ramblings was a US television series shown intermittently and at odd hours on the local ITV station, Granada. When people consider the artistic cauldron of the North-west in the 1960s Granada TV, based in Manchester but serving the entire region, innovative, liberal and creative but always populist, pioneering investigative documentaries, US comedies and ground-breaking dramas, often gets forgotten. But I grew up in an area that effectively had two BBCs. Though it was true that Granada, with their eccentric scheduling, could make you work hard for what you wanted to see. I did sometimes wonder whether I was hallucinating one particular show because it had so few viewers that when I asked other people they said they had never heard of it. Also, in form and content it seemed to have been made specifically for me.

Route 66 was probably the only TV drama series ever to be filmed entirely on the road with not one scene shot in a studio. It concerned two enigmatic young men named Tod and Buz who travelled around the USA in one of the greatest cars of all time – a Chevrolet Corvette convertible powered by the 327 cubic inch 'Small Block' V8, getting involved in existential adventures and speaking to each other in a hyped-up quasi-hipster English. The show clearly had a liberal, progressive agenda and dealt sympathetically with stories about mercy killing, the threat of nuclear annihilation and teenage runaways. Tod and Buz were also always running into isolated nihilistic loners living in tumbleweed-infested ghost towns.

Though I was unaware of it at the time, *Route 66* gave work to emerging directors such as Sam Peckinpah and Arthur Hiller and featured guest stars of the calibre of Rod Steiger, Martin Sheen, Buster Keaton, Robert Redford and a young Robert Duvall playing a heroin addict. In the episode with Robert Duvall, Buz revealed that in the past he had had his own problems with the White Horse, the Brown Sugar, the old Yam Yam, which seemed like a really cool thing to me. Not that I ever wanted to take heroin, which frankly looked like it was a lot of hard work, appeared to be quite uncomfortable and meant you had to listen to jazz music. Rather, I wondered if it might somehow be possible to just jump straight to being the sort of world-weary, wise person who had once been a junkie without ever going to all the trouble and mess of actually being a junkie. When I drew myself in biro in my MGTF driving to London I was trying to capture the same restless spirit that informed *Route 66* or *On the Road*. Me as the loner, the free spirit, a man with a complicated past, steering his sports car wherever the mood took him, to romantic places such as Runcorn, Bedford and Dunstable where he would have adventures that ended with a liberal conclusion.

After the botched surgery on his foot Joe was on sick leave at home for several months. At first he remained up in the bedroom sleeping all day. It might have been unsettling having this silent presence above your head, but it was possible to tell yourself that the situation wasn't any different from the time before the operation, when Joe had been doing shifts as a guard. Then too he had been in bed the whole day long while other men were at work.

When he did return to the railways it was on light duties, part-time, as a ticket collector at Liverpool Central Station. My parents decided that because he was still recuperating Joe might not be up to travelling across eastern Europe, so at the Boxing Day holiday meeting we chose for the summer of 1965 to take a nice restful holiday on our boat.

I'm not sure I had a vote at these meetings, because for me there was a long list of things that were wrong with a holiday on the boat. I have no idea what Molly and Joe thought they were going to get out of this vacation, but then again Communists like us often seemed to make dubious life decisions. Perhaps if you believe at the very core of your being that violent revolution, state repression and forced eradication of unwanted classes of human beings is likely to bring about peace amongst all mankind, then thinking that two weeks in a cabin cruiser on the Shropshire Union Canal might be good for your health isn't such a stretch.

I hated the whole idea from the start. For example, when we visited Czechoslovakia or Hungary we were treated as if we were truly remarkable people: fleets of black limousines usually waited for us on the forecourts of our luxury hotels, and enormous dinners were held in our honour. In slightly creepy rituals, I was made an honorary member of quasi-fascist organisations. And when I returned to Liverpool I had all these stories to tell that nobody else at school could match. Besides, I was beginning to get that teenage obsession with looking cool at all costs and caring about how others saw me above everything else – and a holiday on a canal with your parents was unlikely to be considered cool. Kerouac's drug-fuelled beat odyssey was not called 'On the San Francisco to Tijuana Grand Union Canal'. Tod and Buz had not chosen to travel the United States being enigmatic on a narrowboat.

At this time the cabin cruiser was still moored on the Chester branch of the Shropshire Union Canal, so at least we didn't have to carry our gigantic outboard motor with us along with two weeks' luggage and Bruno the dog. This canal had been built to bring goods, especially salt, from the south Cheshire town of Nantwich to Chester and then onwards to the sea via the Dee estuary. We planned to travel the other way, imagining perhaps that we would tie up each night beside rustic pubs where we would buy eggs and milk from a friendly farmer's wife. In all the millions of words

Karl Marx wrote about bringing the workers' state into existence – the *Communist Manifesto*, his *Eleven Theses on Feuerbach*, the *Critique of the Gotha Program* – when he tried to imagine the world as it would be after the dawn of Communism, which was after all the point of all this furious scribbling, he was only able to come up with a feeble bucolic fantasy involving smocks and cowherds who played the flute in the evenings.

It was the same with all the 'progressives' I had encountered: their vision of the world to come was either a brutal, uncompromising futurism or camp pastoralism such as that which inspired the garden city movement and its deformed child, the new towns. Nowhere across the whole spectrum of the left did there seem to be any appreciation of anything that was worn, anything that was industrial, in fact anything that was working-class. So that summer we weren't on a boating holiday, we were searching for the shape of things to come on our cabin cruiser *Potemkin*.

And I have to admit that sometimes it could be tranquil. In the mornings I would sit at the prow watching the fields slide past, listening to the purr of the engine behaving itself as the bow cut through the shallow clouded water. But all too soon disaster would strike, and Jewish hysteria is not suited to marine emergencies – screaming and shouting do not help when you are heading backwards towards a weir. The situation wasn't assuaged by an angry and self-conscious teenager and two adults being crammed into a space that, if it had been a gaol cell, would have been condemned by the chief inspector of prisons. It's hard to express the claustrophobia I felt. Swept by the solar winds of puberty, the last thing I needed was to be stuck on a boat with my parents.

At one point we crashed into a bank in some remote spot where there were overhanging trees, their tangled roots reaching into the water, and cows staring sardonically at us from the other side of an old metal fence. The boat became wedged in the mud – the Evinrude was great at getting you stuck into places, but less cooperative when you wanted to get out again. I tried putting the outboard into reverse until blue smoke began to pour from under its cover, but nothing else happened. Since his operation, in moments of crisis Joe, rather than taking charge as he once might – perhaps jumping off the boat and going to look for helpful Communists – seemed to fold inside himself, just standing passive and blank, while Molly thought the power of yelling might get us off and the dog, unusually for him, joined in, barking furiously. In the end I jumped over the side fully clothed; the water only came up to my waist. 'Lexi! Lexi! What are you doing?' Molly shouted. 'My child! My child's in the canal! There's probably rats! If you ruin those trousers I'll fucking kill you!' And then by myself I pushed the boat until it came free. And perhaps the way our holiday turned out was closer to the reality of Communism than Marx's sylvan prophecy.

One of the better things that came out of our vacation on the Shropshire Union Canal was that I won a prize for a drawing of the view from our boat. I was a member of something called the Little Woody Club, which was run by the Littlewood's stores, catalogues and football pools organisation. The Little Woody

Club was a juniors' club, an attempt to attract younger people to the company's products. Little Woody himself was a rather frightening figure with a grinning face set in the centre of a jagged piece of wood that had sprouted arms and legs. The company held an annual art competition and I sent in a biro drawing of a stone bridge near where we moored, as seen from the roof of *Ty Mawr*, done one late summer morning. I was awarded a badge of creepy Little Woody and a very elaborate pencil set in its own case. I imagine the judges were impressed by the unusual darkness and suffering expressed within a rendition of a bucolic scene, in many ways reminiscent of the later works of Vincent Van Gogh.

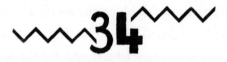

A Week in Southport

A child in Liverpool grows up understanding comedy in the same way that a young Mongolian nomad grows up knowing his way around a horse. Apart from shipping and its attendant industries, comedy was what we did. Many of the most successful comedians of the immediate post-war era came from Liverpool: Arthur Askey, Ken Dodd, Tommy Handley, Ted Ray and Robb Wilton, and we could claim at least a quarter share in such Lancashire comics as George Formby, Jimmy Clitheroe and Frank Randall. After lunch on Sunday every family in the city, along with the rest of the country, would listen to popular radio comedy series such as *Round the Horne*, *Hancock's Half*

Hour and *The Navy Lark*. But in Liverpool it was a good idea to have a pad and a pencil handy to jot down notes, because the analysis next day in the playground could get pretty competitive.

I found from very early on that I was super-critical even by the exacting comedy standards of my classmates. If they liked a show they tended to like everything about it whereas my tendency was to pick it apart, to say, 'Well, that bit worked but that other bit didn't.' Which just seemed to confuse the other kids. And if my classmates disliked a show or a performer they just ignored them, barely acknowledging their existence, which was the sensible thing to do. But for me it was the things I hated that drew my attention the most. I could get furious over the oily charms of game show hosts like Hughie Greene and Michael Miles and the bovine compliability of the participants, and comedy shows I disapproved of could send me into a blind rage. At 6.30 every night Granada would show imported American comedies such as *The Dick Van Dyke Show* or *Car 54 Where Are You?*, which I more or less enjoyed along with everybody else. But there was one called *My Mother the Car* that drove me absolutely nuts.

The plot of *My Mother the Car* was that an attorney played by Jerry Van Dyke (Dick's talentless younger brother) ends up buying a vintage car that happens to contain the soul of his dead mother, who talks, only to him, through the car's radio. My parents couldn't understand why I would go on and on about this show.

'But don't you understand?' I would yell. 'The car is his dead mother! It's insane! And that scene where he puts petrol into it with a hose is disturbing!'

'Well, if you don't like it don't watch it then.'

'Oh, you don't get it, do you? That's what they want me to do!' And I would run out of the house, slamming the door.

The first radio series I tuned in to on my own, in my bedroom under the covers using Joe's blue and white transistor radio, was *I'm Sorry, I'll Read That Again*. I don't know why I listened under the covers, since Joe and Molly wouldn't have been bothered. I assumed, since it was what everybody said they did, that having a blanket on top of the radio improved reception. *I'm Sorry, I'll Read That Again* was the first TV or radio show which seemed aimed at my generation and actively excluded older people with its noisy and irreverent humour. It originated from the Cambridge University Footlights revue and featured young talent such as John Cleese, Bill Oddie and Tim Brooke-Taylor. One day towards the end of the spring term of 1966 I was in the playground analysing the latest edition of *I'm Sorry, I'll Read That Again*. I was saying, 'I find that Bill Oddie's Angus Prune character can slip into the bathetic if he doesn't restrain his more sentimental tendencies . . .' when I sensed my audience's attention slipping – it was the oddest experience. A rumour was going around the playground, and you could actually see it travel from group to group until it finally reached the little gang of boys of which I was a part. The news had leaked that after the summer holidays Alsop Grammar School would be 'going comp'. This meant that our school was going to join the comprehensive system and would amalgamate with the larger and more modern Anfield Comprehensive School half a mile away on County Road.

The crumpet-toasting fops in the Rectory were particularly

worried about what this news would mean, but all of us had our concerns. The kid who had the most to worry about was the boy who was considered to be the best fighter at Alsop and was therefore known as the Cock of the School. Our Cock was some tall blond lad who played in the first footie eleven, was good at boxing and might have smoked a pipe, while the 'Cock' of Anfield Comp was a squat gingery thug. The story went that when he was eleven he was stopped by the police while at the wheel of a huge articulated lorry. When the coppers asked what a schoolboy was doing driving a large commercial vehicle, his answer was: 'Me mate give it me.'

As it turned out, the amalgamation did not cause too many problems. In the first week of the new academic year our Cock met their Cock after school in Walton Hall Park on the other side of Queen's Drive and was quickly battered into unconsciousness. Thereafter we all knew where we stood and peace reigned. I liked the idea that I was now attending some hard-case comp rather than a prissy grammar school, but we weren't inconvenienced by mixing too much with the more proletarian kids from the other school.

That summer, as if to make up for the previous year's boating disaster we had two holidays. The NUR AGM for 1966 was to be held in Southport, just fifteen miles north of Liverpool. Even though it was only forty minutes away by electric train, we decided to spend the week in a boarding house just behind the promenade. By the time we got to Southport I was thirteen years old, nearly fourteen, and I was beginning to seriously wonder about the advisability of going on holiday with my parents. After all, the year before, following two weeks on a boat with them I had literally thrown myself overboard. Some of this was the natural inclination of the teenager to separate from his or her parents – it is a biological imperative that you find your mother embarrassing from time to time, so that you forge your own personality. But mine, with her propensity for screaming in public and loudly holding unconventional opinions ('Lexi, why's everybody fucking standing still?' 'It's Winston Churchill's state funeral, Mother.' 'Churchill – that drunken bastard!'), made you not just want to forge a personality but take on a whole new identity and move to Norway.

Less understandably, I also began to find Joe's geniality embarrassing. Judgemental little bastard that I had become, I would sometimes recoil when I saw him telling terrible jokes at the centre of a crowd of railwaymen. I had this idea that the best people were the ones who lounged in a corner sneering.

After nearly a week I had become heartily sick of Southport. It was an odd town. The main shopping street, Lord Street, was a long and elegant boulevard, full of expensive shops and refined tea rooms, tree-lined and covered with a continuous glass canopy supported on wrought iron pillars. But right behind were narrow streets stuffed with shops and cafés that catered to the holidaying masses of Merseyside and Lancashire, selling buckets and spades and lunches that came with sliced bread and a cup of tea. This collision of styles, of refined spa and northern seaside resort, made it seem as if Baden Baden had by some gigantic feat of engineering been literally twinned with Skegness.

It was at heart a rich town, rich and old, and had a very

ambivalent attitude to the working-class hordes that descended on it in the summer months. Every year on 12 July the Protestant Orange Lodges would travel from Liverpool to celebrate the Battle of the Boyne by marching up and down to fife and drum bands. Pale and undernourished-looking boys and girls from the streets, tower blocks and tenements of Liverpool sat on huge carthorses, dressed as King Billy and Queen Mary. I saw a shop-girl in Woolworth's bringing out the special price label that they must have kept just for the 12th that doubled all the prices for the day.

By the edge of my fourteenth birthday I could, at least in appearance, pass as an adult. I had long black hair flowing over my collar and the beginning of a beard, but though I didn't wish to spend time with my parents I didn't know how to occupy myself as a grown-up would. So instead I wandered through the sand dunes and pine woods that stretched from the edge of town to Ainsdale, I meandered up and down the streets of Birkdale with its huge Edwardian villas, I walked round and round the town centre till I was dizzy, and I strode up and down the wide beach where on a very clear day you could see Anglesey and the Welsh mountains in Snowdonia to the south and Blackpool Tower further up Liverpool Bay to the north.

Having said that what we did on Merseyside was comedy, there was one other related thing which was music. Again, even before the Beatles and all the other Merseybeat groups I was vaguely aware that we had had fifties' heart-throb crooner and Jewish Liverpudlian Frankie Vaughan, singer Michael Holliday and rock and roller Billy Fury, but by and large the city's music scene passed me by. According to those who were in the know, music was everywhere in Liverpool – it leaked out of every basement and attic. But when they started showing films on television about the Cavern Club I was astonished to learn that there were such places in Liverpool city centre. As far as I was aware there were only the big shops in Church Street, the Pier Head where you went for demonstrations and to get the ferry, and Unity Theatre where you went to see black and white Eisenstein films and plays written by Arnold Wesker about angry Jewish people. The live music I had encountered on the left was either the humourless folk ballads of Pete Seeger, all about mining disasters or sneering at people who lived in the suburbs, self-pitying Irish rebel nonsense or trad jazz. No wonder I wasn't interested in live music.

But the effect of the Beatles went far beyond music. John Lennon had just introduced the world to 'the John Lennon cap', a jaunty item of seaman's headgear that, like National Health specs, he had made into an unlikely fashion object. I desperately wanted one, but the closest I could get to it was a dark blue Wild West-era US 7th Cavalry soldier's cap that I bought in a souvenir shop off Lord Street. This seemed close enough to me because at that point I had great difficulty differentiating the nuances in things – for example, leather and plastic, which, both being shiny and black, I couldn't tell apart. I had a mac which was clearly made of plastic, but I was never sure it wasn't leather. It was only when I leaned against a hot radiator and my mac burst into flames that I began to see the difference. Similarly with this cap. It was round and had a peak, so I thought it was identical to John Lennon's. I took the plastic crossed silver swords off the front of it and, regarding my reflection in shop windows, considered myself really cool and trendy. In fact I looked like an angry man who was wandering around town wearing a kid's toy hat.

I had one very nice afternoon with Joe. He must have taken time off from the AGM because we went to see *Von Ryan's Express* at the big ABC cinema in Lord Street. I loved this movie, in which a group of Allied prisoners, led by Frank Sinatra as Colonel Ryan, who have been captured by the Germans in Italy manage to seize control of the prison train they are on. Despite being caught in an Allied air raid, negotiating uprooted tracks and enduring attacks by the Luftwaffe, they succeed in steering the train to neutral Switzerland via Florence and Milan – though Ryan is shot in the back and killed right at the end. Shot in Panavision and using Ektachrome stock, giving it a pleasing cool blue tone rather than the gaudier Technicolor, the film, with all the jumping on and off and the confusion, reminded me and Joe of our rail holidays in Europe. And all the shouting reminded us of Molly.

But the thing that came to obsess me while I was in Southport was the idea that I was so close to home yet I was sleeping in a narrow bed in a damp boarding house. All the things that were familiar to me were just a few miles away, yet here I was bored out of my mind. On the Friday I told my mother I was going for yet another walk, but in fact went to the station and caught a train to Liverpool. From the moment the train left the station I felt like I was on the most amazing adventure, because I was heading for our empty house back in Anfield. It was almost like I had found a new way to be on a journey – the complete pointlessness of it was dizzying. At Exchange Station I took a bus, and within twenty minutes I was unlocking the front door of our empty and silent house. It was the most incredible experience. I sat in the armchair in the living room and wondered what to do next. Nobody knew where I was and this was the last place they would ever think to look for me. After all, what kind of an evil genius would leave Southport just to sit in an armchair in an empty, cold house?

I had recently read a Ray Bradbury short story in one of the American science fiction magazines I bought for a shilling each from a secondhand bookstore. In this story the *Twentieth Century Limited* stops at a desert town where the train has never stopped before and a man gets off. The man intends to murder a stranger at random, but there is another man in the desert town who has sat for years watching the train and waiting for it to stop because he knows that one day the *Twentieth Century Limited* will stop there and a man will get off intending to murder a stranger at random. The two men then hunt each other through the desert town. I thought to myself, 'That's me. I could show my bottom to the woman in the pet shop and she wouldn't believe it was me. She would just say to the police, "It couldn't have been Alexei Sayle even though it looked just like him, because he's in Southport with his parents." And the police would reply, "Well, yes, but Southport isn't that far away." But she would say, "Certainly that's true. But he's on holiday with his parents. Why would he come back? The thought of him coming back here from Southport is literally impossible." And the police would be forced to agree.'

So I thought of doing that, but then I looked at my watch and saw that if I didn't get back up the coast I would miss the annual dinner dance, so I took the train back to Southport and never told anybody I had been at home for the afternoon.

35

Odd Behaviour

The second holiday we took in 1966 was a few months later, towards the end of the summer: two weeks in Bulgaria. Though Bulgaria was a Communist country the trip didn't resemble our previous visits to the Soviet Bloc because for the first time in our lives we were on a conventional package holiday. Me, Molly and Joe would be spending two weeks at a resort on the Black Sea called Golden Sands and, rather than taking days on the train to get there, we flew from Gatwick to the airport at nearby Varna in a four-engined turboprop Ilyushin IL 18 airliner of Balkan Airlines.

Molly and Joe were completely relaxed about flying, but I was more anxious. The interior of the IL 18 was fitted out with rows of seats that had frilly antimacassars on the headrests, net curtains hung from a plastic-covered wire at the porthole windows, there were open luggage racks above the passengers' heads, and a line of round Art Deco-style light fittings set in the ceiling ran the length of the passenger compartment. If I was going to travel through the air at thirty thousand feet I wanted to be in something that looked like a futuristic spaceship rather than an Edwardian saloon bar or a railway station buffet.

Our refreshment room came in fast and low over a cornfield before bumping down on to the tarmac, engines screaming in reverse as we hit the runway. On arrival at the tiny terminal building it felt odd that we weren't met by a delegation from the Bulgarian Communist Party but had to get on a coach with all the other tourists. On the other hand, at least we didn't have to visit any locomotive factories or the sites of Nazi massacres.

Golden Sands had been constructed as a resort solely for the use of foreign tourists. The only way you could eat in the restaurants or drink in the bars was by using Western currency to buy coupons, which you then exchanged for food and drink. In effect it was a town built along the lines of the crappy shops at the border between the Soviet Bloc and the West. Despite this, Golden Sands provided a reasonable holiday for the Western visitor, if not for the Bulgarians. Local people were free to come into the town and watch Westerners enjoying themselves but couldn't legally buy a single thing in this segregated part of their own country.

The hotels we stayed in were all low two-storey buildings, linked by paths lined with highly manicured flower beds. These flower beds were sprayed every night with insecticide to keep the mosquitos down. At night, once the insecticide trucks had gone, in these patches of vegetation there lurked men who would hiss at you, offering local currency in exchange for pounds, marks or francs at much higher rates than were provided by the government. They didn't get many takers because there was nothing to buy, no matter how many zloty you had.

The local teenagers who came into the town didn't want money. What they longed for was information about one thing – pop music. A group of boys sat next to me on a bench asking if I had any Beatles music. I don't know why they thought I would be carrying records around, but before I could answer a policeman walked past and they became very nervous, pretending they had nothing to do with me. I realised that, in all the time we had spent in the East, up until then we had only ever mixed with people who were part of the system, who were loyal to the party and its allied organisations. This was the first time I had encountered kids my own age who weren't running their own railway. Clearly there were tensions, but you didn't get to be a Communist without learning to ignore what was in front of your face. I put the youths' willingness to risk being seen talking to a Westerner down to the unstoppable power of the Beatles. In that year of 1966 it was impossible to overstate how big they were, and on their backs how big Liverpool had become.

During the day I hung around a wooden jetty that stretched out from the hot, silky sands into the Black Sea. This was where the teenagers congregated, away from the adults. These young people had come to Bulgaria from all over Europe, and there were even a few from the United States. Sun-tanned girls in bikinis floating in the cobalt water would ask me, 'So are you, like, really from Liverpool?'

'Yes,' I would reply.

Then, wide-eyed and excited and looking at me in a way I

didn't quite understand, they would say, 'Wow! So do you know the Beatles, then?'

'No,' I would reply.

There was one girl, a couple of years older than me, called Julie who was on holiday with her mother. She was from Ealing in London and she seemed absolutely lovely, droplets of water glistening on her skin, the sun reflecting off her white bikini. The closest I got to expressing my adoration was to suggest I swim along the bottom of the sea, then come up between her legs so she would be sitting on my shoulders, and then we would topple sideways as I had seen others do. But she declined, perhaps fearing dreadful injury apart from anything else. I would try and sit next to Julie in the evenings when we ate, looking devotedly at her.

Many of the restaurants in Sunny Beach were open-air – tables arranged around a dance floor, with a band in dinner jackets playing on a small stage and a bar under a canopy strung with coloured lights. The night was scented by the nearby pine forests and the lush flower beds, cicadas chirped in the grass and insects fluttered on the warm breeze until the insecticide lorry came along and killed them all. One night we were sitting with a group of other British tourists when Joe offered to go to the bar to buy a round of drinks. He collected everybody's coupons and headed off into the crowd of dancers. He didn't return for nearly an hour, and when he did, smiling to himself, he didn't have any drinks with him. On his way to the bar Joe had got chatting with the band leader and had ended up giving the musicians everybody's coupons in exchange for them playing the Gerry and the Pacemakers' song and Liverpool FC anthem 'You'll Never Walk Alone'. The other tourists were very annoyed that they didn't have any drinks but their anger just seemed to confuse Joe, who couldn't really offer any proper explanation as to why he had given everybody's vouchers away. After that, wherever we went in the resort any nearby band would strike up Rodgers and Hammerstein's show tune, so that it followed us around for the rest of our holiday as if we were trapped in some two-week-long, Balkan-tinged production of *Carousel*.

❨36❩
'Do You Want a Kiss?'

It's hard to say now what exactly was wrong with Joe. His problems with memory loss and personality change were more gradual and spread over a much longer period than is common with Alzheimer's. Another explanation might be a series of small but undetectable strokes. Whatever the cause, the fact that he was ill was never discussed in our house. I know there were concerned visits to Cyril Taylor, our doctor, but the reason for them and the diagnosis, if any, were never revealed, at least not to me. I suppose there was no answer in any of the places we would normally look. The party couldn't offer a solution. If you looked in the *Daily Worker* there wouldn't be an answer. The National Executive of the NUR didn't have any helpful ideas. So as a family we took an unspoken decision to look the other way, which worked for a while – but it's when you're looking the other way that you get hit by a bus.

I was just left with a fragmentary sense of something wrong and some unsettling memories. One Sunday evening, soon after our return from Bulgaria, we were having egg and tomato sandwiches for our tea and then planning to watch the TV show *Perry Mason*. Before the programme began we would play board games, and on this particular evening me and Joe were having a game of draughts. Until then he had always won, but this time it was as if my father had forgotten the rules of the game because the moves he made on the board made very little sense. As the contest went on I found Joe's behaviour increasingly disconcerting, so somehow, by making stupid moves of my own, I contrived to let him win. Afterwards I could tell that Joe knew I had let him beat me. It was an uneasy sensation, to feel pity for a parent when you're fourteen years old.

After he had been on light duties as a ticket collector for a few months, Joe was finally considered fit enough to go back to work full-time. But the injury to his foot meant he couldn't perform the duties of a guard any more, so instead he was promoted and appointed senior foreman at a railway goods yard at Bidston over on the Wirral. At least as he was no longer a guard Joe didn't have to work shifts, but he would still come home exhausted. And when he did he would often tell us stories of a train that had been sent down the wrong route or an important shipment that had somehow been mislaid. But between them the men at the depot always seemed to save the situation, or at least conceal the identity of who was responsible. I went to visit him there one weekend and found it an eerily remote sort of place. The depot had been built on marshland and tall, slender grasses grew between the tracks, nodding slowly in the salty breeze that blew in from Liverpool Bay. This depot at Bidston was slowly being run down: grey rail lines unused for many years curled this way and that like whip marks across the soil, while on the oxidising tracks rested row after row of battered, old-fashioned, wooden coal wagons that would never move again.

'Who's that?' I heard one of the junior railwaymen, a long-haired youth who had been throwing stones at an old window frame and shattering the glass, ask one of the others, referring to me.

'That's the boss's son,' he replied.

It felt weird that Joe was somebody's boss.

Another realisation which slowly dawned on me as I began to go out and about in the world was that there was something odd going on with men's toilets. If you wanted to use a public lavatory and were walking towards it from a fair distance you wouldn't see anybody going in or out, yet when you got down the steps the subterranean space would be full of men standing silently at the urinals, with only one gap left for the bona fide customer. I wondered whether when you got to the age of twenty or something, like these men were, it took three-quarters of an hour to have a piss, which I wasn't looking forward to. What's more, as you went up the stairs and out into the night you would hear a sudden scuffling back down in the lavatory. What was that all about?

Also, one evening when I was about fourteen and was walking back from the local library along Walton Breck Road with an armful of Sherlock Holmes novels a man stopped me. He said he was a long-distance lorry driver who had parked up for the night and asked if I knew where the best chip shop in the neighbourhood was. I thought for a second, then told him about several chippies in the area, first noting their opening hours and then listing their various merits and demerits, explaining differing prices and comparing cooking techniques. He, however, appeared distracted and not really listening, until suddenly in the middle of a long discourse about batter he blurted out, 'Do you want a kiss?' I told him that no, on balance I didn't want a kiss, and he went on his way leaving me feeling confused. I didn't realise that he was homosexual – I just thought he was a lorry driver who was sexually excited by people comparing chip shop prices. Afterwards, when I did figure out what he was, I was sorry I hadn't known he was gay. It annoyed me that I had missed an opportunity to be liberal-minded towards somebody who was still at that point part of a legally persecuted minority. If I had known he was homosexual I would have been able to express my cloying tolerance towards him (though I still don't think I would have given him the kiss he wanted because he wasn't very good-looking).

A few months later, when I was almost fifteen, the lorry driver might not have found me that good-looking either, since within less than six months my appearance had changed radically. The olive-skinned, brown-eyed boy had vanished completely, to be replaced by this hulking youth with long hair and a wispy beard which I would occasionally augment with black biro, and spots. My mother suggested that the best treatment for pimples was to put calamine lotion on them, so instead of little red spots my face was adorned with huge pink patches.

And along with this change in appearance came a much more focused interest in girls – though this interest wasn't accompanied by any insight into how you might get them to let you do the things you wanted to do with them. I envied the gay lorry drivers of Britain who just seemed to wander the streets asking boys if they wanted a kiss. Somehow that didn't seem possible with a girl, and as far as I knew girls didn't hang around in underground urinals either, conveniently letting you fumble with them in the dark.

Before I was fifteen I had had only a single experience that might have been called a date when I had invited some poor girl, the daughter of an NUR official I had met at a union function, to come and visit our boat with me. Once I had got her there I was completely unsure what to do next – the urge to reproduce is supposed to be irresistible, but in me the urge not to be rejected was even stronger – so I just sat staring at her for an hour and then took her home on the bus. But while I had no idea how to get an individual girl to do what I wanted I discovered that I did have the ability to make a crowd bend to my will.

～37～
Rockin' the Kremlin

One evening on the stage of the NUR social club in Dean Road
Joe was presented with a cheque for the union's Orphan Fund
by the Liverpool players Ian St John and Ron Yeats. It was the
first time I had been around celebrities, and I liked the way
they seemed to drive other people crazy for their attention.
Drinkers tore up cigarette packets that they pleaded with these
big, noble, polite men to autograph. So I got myself cast in
the school play. Our nervy English teacher Mr Johnson was
directing a production of Nikolai Gogol's satire of corruption
set in late nineteenth-century tsarist Russia, *The Government
Inspector*. There may have been something a little pointed in
my being given the one-line part of 'A Jewish Merchant', but I
didn't care – it was showbusiness, baby! The corrupt mayor of
the town was played by Cliff Cocker and the part of Khlestakov,
the foppish civil servant with the wild imagination, by a guy
called Russ Stamp from the year above me. There was much
excitement because some girls were being imported from our
sister school, Queen Mary, to play the female roles, and one of
them actually had to kiss Russ Stamp.

My one scene involved a deputation of Jewish merchants
approaching the fake government inspector, complaining about
the mayor's behaviour and attempting to bribe the fraudulent
official with gifts handed over on a silver tray. My single line
was 'Please accept the tray with it', a piece of nothing business

with which I managed to get a huge laugh on every one of the three nights the play ran by employing instinctive timing, some physical comedy and a huge helping of unacceptable racial stereotyping.

Getting that laugh was confirmation of what I had always suspected: I knew how to make a crowd laugh, and I would do pretty much anything to get that laugh. Though my class-mates were more analytical in the way they looked at comedy than they would have been if they had lived in any other part of the country, they still came at it from the direction of well-informed punters, in other words as amateurs. When I looked at the performance of a comedian on the TV or the radio it was as if I could see inside it, know what the comic was attempting, what would be coming next; also I would sometimes hear or see something that got a laugh and yet I would feel that the response was undeserved, on account of it being obtained through some trick or because the audience were too coopera-tive, too willing to laugh uncritically. Not that I loved humour or anything. I didn't start collecting George Formby records or going to see comics in working men's clubs, I didn't even particularly try and watch comedy shows when they came on the TV. It was just that I knew with absolute certainty that I was fluent in the language of that country and I might go and live there one day.

It was odd for me to have such a complex relationship with humour at such an early age, since neither of my parents were at all sophisticated in that department. Joe liked terri-ble puns and being jolly and everybody getting along, which I didn't value at all, while Molly's concept of comedy was wholly Jewish, straight out of the nineteenth-century shtetl; and they both liked awful, sentimental, bloody Charlie Chaplin. In 1963 a famous tour had come to the Empire Theatre in Lime Street, featuring Roy Orbison, the Beatles and Gerry and the Pacemakers. We hadn't gone to see that or even been aware of its existence, but we had that same year been in the audience for something called the Red Army Ensemble – the official choir of the Russian armed forces. This group of folk dancers, musicians and singers toured the world improving the image of the Soviet Union by having fat men in jodhpurs sing 'The Volga Boatmen's Song', 'Ave Maria' and 'Kalinka'. The Empire was completely packed for the show with an audience as excited and expectant as that which had greeted the Beatles, but a lot older and with many more of those Russian-style astrakhan hats. There was a lot of heavy-handed humour in the show, such as when these gimlet-eyed killers sang as an encore a comical version of 'Roll Out the Barrel'. This cracked my parents and the rest of the audience up, except me. The two of them loved these ponderous agitprop jokes that Communists told each other, whose punch-line was usually something to do with the President of the United States being a bastard. That and people falling over.

Molly was also particularly poor on the importance of plot development or story structure in fiction. If I left one of the novels I was reading lying around – *Catch 22*, *L'Etranger* or *The Hound of the Baskervilles* – she would pick it up and then start reading it backwards, beginning with the last page. Then she would refuse to let me have it back, spending hours happily engrossed in a story whose outcome she already knew, watching characters' personalities unevolve.

Through appearing in the school play I at last became good friends with Cliff Cocker. Well, I say friends, but in some ways Cliff treated me like a wild boy he had found living in the woods. By then he was in the sixth form and intending to become an actor. Cliff's group had their own form room which as a fourth-year I supposedly wasn't allowed to enter, but he would sneak me in and encourage me to sing, do impressions of the staff and swear for the other, older boys. I used to sing the Foundations' 'Build Me Up, Buttercup', which for some reason killed every time.

Cliff was always pointing out how handsome he was, just like his namesake Cliff Richard, and certainly he had been a bit of a heart-throb with the girls from our sister school during the run of *The Government Inspector*. I came to think of myself as another member of the Cocker family and took to spending a lot of time round at their house. They were an extraordinarily good-looking family, which is why Cliff had to keep saying how handsome he was. Cliff's father, Len, was a strikingly tall, upright man who had been in the Palestine police throughout the Second World War serving in the British Mandate, where he had developed a great sympathy for the Arab cause. His mother, Maeve, was remarkable too, elegant and dark-haired and unmistakably Irish in her looks. Cliff also had a sister, Penny, and of course there was his older brother Glen, who had lost his virginity on the Aldermaston march.

Now in his early twenties, Glen had been at Liverpool Art

School studying graphic design at the same time as John Lennon and in many ways bore a strong resemblance to the pop star. Glen had the same wiry looks, fervent opinions, quick surreal wit and ironic manner. He was also short-sighted like Lennon, though Glen's glasses always seemed to be held together with sticky tape. Unfortunately Glen couldn't sing or write songs.

There was also an autocratic granny who lived in the same neighbourhood with her other son, Uncle Billy Cocker. Though Len and Maeve were both in the Communist Party they owned their own business: they and Uncle Billy were printers. Operating a press in those days was a true craft that required a great deal of skill and a degree of artistry. The local printer was a vital part of the life of a community, and invoices, posters for church events, business cards and stationery all flowed from their shops.

The Cockers lived in a two-storey flat above their shop in Granby Street right in the heart of Liverpool 8, Toxteth. Though Liverpool had the reputation of being a racially mixed city the African and Afro-Caribbean population were in fact very much confined to the Toxteth neighbourhood in the south end of the city, known as 'The 8' or Tokky. Black Liverpudlians were often not even welcome in pubs and clubs in the centre of town. Granby was a wide street of two- and three-storey brick buildings, shops with flats above. A number of the shops were run by Pakistanis, Somalis or Arabs. They stocked strange fruit and vegetables unknown in Anfield (which pretty much meant anything apart from potatoes) and peppers, aubergines, mangoes and melons tumbled on to the pavement. These shops also stayed open well past five o'clock in the evening, the time when all other shops gleefully closed whether anyone wanted to buy something or not. Along Granby and down the side streets old Jamaican men sat in open doorways noisily playing dominos.

The BBC had a television drama strand called 'The Wednesday Play', featuring innovative and challenging dramas that people had to watch because there was nothing else on. One of these plays was a priapic fantasy about a Liverpool postman who won a thousand pounds on the Premium Bonds and moved into a bedsit in Cliff's neighbourhood, Liverpool 8, where he had all kinds of bohemian adventures with free-spirited girls, became an artist and hung out with black people (referred to by him as 'spades', which they didn't seem to mind at all in the play). I would like to have been like that postman, but found all this vibrancy in real life a bit intimidating and overwhelming. It was all right when it was Communists abroad doing it and I was one of the privileged few who saw it, but all this vigour seemed too free-form and out of control and it was happening just a bus ride away from our house. So I would hurry past all the colourfulness to get to the Cockers' flat.

There was another Wednesday Play written by a man who I'm sure was called Barry Blancmange, shown, I think, in 1967 or 1968. It had only one set, a smart room in which a group of people sat at a fashionable dinner party making polite chatter, while in a corner, unwatched, a television played footage of the Vietnam War. From time to time the camera would cut away from the guests to the TV, and when it came back to the dinner party one of the diners would have burst into flames and was now reduced to a smouldering, black stump. It went on like this for an hour of prime-time broadcasting until there was nobody left at the dinner party and probably nobody watching either who wasn't a blackened stump themselves.

Though they lived in this cosmopolitan quarter there was something quite austere about Maeve and Len's Communism. They, and Cliff too, were very staunch and uncritical members of the party and completely unquestioning of the actions of the Soviet Union. Though they attended to all the other rituals such as paying party dues, going to see the Red Army Ensemble and shouting at the television, by this time Molly and Joe had both stopped attending actual party meetings. I suspect that Len and Maeve found something a little untrustworthy in my parents' politics, which was fine by me.

Glen was less political than Cliff, who shared his parents' beliefs, and a less restrained character. I was very honoured to be invited to a small party in their flat to celebrate Maeve and Len's twenty-fifth wedding anniversary. Apart from me there were only family members present, except their oldest son who was nowhere to be seen. Then, just after 10.30 when the pubs closed, Glen turned up drunk with three or four straggly-haired, whey-faced hippies. There were three pubs in Liverpool where everybody drank, O'Connors, the Crack and the Philharmonic Hotel, and when the barman started shouting last orders there at 10.15 somebody would always say, 'Hey, man, does anyone know where there's a party, man?' To which on that night Glen had replied, 'Yes, man, I know where there's a party, man.' The hippies brushed past Cliff's granny and headed straight for the drink and the cocktail sausages. In a very quiet voice Cliff said to his brother, 'Glen, could I have a word with you out on the landing?'

'Sure, man,' said Glen.

He followed Cliff out of the room, and the next sound we heard was the smack of somebody being punched very hard followed by the sound of them falling down a long flight of stairs. After a second Cliff came back into the room and said to the grazing hippies, 'Right, you lot, fuck off out of it!' Which they did, moaning to themselves about people being 'downers, man'. Then the party carried on as if nothing had happened, and after a while Glen came back into the room rubbing his head.

Too Many C2s

During the long period of recovery following Joe's botched surgery, when he had been convalescing, then working part-time on light duties, Molly had herself gone back to work part-time. She spent three days a week at the Vernon's Pools company, with thousands of other women, combing through the coupons each week for a winner. And when Joe returned to work as a foreman he was still not making the money he would have made doing shifts as a guard, so she continued to go to work. She enjoyed getting out of the house and valued the comradeship she found at Vernon's. Indeed, Molly enjoyed herself so much that in all the time she was at the pools firm she never organised a strike.

Up until that point the only employment my mother had had during her marriage was doing what we called 'the surveys'. Our family's connection with opinion polling had begun in the 1930s when Joe had carried out some research for the left-wing newspaper the *News Chronicle*, performing surveys which involved asking people in the street questions on political choices, shopping patterns and reading habits. In time he began to do the same thing on a part-time basis for the Gallup organisation, and after they were married Molly took over this work. When I was young Molly and I once went to the Isle of Man in very stormy seas to spend a couple of nights in budget boarding houses. During the day we would stop people on the rain-lashed promenade to ask them what they wanted out of a holiday on the Isle of Man, which was mostly for the rain to stop.

When Molly went to work for Vernon's, she suggested I might want to earn a little money during the long summer holiday doing the surveys myself. This was the second time it had been suggested that I needed to find employment. I had briefly, via a friend from school, done a little part-time work sweeping up in the Grafton Bingo Hall in West Derby Road, but they had had to ask me to go and hide in a back room after complaints that my bizarre manner and unusual appearance were frightening the old lady customers.

I imagine that, as well as getting a bit of pocket money, my parents thought that doing the opinion polling would teach me the virtues of meticulousness, responsibility and reliability, but it didn't turn out that way. One of the requirements of doing surveys was that you were supposed to ask your questions of people in every one of the socio-economic groups. Socio-economic grouping, a system commonly used in market research, ran from A to E and classified a household according to the job of its main wage-earner. A was a professional person or somebody at director level; B was senior management; C1 was junior management or clerical; C2 was skilled working class; D was unskilled working class, manual labourers and so on; and E was those reliant on the state such as pensioners or the unemployed. This was a problem. It was easy enough for me to find C2s since that was everybody's parents, and there were also plenty of Ds and a few Es around our way. But I'm not sure an A had ever been in Anfield, and even if they had they had never hung around long enough for me to go up to them and ask them for their views on detergents, soup or skiing holidays.

I'm sure that somebody more suited to this type of work would have found a legitimate way to locate members of every socio-economic group, but as soon as I set out to do the surveys I discovered that I had several failings which militated against me doing the job effectively. At the outset there was my inability to be systematic. My very first job was a survey on chemical fertiliser. A more organised person might have contacted the farmers' union, got a list of members, phoned ahead and made appointments, then travelled to their farms and conducted the survey.

What I did was catch a ferry to Wallasey. I was certain they had farms on the Wirral because I was pretty sure they had countryside out there somewhere – I had seen it from the train on the way to Chester. Then from the Wallasey landing stage I walked up the ramp to the bus station and went from unfamiliar bus to unfamiliar bus asking the conductors, 'Do you go anywhere in the country where they have farms?' Finally I found one who said that they did go to the country and that was where they kept the farms, so I caught his bus and got off where he told me to, which was certainly in the middle of the countryside.

I stood in a lane with cowslips dotting the hedgerows and watched the bus disappear into the distance. Then silence descended, nothing moving in the warmth of a spring day. After a few moments of indecision I decided to carry on trudging up the lane in the direction the bus had vanished in, until eventually I came to a rough track that seemed like it might lead to a farmhouse. Following ten minutes of walking I was attacked by a dog and had to run away. I found a path, stumbled through a wood and found another farmhouse, but the farmer's wife was extremely annoyed at being disturbed in her chores by a long-haired youth mumbling about her preference in nitrates. Then I said to her, 'Oh, before I start I need to know, would you describe yourself as a C1? Or would you say you were a B? You're not a C2, are you?' At which point I had to run away again. As far as I could tell the most common animals in the countryside weren't sheep or chickens but angry dogs. Finally a farmer did speak to me. He pointed out that I was in an area devoted entirely to dairy farming and they had no use for chemical fertiliser.

I was astonished at how bad all this made me feel – I hated

how out of my depth I was, how alien and confusing those country lanes seemed and how much of a failure I felt. There was a raging compulsion in me to succeed, to gain mastery over the situation, and yet I couldn't seem to go about it in the way that anybody sensible would. And I didn't like talking to people I didn't know, either. It was like being on the date with the girl on the boat. What did they want? What did they think of me? Why weren't they saying anything? Would they like it if I sang 'Build Me Up, Buttercup'?

I got back to Anfield late in the evening, hot and dusty. Giving vague replies to my parents' enquiries as to how it had gone, I went up to my bedroom and sat at the little desk where I sometimes did my homework. After a few minutes of staring at the questionnaire forms I began to write. I invented addresses, made up names and of course faked entirely the answers to questions about chemical fertiliser – just like Volunteer Marek in *The Good Soldier Schweik* writing articles about imaginary animals for the natural history magazine he worked for. I sent my survey off and in a few weeks received a cheque and another assignment, this one about chocolate bars.

In the autumn, because they were so pleased with my work I was getting sent many more opinion polls to carry out and beginning to feel overwhelmed. When I returned to school after half-term I got my fellow pupils involved. At first I just asked them to pretend to be their parents and give the answers they thought their parents might give, but after a while I simply handed out the forms and left them to it. They in turn now started to get carried away and began inventing identities, claiming to be a Dutch pilot who owned a string of racehorses or, more worryingly, a female ballet dancer with a great liking for rugby players. In many ways it was more creative than the English lessons we sat through. During the lunch break the whole class would be quietly working away, compiling false information which I sent off to headquarters and which was then used to formulate government transport and housing policy, predict shopping trends and analyse how the public felt about the politics of the day for articles in newspapers and magazines.

Bicycles to Vietnam or Somewhere

At the age of fourteen going on fifteen my dance card was as full as that of a debutante doing the London season. I had good pals my own age at school; I had Cliff and his mates, all older boys; I spent a great deal of time with Cliff's family as well as my own; and I had begun to get involved in organised revolutionary politics. In 1966 I joined the youth wing of the Communist Party – the Young Communist League, generally referred to as the YCL. There was no pressure from my parents to do so, it was just a natural and timely thing as if I was seamlessly moving into the family business. I always thought that if we had had a van it would have written on the side in big letters: 'Joseph Henry Sayle and Son – Revolutionaries. Estimates given. No Kalashnikovs left in this van overnight.'

The first meeting of the YCL that I attended was at a small, early nineteenth-century terraced house on the other side of Oakfield Road, one of the poorest type of workers' cottage with a front door that opened directly on to the street. The house was owned by a man called Eric Savage who, though he might have been a Communist, certainly wasn't young. I learned at the meeting that this was quite normal. Though the membership of the YCL consisted of boys and girls between fifteen and twenty years of age, the leadership of the Communist Party didn't trust them to run their own affairs. So the secretaries of the local groups were generally middle-aged men who had been vetted by the CP hierarchy – though solely for doctrinal obedience. Eric Savage shared the house with two young women who were both in the YCL: one was called Fizzy and the other Sheila. He had been a member of one of the lesser Merseybeat bands in the early 1960s and owned two giant Alsatian dogs who were eating the walls of his home and finally broke through to the house next door.

My first meeting involved rehearsing in the road for a piece of street theatre that the group were planning to put on at a Vietnam demonstration at the Pier Head. We stood around outside Eric's house and somebody pretended to be an American soldier stabbing a peasant woman with a bayonet. That was as far as we got, because everybody appeared to run out of energy after that point. It seemed extraordinarily lame.

Much as another household might hold in high esteem a religious personage, a popular singer or some local sports team, the Soviet double agents Philby, Burgess and Maclean were much-revered figures in our home. We admired the way they had managed to deceive the British security services for so many years while working for the cause of Communism, we valued the damage they had caused to the reputation of Britain and the hundreds of British agents they had effectively killed, and we applauded the way they had evaded punishment, escaping from the West to enjoy what we supposed were full and fulfilling lives in Moscow and going to see the Red Army Ensemble whenever they felt like it. When Philby published his autobiography, *My Silent War*, I was particularly taken with his description of the moment when he first joined MI6. So incompetent and chaotic did those around him seem that he assumed he was working for some sort of sham front organisation designed to deceive the enemy. He imagined that at some point, when he had been with them for a while, he would be shown the real, hidden MI6, all cool efficiency and sleek modernity. Only slowly did it dawn on him that the ramshackle organisation he was working for was all there was. There was no better MI6 – this was it.

I felt the same about the YCL. This was the youth wing of an organisation that occupied hundreds of Special Branch spies in the UK. Internationally, Communism controlled something like a third of the world's population – the Soviet Union, China, great swathes of South-east Asia, Cuba, all of eastern Europe – and yet these people couldn't organise the fake stabbing of a peasant woman in the street.

At Eric's house I met a tall red-head, a couple of years older than me, Ian Williams. From time to time I would see him on the political scene at mass meetings or demonstrations, as we shopped around deciding who we would give our revolutionary business to. Ian took the idea of revolution so seriously that he invested in his own crash helmet to wear on demonstrations. It was a cylindrical leather-covered thing with long flaps like the ears of a bloodhound that buckled under the chin, and was of a type that was generally worn by human cannonballs at the circus.

He never came to another meeting of the YCL, and you could see why. The thing that finally did for me was when they organised a nationwide campaign called Bicycles for Vietnam, an operation orchestrated by the leadership in London. Two trusted members, who were both rather handsome twenty-five-year-old guys, were to drive an ancient removal van round the country collecting unwanted bicycles which they would then take down to Marseilles for transshipment by Cuban freighter to the North Vietnamese port of Haiphong. When the bicycles arrived in South-east Asia they would be employed in the war against US imperialism. We were already aware that for the Vietnamese the bicycle was a mighty weapon – the Vietcong would reputedly transport up to a ton of munitions along the Ho Chi Minh Trail on a single machine. For me, though, this confirmed that the YCL didn't know what they were doing. This scheme was just a piece of make-work nonsense, designed solely to distract fractious members like me who were becoming disenchanted with the group and their elderly, rubber mac-wearing leadership. My guess was that the Vietcong had their own bicycles, sturdy Chinese-style machines, and had no need for bikes designed with the European market in mind, models that folded in the middle or pink ladies' bikes with shopping baskets attached to the front handlebars.

When the guys turned up at Eric's house they acted all Southern, arrogant and snotty in their leather jackets and stubble. Then they both got drunk on cheap red wine and I think they slept with both Fizzy and Sheila, which I would like to have done, but worst of all I saw them casting covetous glances at my brand-new second-hand Raleigh Equipe racing bike with five Campagnolo Grand Sport gears and Brookes leather racing saddle. The last I heard of these two men and their truck full of bicycles was that, after careering all over the UK causing chaos and sleeping with members' girlfriends, they had crashed into a ditch outside Boulogne and abandoned the van. It didn't seem a very effective way to fight the forces of US imperialism.

o– 40 –o
The Brightest Heaven of Invention

Despite being a noisy show-off, up until my fifteenth year I had never been in any disciplinary trouble at school. But all that quickly began to change. Apart from anything else I felt free to challenge the staff and their rules because I was certain that I wasn't going to get punished in any significant way. Another child might have resented his mother turning up at the school complaining or fighting his battles for him, but early on I had realised there was no way I could deflect Molly from interfering in my life and so I might as well use it to my advantage. One of the favourite stories from my childhood that Molly would tell about herself concerned a kid from another street who had been pushing me around outside our house. Hearing the commotion, Molly and our dog Bruno had come roaring out of the front door and chased the kid away, pursuing him to the corner. The next time I saw the bully, he was full of admiration. 'Your mum should be in the Olympics,' he said. Molly loved that story.

So fear of Molly was probably why, despite all the things I did, I was not once caned. Corporal punishment wasn't that common at our school but it was used on occasion and though, particularly later on, I committed several offences that would have earned another boy six strokes on the hand I never got them.

I started to argue more fiercely with the teachers in class and I began to take liberties with the school uniform. Rather than the regulation striped tie, I wore a thin black knitted one. I wore high cuban-heeled boots rather than the official sensible brogues, and after my plastic mac caught fire I bought another one, bronze-coloured, which drove the staff into paroxysms of anger with its gaudy iridescence.

They tried to discipline me. I got a lot of lines, I had to write out various scientific laws hundreds of times so that I could recite them without knowing what they meant, and I was given tons of detentions. From time to time I was also required to do my homework while sitting outside the head-master's office. But I never got the cane. And the fact that the other kids saw me getting away with stuff that they were getting beaten for only served to increase the idea that there was something special and mysterious about me – at least that's what I thought. 'Why didn't Sambo get the cane?' kids would say in aggrieved tones, rubbing their stinging palms. 'He was there when it caught fire. In fact it was his idea to set it alight.' But Sambo said nothing. He let the impression grow that he was the headmaster's illegitimate son or that his Communism gave him magical powers. He certainly wasn't going to let on that he only got away with stuff because the staff were frightened of his mum.

After the betraying of Peter Pemberton it had taken me quite a long time before I made another best friend my own age, but after a while I became close to another boy at Alsop. His name was Leo Scher and one or both of his parents were Swiss. For a couple of years we were very good friends. He lived in the Wavertree district of the city where I would visit him on a Saturday. We would go to the swimming baths or take his dog for a walk in the park; then I would be home by five-thirty or six and I'd be in from then on. Then one day, I think it was a Saturday, it was as if I thought to myself, 'Sod this!' I never spent another night in, and I didn't spend any more time with Leo Scher.

There was a different group of boys from my class that I started hanging about with. One of them, Sid, was on probation for committing some minor crime. He said he got to talk to his probation officer about whatever he wanted for an hour a week. I thought having somebody who had to listen to you for a whole hour sounded brilliant. And he said he was given a transistor radio by the probation service as a Christmas present.

We were doing *Henry V* for O-Level and as there was a

production at the old Hope Hall, now renamed the Everyman Theatre, the school gave us the afternoon off so we could go as a group to see the play in the evening. Sid spent the afternoon drinking, and when the Prologue came on at the beginning of the play and said, 'Oh for a muse of fire that would ascend the brightest heaven of invention . . .' Sid jumped up and shouted, 'Ah, fuck off. . . .' To his credit Roger Sloman, the actor playing the Prologue, paused, looked directly at Sid and said, 'Right, I'll come on and do that again then', which got a big laugh and took the heat out of the situation – a lesson in comedy I made a note of. The play progressed with ushers chasing Sid all over the theatre, which only added to the Elizabethan atmosphere of the event.

I had had my first drink on a Vietnam demonstration. When I was not quite fifteen I had persuaded another boy from school called John Burrell, who was a Mod, to come down to London with me to go on a demo. The final destination must have been St Paul's Cathedral, because we ended up in a pub at Ludgate Circus where I think I asked the barman for 'A half of a beer'. At first I couldn't understand what anybody saw in this odd stuff, but I forced myself. As Communist literature constantly pointed out, sacrifices had to be made if you wished for freedom.

A gang of us started going out drinking together at the weekends and sometimes even early on a week-night. Neither Molly nor Joe drank much – strange bottles of plum brandy given to us by the Hungarian Minister for Railways would lie

for years in the Secatrol untouched, and my parents never ever
went to the pub, 'Dreadful smoky places,' Molly said they
were. So I figured that would be a good place to hide from
them.

There was no moral panic back then over young people
drinking and there was never a problem concerning our age
– if you wore a suit and tie and didn't misbehave you could
drink in a pub from about the age of six. We frequented pubs
in Anfield and Everton and drank pints of dark brown mild
ale mixed with a bottle of pale ale, a drink which was called
a Brown Mixed. I loved those pubs. Each was divided into
several bars, a snug, a public and a saloon bar being usually the
minimum and often there could be more, all of them equipped
with copper-topped tables and seating covered in a sort of red
linoleum – and my parents weren't in any of them. There were
many local breweries – Higson's, Walker's Warrington Ales,
Threlfall's – and one called Bent's whose pubs were tiled like
lavatories and sold their own brand of wine they called Bentox.

At the weekends, if the gang weren't available, rather than
stay about at home I would go into the centre of town and
just walk about. I didn't walk about with any purpose – just
walked. I didn't even stop for coffee or a sandwich or anything,
being unsure how you bought such things. When I was with
a group of people I knew how to act; I had a sense of what
my purpose was within the pack, which was basically to clown
around, carry on and make trouble. And if you were in an
unfamiliar place there would always be somebody else in the
group who understood the rules of the place – or if you got
thrown out you got thrown out together. When I was on my

own a paralysing uncertainty took hold of me. I would think to myself, 'Do you go up to the counter and order your sandwiches, or do you wait to be served?' So in the end I didn't have a sandwich.

I also began to develop a paranoid dread that I would be thrown out of places because of the way I looked, which was a reasonable fear. Along with my long hair I was now experimenting with hippy clothes. I often wore a denim jacket that Molly had lined with rabbit fur bought at a *Daily Worker* bazaar, beads round my neck and of course my toy hat. With my clothes I was ineptly attempting to emulate the bands I saw performing on *Top of the Pops* or whose pictures I saw in the music papers I sometimes bought. The boys I hung out with wisely stuck to suits and ties when they weren't in their school uniforms. People might wear fur coats and beads on the King's Road, Chelsea, but in Liverpool the wrong kind of shoelace could still get your head kicked in.

So I mostly hung about in places like the Walker Art Gallery where they had to let you in and where it was unlikely, though in Liverpool not guaranteed, that you would get into a fight. There was a Rembrandt self-portrait that I used to spend hours standing in front of, and a Lucian Freud painting of a man in a mac standing by a door in a bedsit in Paddington that particularly attracted my attention. 'That's what I want to do when I'm older,' I thought to myself. 'Be painted standing by a door in a room in a seedy part of London.' I also enjoyed many of the Pre-Raphaelite paintings that the Walker owned, paintings which I imagined would echo the trippy colours of a hippy lightshow if I ever got to see one.

I also spent a huge amount of time in Liverpool's two cathedrals, not attending services or anything but just sort of standing there. One thing that had really stuck with me and which I never questioned was my parents' violent atheism. Whenever we were told Bible stories at school my mind had shut down like a shop on a Sunday. So with places of worship there was not a whisper of religious awe in the way I regarded them – to me they were just big, complicated buildings. The Neo-Gothic Anglican cathedral at one end of Hope Street, designed by the twenty-two-year-old Giles Gilbert Scott, seemed like the most gigantic and elaborate Victorian pub in the world – the same stained glass, the same highly polished brass and stone-flagged floor, even the side chapels were like the subsidiary bars you found in an alehouse (the ladies' bar, the snug and the saloon). Its foundation stone had been laid in 1904, but it was still unfinished in the 1960s. There was also a magnificently spooky and overgrown graveyard that I liked to lurk in. The cathedral was surrounded by little streets of terraced housing, which provided a counterpoint to its bombastic bulk.

By contrast, the building of the Catholic cathedral at the other end of Hope Street began in October 1962 and was completed in May 1967. I spent a lot of time there too. In those days there was a chain of restaurants called the Golden Egg which employed a very similar design aesthetic to Liverpool's Catholic cathedral. They both made liberal use of handmade ceramics and modern materials such as coloured plastics and back-lit fibreglass panels. One day while wandering around the Catholic cathedral I came upon the most peculiar thing. Beneath the plinth on which the space capsule-shaped modern building rested, there was an older building. I didn't know it then, and there were no explanatory signs, but this was the crypt of Sir Edwin Lutyens' massive classical/Byzantine cathedral which was begun in 1933 and then abandoned – a building which, if it had been completed, would have become the second-largest church in the world with the world's largest dome. As it was, it looked as if the modern cathedral had stolen an older one and was then sitting on it.

Morning Assembly

Staying out till all hours meant I was frequently late for school. One day, long after assembly had begun, I was trying to sneak on to the premises unnoticed when I saw another dark-haired boy the same age as myself strolling through the gates, hands in pockets, whistling happily to himself. I followed this boy to a classroom where he joined a number of other boys who were sitting about in a relaxed fashion, reading magazines and comics or chatting happily together.

A prefect walked past and I said to him, 'Hey, who are those kids in that room?'

'Those are the Jews,' he replied.

'The Jews?'

'Yeah, they're Jews. Morning assembly involves a lot of

Christian hymn singing, so because of their religion they don't have to attend. They can more or less come in when they want as long as they get here by the beginning of classes. Unlike you, Sayle. You're on detention . . . again.'

When I got home that evening I angrily asked Molly why she hadn't got me excluded from religious assembly because I was Jewish.

'I didn't want you to be left out,' she replied.

'So let me get this right,' I said. 'You called me Alexei when everybody else was called Sidney, you took me to see *Alexander Nevsky* and *Ivan the Terrible* rather than *Bambi* and *Pinocchio*, you made me wear peculiar trousers . . . .' My trousers were a big area of contention between me and Molly at the time. Since I had been a child Molly had always made my trousers on her sewing machine. This had been fine when I was young and unselfconscious and in shorts, but once I moved up to proper trousers at the age of eleven or so it slowly began to occur to me that there might be something a bit off about my pants. By the time I got to fourteen I was certain that the trousers I was wearing possessed all kinds of strange bulges, weird pouchy bits in the seat and twisted seams that ran all over the place, and one leg always seemed to be at least six inches shorter than the other. Molly, on the other hand, was convinced that there was absolutely nothing wrong with her handiwork. I remember standing on a stool with her sticking pins in me and me screaming at her, 'I bet you were a lousy tailor.' And she replied, 'Yes, I was,' and she laughed, which made me absolutely crazy. The weird thing was that neither of us ever thought of going to a shop and just buying some proper factory-made trousers.

I continued with my diatribe: 'You forced me to see the Red Army Choir rather than the Beatles! You told me Lenin came down the chimney at Christmas with my presents! And yet, and yet, the one time when me being a bit different could have got me another half an hour in bed, you didn't want me to feel left out!'

'Oh, fuck off, Lexi,' she said.

Spending five years at forced Christian worship did at least make me one of the few atheist Communist Jews who knew all the words to 'All Things Bright and Beautiful' and the Lord's Prayer. I consoled myself with the thought that if the National Front or some other Nazi organisation ever gained power in Britain and their version of the Gestapo came for me I might be able to pass myself off as a Christian by enthusiastically singing every verse of 'Oh God Our Help in Ages Past'.

Having managed to put a bit of physical distance between me and my parents the time now seemed right to try and put a degree of ideological space between us too. Most teenagers rebel against their parents, try and become different from their mother and father, preferably adopting some way of life that really annoys them. But for me breaking away was more problematic because I really liked being left-wing and I really liked left-wingers. Being a Communist amongst Communists was what defined me – it was my thing. So in the end the form my teen rebellion took was that I didn't do the obvious thing and become self-interested and reactionary and a little Tory, or, even worse, become self-interested and reactionary and join the Labour Party. I didn't even stop being a Communist. I just became a different kind of Communist.

Up until the late 1950s the two biggest socialist states, the USSR and the People's Republic of China, had seemed to be close as close could be. But towards the end of the decade splits in the relationship began to appear, until in 1961 Mao and the Chinese Communist Party openly denounced 'The Revisionist Traitor Group of Soviet Leadership'.

The dispute was really about national interest, access to nuclear technology and people simply not liking each other, but the ostensible reason for the fracture was disagreement over who was truly the heir of the Soviet Revolution. In 1956, in his 'Secret Speech' to the 20th Party Congress, Khrushchev had denounced the 'cult of personality' that surrounded Stalin and had revealed some of the terrible crimes committed during the Great Purges. Over the next couple of years Khrushchev attempted to reform the Soviet system, placing more emphasis on the production of consumer goods over traditional heavy industry and liberalising, a tiny bit, the repressive Soviet attitude towards any form of dissent. Though slightly assuaged by the crushing of revolts in Hungary and East Germany, many in the West's Communist movements were uneasy with this liberalisation. They didn't like the idea of a Communist society allowing its citizens to express their opinions freely or to have a choice of more than one type of hat. Yet they had nowhere to take their disaffection until the Sino–Soviet split offered these puritan characters a choice of an extra-dour kind of socialism more in keeping with their sententious inclinations.

So I became a Maoist, while my parents remained devoted to the Soviet Union. Soon violent arguments erupted over the breakfast table in 5 Valley Road, Liverpool 4.

'Don't you dare call your mother a Bureaucratist Capitalist Roader, Alexei!'

'Well, she is, Dad! Anyone disassociating themselves from direct manual labour is bound to set themselves apart from the masses, inevitably leading to Bureaucratism. As the Great Helmsman, Chairman Mao, has stated, "There must be no 'sitting in the office', 'no moving his mouth but not his hands'."'

'What are you talking about, Lexi? You haven't done a day's manual labour in your life! And why do the Gallup Poll people keep phoning, saying they need to speak to you urgently?'

'You're a Red Fascist, Molly! A Commandeerist! A One Voiceist! And is my football kit ready? Because we've got double games tomorrow.'

It was on a Vietnam demonstration early in 1967 when I first became aware of Maoism. There was this extraordinary guy walking along by himself; he had long hair, a straggly beard and a floor-length overcoat. Using both hands, he carried in front of him a large poster of Chairman Mao Tse-tung attached to a tube of grey plastic piping. As we passed a Chinese restaurant on Lime Street, all the waiters and chefs piled out of the restaurant cheering him and making the 'waving a little red book' gesture. Which, when I thought about it, seemed a bit odd since most of the Chinese in Liverpool had been in the city for three or four generations, spoke English with thick Scouse accents, were extremely entrepreneurial and held no affection for Communism. Maybe they were just excitied to see one of us parading around with a picture of one of them. This man was Nigel Morley Preston Jones and he was Merseyside's first Maoist.

Mao Tse-tung had launched the Chinese Cultural Revolution in May of the previous year, and for the first time there was a revolutionary movement that was explicitly centred on the youth of a country. Right across that vast nation young people were formed into Red Guard groups and were then encouraged to beat up their teachers, destroy factories and generally parade around like little dictators. It seemed such an obvious idea that teenagers should be allowed to wreck businesses and stop the traffic, many members of my generation wondered why nobody had thought of it before. After all, young people knew all there was to know on all subjects; our certainty and our clarity of thought meant that it was obvious that we should be put in charge of everything right away.

I Was a Teenage Maoist

In left-wing politics there were a number of code words that instantly signalled the ideology behind an organisation. If you were in the know you understood that 'Peace', as in 'Peace in Vietnam' or 'Women's Peace Day', meant 'Communist Party Front', while 'Solidarity', as in 'Vietnam Solidarity Campaign', meant Trotskyist-controlled. Similarly, though all Communists were supposedly Marxist-Leninists, inspired as they were by the economic and philosophical ideas of Karl Marx allied to V.I. Lenin's theories on imperialism and the nature of the vanguard party, if you went on about it, going so far as to include 'Marxist-Leninist' in the name of your group or party, then it meant that you were in fact a Maoist.

The leader of the Merseyside Marxist-Leninist Group was Ian Williams, the young man I had first encountered at the lame YCL meeting. Now a student at Liverpool University, he lived with his girlfriend Ruth who worked in an office to support them both since Ian, because of problems with his father, couldn't obtain a student grant. The MMLG was more diverse than a lot of left-wing groups. Its oldest member was a dock worker from Birkenhead called Wally Sturrock: high-cheeked and dark haired, part-gypsy, he was in his mid-twenties and unlike the rest of us was always well dressed in smart tailored suits, narrow shoes, colourful shirts and stylish slender ties. Another member, Dave, always reminded me of Pasha Antipov as played by Tom Courtenay in David Lean's film of *Doctor Zhivago*. Pasha is the disappointed romantic whose bitterness turns him into a cold-blooded and callous revolutionary known as Strelnikov. It was easy to imagine Dave travelling post-revolutionary Britain in an armoured train, shelling villages and shooting people for ideological deviationism. There was also the man with the picture of Mao on a stick, Nigel Morley Preston Jones. He had met Ian in a pub after some demonstration and, brought together by Nigel's photo of the Chairman, they had founded their own group. Nigel was converted to Marxism-Leninism by a guy he met in Glasgow who was a member of a tiny Scottish Marxist-Leninist party. Like all little parties this group put a great deal of energy into producing their newspaper, whose headline one month read 'Victory for Chairman Mao Tse-tung's Thought in the Gorbals'. After coming to Liverpool Nigel had found a job and a place to live at the Simon Community, a shelter for the homeless housed in a crumbling building just off Scotland Road where it was generally impossible to tell the difference between the clients and the staff.

I found myself in an odd position within the Marxist-Leninist group because, although all these people were older than me in conventional years, I was much older than them in Communist years. I had been around revolutionary politics since I was a baby and so sometimes had the strange sensation of being able to know exactly what they were going to say minutes before they had said it.

Other members were a young couple of social workers from Yorkshire called Barry and Ingrid and a New Zealand woman whose name was Judith Wareham. I don't recall Judith's particular motives for becoming a Marxist-Leninist, but for some reason the sterility and asceticism of Maoism and its Balkan offshoot, Enver Hoxha's hard-line Communist Albania, seemed to hold a particular attraction for Kiwis. Sometimes at night I would tune the little blue and white plastic radio to Radio Albania whose English-language service, judging by the accents, seemed to be staffed entirely by New Zealanders. In reciting their long screeds of Marxist theory they would always refer to the Premier of China, the Great Helmsman, as

'Chairman May-ow', as if he was somebody's pet cat. 'Today in Beijing Chairman May-ow congratulated the Albanian State Metalworks on increasing washer production by two hundred and twelve per cent thanks to the rigorous political analysis of vice president Mehmet Shehu.'

I used to wonder how they lived, these freckly redheads whose words floated to me over the short wave band – young men and women whose romantic obsession with a distant people and a violent ideology had landed them in a Balkan city that regularly ran out of soap. Did the Albanians secretly spy on them and keep them from mixing with the ordinary populace, or were they forced to take Albanian wives and husbands, boyfriends and girlfriends of impeccable revolutionary character? Were they allowed to go home if they changed their minds about Marxism-Leninism, and did they manage to get the latest rugby scores?

The weekly meetings of the Merseyside Marxist-Leninist Group were held at Ian and Ruth's place in Huskisson Street in Liverpool 8, where they lived in a high-ceilinged first-floor flat above a Jamaican drug dealer named Beaver. In becoming a Maoist I felt I finally belonged to something that was truly mine; for that brief period it was the height of fashion to be in a revolutionary group. I was also mixing on equal terms with people who were much older than I was – at fifteen I was by far the youngest member, quite a few of them were in their twenties. I thought myself very sophisticated and worldly to be hanging out with people such as these. There was a very nice girl called Chris Walker doing postgraduate work in psychology at Liverpool University, who joined the group a little while after me. Chris would walk me to the bus stop every week after the meetings and wait with me until the bus came. I thought she must live nearby or fancied me or found what I had to say about armoured fighting vehicles so fascinating that she wanted to spend every available minute with me, while in fact she was just making sure I got safely home to my mum.

My only real problem with being a Marxist-Leninist was that I didn't believe a word of it, or rather I both totally believed it and totally didn't believe it, all at the same time. The trouble with any kind of fundamentalist organisation is that it cannot be big on subtlety or nuance. The Nazis did not say, 'Well, some people don't like Jews, but live and let live is pretty much our attitude.' So it was a requirement that you switched off the critical part of your brain for meetings and pretended that China acted only in the interests of international socialism, or that the oppressed peoples of the world were inevitably virtuous and decent and generally good at singing. I suppose I should have said some of this, at least to myself, but apart from a couple of exceptions my comrades seemed like nice people, were genuinely disturbed by injustice and bought me drinks, so I kept quiet.

Unfortunately your mind will not allow you to get away with the kind of split-brain thinking I tried to stick to. Psychological tensions rise to the surface and tend to find an outlet in erratic behaviour. In this I was no different from the seemingly pious Jew who secretly gorges on bacon sandwiches, the devout Muslim who drinks or the Evangelical preacher who dresses up as a cowgirl at weekends.

I sometimes thought that my feelings about being a

Communist were so ambivalent that I would have made an excellent double agent, a Special Branch spy, like the several hundred who were at that time infiltrating themselves into the top echelons of major trade unions such as the National Union of Mineworkers as well as many of the left-wing groups and parties. I thought of myself as someone who could pretend to be left-wing but in fact was working for the government, motivated by bitterness, ambition or extreme reactionary faith brought on by resentment of their parents. But then I thought I wouldn't really have made a good spy because the government agents always presented themselves as humourless ideologues who slithered their way to the top of the union or the party. They didn't suddenly run away from demonstrations like I did, throwing their placard in the gutter or sit at the back at meetings absent-mindedly making strange hooting noises.

The main activity of the group was running a bookstall every Saturday morning in Great Homer Street Market, better known as Paddy's Market, which was maybe three-quarters of a mile from Valley Road. The neighbourhood had until recently been a network of terraced streets radiating from a mile-long road on which there had been an astounding variety of shops – butchers, greengrocers, fishmongers, bakers, household equipment, clothing, confectionery, tobacco and sweet shops, a number of bicycle shops, a herbalist, a local department store called Sturlas, a Woolworth's and a cinema. All this had been demolished a few years before, and the former shops and houses replaced with a number of bleak tower blocks and a shopping precinct of extraordinary tawdriness and such flimsy construction that it looked as if it had been made out of the paper the architects had done their optimistic drawings on.

The weekend open-air market was held behind this precinct and, though all trace of the old area had been expunged, the former shoppers still came. In the Sherlock Holmes mysteries I read, if there was an indeterminate brown-skinned character he would inevitably be referred to as a 'Lascar'. Paddy's Market was full of Lascars, seamen from boats moored in the river who had been coming to the market for over a century to buy secondhand woollen clothes that they would unravel and take back home with them, presumably to make into new garments.

'Five shilly, Johnny,' the old women who ran the stalls would say to them as they haggled over some moth-eaten jumper. 'Five shilly, Johnny.'

'Two shilly?'

'Four shilly, Johnny.'

'Three shilly.'

And once they had finished buying old overcoats and worn out socks the Lascars could come to our stall and purchase copies of Lenin's *What Is to Be Done?*, Karl Marx's *Grundrisse: Foundations of the Critique of Political Economy* or Stalin's *History of the CPSU*.

The stall itself had been made from an oak door that somebody had salvaged from a building site and was incredibly heavy – it took four of us to carry it the half-mile from the Simon Community hostel where it was stored. We didn't know anybody who had a car. However, once we had put it up, Liverpool being the sort of place it was the stall did a reasonable amount of trade – better than some of the others that only seemed to sell twisted wire, broken fish tanks and rusted-up fuel pumps. There would always be some little old bloke in a flat cap coming up to us and saying, 'Ere, son, do you have Friedrich Engels' *The Holy Family*, the critique of the Young Hegelians he wrote with Marx in Paris in November 1844?'

'No, but we do have Engels' *The Condition of the Working Class in England in 1844.*'

'Naww, I've already got that.'

'Make a lovely Christmas present for a family member.'

'Eh, I suppose you're right there. Give us two copies then, son.'

The Unknown Vacuum Cleaner

Molly was not the most domestic of mothers. When attempting to clean the house she deployed a great deal of violence but to very little effect, moving the dirt around rather than actually picking it up. She used to store the vacuum cleaner at the top of the flight of stairs that led down to the cellar, and when she had finished using it, knocking the furniture about and frightening the dog she would just open the cellar door and throw the vacuum cleaner in so that it inevitably tumbled down the wooden stairs. Quite soon, due to this rough treatment the cleaner would stop working. Then it would be abandoned where it had fallen in the dark cellar and Molly would buy another, which she would throw down the cellar stairs like its predecessor. In time that cleaner would join its fallen comrades until after a few years there was a large pile of broken vacuum cleaners in our cellar with the one working cleaner lying on top.

Molly's biggest cleaning or recycling problem, though, was connected not with the accumulated dirt or rotting kitchen waste but with the *Soviet Weekly*. This was a Russian state-subsidised tabloid paper published in full colour which was crammed full of propaganda about the Communist workers' paradise. Lies about industrial production and the grain harvest would be accompanied by photos of smiling agricultural workers and industrial labourers, there were editorials and articles ranting against the West, and there was always a big spread on the latest African dictator being feted by Moscow. At some point in the distant past Molly and Joe had agreed to take six of these things each week and so they arrived every seven days, month after month, year after year, thumping on to the mat each Wednesday, a tightly rolled log of six *Soviet Weekly*s, like a slow ticking clock marking out the decades. From time to time the head office in Moscow would send us a bill, stating we owed them first fifty pounds, then a hundred pounds, then five hundred pounds, but they never attempted to collect the money and they never stopped sending the *Soviet Weekly*s.

It would have been all right if Molly hadn't felt that, though we had stopped reading them or even unwrapping them years ago, she couldn't bear to throw them out – she felt in some incoherent way that to do so would be a betrayal of the international struggle for freedom and justice. So instead of putting them in the bin she began to store them all over the house. Next to the front door was a coat rack mounted on the wall, and Molly would often pick up the roll of *Soviet Weekly*s as they came though the door and stuff them in the pocket of the nearest coat. If you left your coat hanging there for a few weeks you would find when you returned to it that every single pocket was stuffed with rolled up newspapers. People who came to visit would frequently go away with their coat or jacket feeling oddly heavy and bulky.

Finally, after years of this, Molly wound herself up to cancel our subscription. But on the very week she was planning to do it Soviet forces invaded Czechoslovakia, smashing Dubcek's Prague Spring, and she felt that the Russian government would take it as a criticism of their actions if she stopped taking their publication now. So they continued to arrive through our letter-box for years to come, bouncing on to the lino in the hall until the very day when the Soviet system itself collapsed.

The only daily newspaper we had ever taken at 5 Valley Road was the *Daily Worker*, the official organ of the Communist Party of Great Britain. While other households read papers which indulged in salacious tales of vicars and their misdeeds or bloodthirsty accounts of murders or showbusiness gossip or investigative journalism or humorous parliamentary sketches, everything we read had to be contorted to fit in with a document called *The British Road to Socialism*, which was the programme of the Communist Party of Great Britain and of the Young Communist League.

Organisationally, the Communist Party was a theocratic organisation very much like the Catholic Church. As with the

Church of Rome the mass of worshippers were actively discouraged from studying the sacred texts, in our case the works of Marx, Engels and Lenin, themselves. Instead the interpretations of the holy books were handed down to the party members from on high, after the line had been decided, first in Moscow and then in London by the party's theologians. For many years the leading 'theorist' had been an Anglo-Indian called Rajani Palme Dutt, whose many dull books resided in our front room. But for the ordinary member or sympathiser the main way in which the party line was received was via the *Daily Worker*, which did not make for the most thrilling read over the breakfast table.

Because it was supposed to be a daily paper rather than a theoretical journal the *Daily Worker* was required to have some of the features of a more mass-market publication. Most famous of all was their racing tipster, 'Cayton'. In 1959 he had spectacularly tipped the winner of the Grand National, Russian Hero, at 66–1 and over the years he generally came out well ahead of all the other tipsters on more capitalistic newspapers. My parents held this up in some vague way as being a triumph of Marxist-Leninist thought, without going into the specifics too deeply. The *Daily Worker* also had its own comic strip entitled 'The Adventures of Pif'. This cartoon featured a patched, ideologically correct dog called Pif and a black and white cat called Hercules. 'Pif' was actually reprinted from the French Communist Party newspaper *L'Humanité*, and though his words were translated into English the characters that he met, policemen, shopkeepers and so on, were unmistakably French in their dress. I don't know if 'Pif' was funny in his native language, but he sure as hell wasn't funny in

English and frequently didn't even make any kind of sense. As I became fascinated by existentialism I sometimes wondered whether leading French Communist philosophers such as Jean-Paul Sartre hadn't taken a turn at doing 'Pif', so arcane did his adventures seem.

In 1966 the *Daily Worker* was relaunched as the *Morning Star* in a supposedly more accessible tabloid format, but the problems with content continued. 'Pif' was still there, as was 'Cayton'. One improvement that did occur, though it didn't appeal much to the old Stalinists, was that, because there were a number of talented young people writing for the paper who were tuned in to the emerging progressive music scene, the *Morning Star*'s coverage of gigs and albums by groups such as the Incredible String Band, King Crimson, Yes, Genesis and Soft Machine was often much better than that of the dedicated music papers. This could sometimes lead to some incongruous juxtapositions, for instance the review of a gig by Emerson, Lake and Palmer at the St Martin's Lane Arts Lab, describing their 'freaky light show', might appear next to Soviet Premier Leonid Brezhnev's latest pronouncement on the best grain harvest in the Urals ever.

Another feature that carried over from the *Daily Worker* was the 'Fighting Fund'. Both papers were always continually in financial difficulties. The *Morning Star*, like its predecessor, carried little commercial advertising apart from Au Montmartre and that boarding house where we used to stay in Belgium. Car makers and manufacturers of expensive watches were not interested in the Communist market, and the cover price did not even meet print and distribution costs. So every day the paper ran its Star Fund appeal. The prominence of the Star Fund appeal waxed and waned depending on how much trouble the paper was in. It told the readers how much money they needed not to go under that month and how short they were from achieving their goal. This always lent a slightly hysterical tone to the front page, as if it was some dumped girlfriend who was constantly threatening suicide.

All those who were regular subscribers to the paper also knew that these threats contained a large element of pretence, since we were certain that the *Morning Star* would always, in the end, be rescued by the Soviet Union. Everyone was convinced that the paper was massively supported by Moscow in that the authorities there took bulk orders for which they had no conceivable use. I imagined that somewhere in the vast expanse of the Ukraine there was a house which in my mind's eye had a front door just like ours, and that every week twenty-four copies of the *Morning Star* would flop on to their doormat and every week the mother would pick them up and stick them straight into the pocket of a nearby overcoat.

44
But I'm a Member

Being old-school Communist Party Cliff Cocker really disliked Ian Williams and my new Maoist mates, but for me the more places I had to go, the more people I knew, the better. I found that if I had time to myself, especially in the evenings, if I wasn't drinking with Sid and my classmates or at a meeting or seeing Cliff a terrible chasm of panic opened up in my mind and I had to run around town until I found somebody to talk to, somebody to distract me. Fortunately via the Marxist-Leninists I had finally got to know the world of Liverpool's radical pubs.

All the bohemians, the artists, the poets and the left-wingers drank in three or four boozers on the edge of the town centre. At night, the town itself was the province of people who didn't know who Friedrich Engels was and had never heard of the Foreign Minister of China, Chou En-lai – clerks, Mods, rich Jewish kids, businessmen, secretaries, nurses. After the pubs closed at 10.30 these people went on to clubs such as the Mardi Gras where Marvin Gaye and Otis Redding performed before they were stars – the Blue Angel, the Odd Spot and the Cavern. But the people I mixed with stayed out of town at night. We drank in the Philharmonic Hotel, a monument of Victorian exuberance with dark wood-panelled walls, copper reliefs, Art Deco lights, a mosaic-covered floor and a bar with a huge golden eagle watching over the drinkers. Alternatively we met up in the Crack, which was the pub favoured by the art students and consisted of lots of little rooms each with weird paintings on the walls.

O'Connor's was the druggiest pub. A former chapel with doors at each end, it allowed the dealers to run out of one door when the police came through the other. And finally there was the one favoured by the Marxist-Leninists, named the Grapes but called Kavanagh's by everyone. Wally, Dave, Ian and the rest drank in what was effectively a corridor, though there were two snugs, with old murals on the walls and unusual round tables supposedly taken from a sister ship of the *Titanic* and fireplaces which blazed with warmth in the winter. I would get the bus into town and then walk up Renshaw Street to O'Connor's. If there was nobody I knew in O'Connor's I would go to the Crack and then to the Philharmonic until I found somebody I knew, and perhaps somebody who might buy me a drink if my pocket money had run out.

All these pubs, especially Kavanagh's, were full of 'characters' – men with strange quirks of behaviour which a lot of people found enchanting and bohemian but whose manner I thought was contrived or self-conscious or just plain stupid. There was one Irish guy who hung around with us. In Ireland this man had been a member of a Communist/Nationalist group called Saor Eire and he was now on the run after being involved in several fund-raising bank raids. He was trying to keep his identity secret but everybody called him Irish John or alternatively 'Irish John Who's Been Involved in All Those Bank Raids in Ireland'. He tried to pay for his drinks with hundred-pound Irish banknotes, then was quickly arrested and shipped back to Dublin. His real name was Simon.

Even more exciting than the pubs, but more intimidating too, were the shebeens, the after-hours clubs that everybody decamped to at 10.30. All these clubs were run by Liverpool's various immigrant communities. We had among others the Chinese Nationalist Seamen's Club, the Niger Club, the Ghanaian Club and our favourite, the Somali Club in Upper

Parliament Street, which had a restaurant upstairs that served a yellow curry that you could never get out of your clothes if you spilt it. The club was downstairs in the basement; they played reggae music at a time when it was unknown outside the ghetto and sold bottled beer from a rickety bar.

Oddly, if you were white you had no trouble getting into any of these shebeens, but if you came from one of the other immigrant communities it was impossible. If you were from Jamaica you couldn't get into the Yoruba, if you were Somali they wouldn't let you into the Niger, and vice versa. And they weren't that keen on letting me into anywhere. It wasn't that I was under-age – nobody ever commented on that – but there was just something about me, some aura which emanated from my personality that got on the nerves of door people. However, early one evening I had a spot of luck. I had managed to get into the Somali because it was almost empty, when suddenly the phone behind the bar rang. The owner came out to announce that the call had been from the police, informing them that there was going to be a raid in ten minutes. Some people left right away, but for those of us who remained they dragged out a box covered in dust and proceeded to give everybody member-ship cards which looked like they had been printed in the nineteenth century and which we all signed.

The next time I went to the Somali the man on the door stopped me, so I said, 'But you have to let me in. I'm a member.'

'What do you mean you're a member?' he asked incredulously.

I pulled out my membership card and showed it to him. 'I've never seen one of those before,' he said, and waved me in with a pained expression on his face.

One other place was the Gladray Club, which charged a shilling whenever there was a stripper on. It was always full of uniforms, postmen in uniform, busmen in uniform, policemen in uniform and sixth-formers from the Liverpool Institute in uniform – but they would never let me in, even for a shilling.

Apart from introducing me to pubs and African shebeens the other great thing about the Marxist-Leninist Group was the theory study classes which were held once or twice a week. Unlike the policy of the old CP, members of the MMLG were encouraged to study the sacred texts themselves rather than have them interpreted by a crotchety Anglo-Indian and the gnomic statements of a French cartoon dog. Though, under the influence of the Red Guards, the rest of the Chinese economy was collapsing into chaos the country was still managing to produce huge numbers of the Marxist classics which they then sold around the world at a subsidised price. These books were rather elegant in a utilitarian way: a uniform edition with a cream-coloured, thick paper cover and a slightly blurry old-fashioned typeface. It was Ian who led these discussions, and they followed a pattern of study which had existed since the first editions of Marx had appeared and working people all over the industrialised world had seized them and tried to prise open their meaning in rooms above pubs, front parlours and Mechanics' Institutes. The group ploughed through *The Communist Manifesto*, *Wages, Prices and Profits* and Stalin's *History of the CPSU* at the speed of the slowest and dimmest-witted member of the group, which was usually me.

For a bit of light relief we would sometimes perform 'The Great Money Trick' from Robert Tressell's novel *The Ragged Trousered Philanthropists*. This book, first published in 1914, is widely regarded as a classic of British working-class literature. It is based on Tressell's experiences of the building trade in which he worked and the poverty, exploitation and terror of the workhouse he found there. Tressell died the year before the book was published and was buried in Walton churchyard next to our school.

In the chapter entitled 'The Great Money Trick' the hero, Frank Owen, organises a mock-up of capitalism with his workmates, using slices of bread as raw materials and knives as machinery. Owen 'employs' his workmates to cut up the bread to illustrate that the employer – who does not work – generates personal wealth while the workers effectively remain no better off than when they began, forever swapping coins back and forth for food and wages. This is Tressell's practical way of illustrating the Marxist theory of surplus value, which in the capitalist system is generated by labour. We would endlessly cut up bits of bread and then pretend that we understood the theory of surplus value, though really it was no clearer now than it had been before. But it did make a change from Marx's argumentative, dense and grumpy writing.

After attending those study groups for something like a year a remarkable thing happened. The way in which we were taught history at school presented the past in one of two ways. Either it was rendered as an endless list of anglocentric facts about seed drills, Bessemer converters, steam-driven lathes and the Treaty of Potsdam, or we were fed the idea that the world changed, moved from stage to stage simply because various powerful or visionary personalities such as Abraham Lincoln, Henry VIII or Julius Caesar decided to do things and everybody went along with it because they made really convincing speeches. That and the notion that groups of people fought each other simply because they didn't get on. So the English Civil War was just an argument between two groups of people with different opinions about whether frilly shirts looked good, and the industrial revolution happened first in Britain because we were cleverer than everybody else and had a lot of coal. I had always struggled with this interpretation that the past was random and incoherent, that after Britain enthusiastically pursued slavery for a couple of hundred years Wilberforce came along and pointed out that it wasn't nice and everybody went, 'Oh, blimey you're right!' and stopped it except in the Southern States of the USA where they were confused because the sun was hot and they talked funny.

To me history as taught at school was like all those memories of galleries, castles and historic monuments that I didn't have. There was the same sense that if there was only some matrix, some philosophical framework to which I could attach all these facts then they would all make sense and they would all stay with me. And then halfway through Marx's *Wages, Prices and Profits* I suddenly thought to myself, 'Fuck me! This shit is actually true.'

Nobody was more surprised than me at this unexpected turn of events. Up until those study groups I had been like some Ulster Protestant born and brought up on the Shankhill Road whose faith is a matter of geography and tribalism. Then one day God appears to him and tells him that actually, yes, as it happens the Pope is the Anti-christ, Glasgow Rangers are the greatest football team in the world and the best way to worship Him, God, is to march about the streets wearing a bowler hat, holding a rolled-up umbrella and riding a white horse up and down the front at Southport on 12 July.

Though I hadn't seen it clearly until that moment, the truth was that like the Orangeman or the Sunni Muslim or the Southern Baptist I had been born into my faith. I had been brought up knowing nothing else, and the people I responded to broadly believed the same things that I did. The only difference was that what I believed, what my parents believed, appeared to be demonstrably correct. Once you understood Marx all the apparent chaos of human existence resolved itself into a coherent and comprehensive pattern. People fought not because they differed about how to wear a shirt but because they represented economic classes whose interests conflicted. The Cavaliers were landed aristocrats and their allies who wanted to hang on to a way of life being superseded by Cromwell's merchant class. Slavery was abolished not out of some idea of 'niceness' in the Northern states but because the industrial factory owners of Chicago and Detroit wanted the blacks to work in their factories, to be 'wage slaves' rather than actual slaves, though often the improvement in their physical conditions was marginal. The British Empire wasn't some project designed to bring enlightenment to ignorant savages, but rather a brutal and rapacious exploitation of peoples who were often more humane than us.

You can imagine, armed with this philosophy, how full of myself I now became. Even when I hadn't had the secret of human history in my grasp I had been a mouthy little bastard in class. Now I was unstoppable.

45

1968, a Year of Upheaval

When Joe was issued with his new British Rail, white-heat-of-technology-style uniform he put it on at home for us to see. Gone were the serviceable, dark blue serge trousers, peaked cap of timeless design, waistcoat and jacket with brass buttons. In their place he was now going to be forced to wear a short bum-freezer jacket made of some sort of polyester that was more commonly used to line the engine compartments of sports cars, with red piping down the sides and a chunky orange zipper up the front. On his head was perched a cylindrical cap with a short peak and ear flaps, also edged in red piping, that could be folded down in cold weather, and for his sixty-one-year-old legs they had given him bell-bottomed trousers. He looked like a very sad and tired Thunderbird puppet.

Since Joe had also been provided with a short cape to replace his long black BR overcoat with shiny brass buttons down the front I took the coat and began wearing it when I went out. It had the look of an old RAF overcoat, which was almost a uniform for hippies, but I gave it my own twist by tying the waist with string. I got a lot of admiring glances from the other hippies in O'Connor's for that coat. At work Joe continued to make mistakes, to confuse or forget things, but the men at Bidston always managed to cover these mistakes up or blame somebody else. In fact, if you didn't know, you couldn't spot that there was anything wrong with my father. Those who did know, me and Molly, were in a permanent state of manic watchfulness and inclined to see examples of memory loss and confusion where there was only normal hesitation and then become hysterical. Fearing a return of that terrifying thing, emotion, I'd go running out of the house looking for any kind of distraction, while my mother's response was to become a thorn in the side of US imperialism.

The Vietnam War, a war we weren't actually fighting in, was to us in the hermetically sealed world of the British left the defining cause of the period, prompting the first large-scale riots on the British mainland since the war and inspiring the plays of Barry Blancmange. Everybody considered it a more or less black and white example of a mighty imperial power (the United States) attempting to crush with brutal military force the aspirations of a small nation (Vietnam). Harold Wilson, the Labour Prime Minister, had managed despite enormous pressure from the United States to keep Britain out of the conflict but that didn't earn him many points from the left.

In 1966 Molly had gone down to London to attend a Women's Day 'Peace' conference. While there she became interested in the Vietnamese struggle for independence and on her return joined a group called Merseyside Peace in Vietnam. That 'Peace' word is there again because the Communist Party line at the time was to call for peace, rather than victory for the insurgent Vietcong and the North Vietnamese which is what everybody else wanted. Eventually Molly became secretary of Merseyside Medical Aid for Vietnam, a group that wasn't closely tied to the party. One of the first big campaigns Molly and her group organised, and which I reluctantly helped out with, was a giant petition-signing campaign. With a crowd of others I went from door to door in Huyton, collecting signatures from Harold Wilson's Liverpool constituents urging him to do a lot more to bring the Vietnam War to an end.

It was the first time I had been anywhere like Huyton, one of the new towns where the working classes of inner city Liverpool were meant to find fulfilment under the flat, sarcastic Lancashire skies. The rows and rows of raw new tenement buildings reminded me of the hen sheds at the Ovaltine Farm outside Abbot's Langley that I used to see from the window of the London train. They were buildings that represented an idea, a false dream, an illusion, rather than something that anybody or anything was truly supposed to live in.

In nearby Kirkby, another 1960s' new town, the Labour council had built at great cost an artificial ski slope. This would have been a dubious asset for the community even if it had been done right, but somebody blundered and they built it the wrong way round so that the slope ended right at the edge of the brand-new M62 motorway. If any of the community had ever used the slope they would have hurtled straight into six lanes of speeding traffic.

A young teacher gave me a lift home from Huyton. She was part of the campaign and had a Renault 4 with the broom-handle gear change. Very excited to be mixing on equal terms with a teacher, I was expounding confidently on my career plans. 'Obviously,' I said, 'I'll get eight or nine O-Levels, then I'll go on to do three A-Levels, then study philosophy at a major Oxford college before a career as the editor of a leading news magazine such as *Time*, *Newsweek* or *Paris Match* – or I might be a car designer.'

He said, 'Well, it's nice to see somebody who's got their career all planned out.' And then he laughed at me! Nobody had ever laughed at me before – not that I could remember, anyway. I didn't like it. It was a taste of what I did to others like Mr Johnson, and it turned out that it felt surprisingly unpleasant. I resolved never to let anybody do it to me again. We finished the journey in frosty silence.

The Catholic Bishop of Liverpool was sympathetic to the cause of peace in Vietnam, and at the urging of Molly's committee helped organise a mass to protest against the war. During the service Molly was unsure what was going on, so when everybody got up and approached the front she went with them. Which was how this atheist, Communist Jew ended up taking holy communion in one of Britain's major Catholic cathedrals. Once the priest's back was turned she spat out the wafer, the literal body of Christ, into her hankie.

Unique amongst provincial British cities, Liverpool possessed a United States consulate. It was in fact the world's first US consulate, and Nathaniel Hawthorne, author of *The Scarlet Letter*, had once been consul here. In the 1960s it made an excellent destination for demonstrators who didn't want to travel all the way to London to throw stones at a piece of US government property. Soon there were enormous anti-war demonstrations taking place in Liverpool most weekends, and Molly was frequently in the poor consul's office shouting at him. Often there were thousands at the Pier Head but, as with all open-air events, timing was crucial. When the Merseyside Peace in Vietnam organised one march for what turned out to be a rainy weekday afternoon, so few people turned up that my mother and the other organisers had a debate about whether to march or not. In the end it was decided that the twelve or fifteen of us who were there would walk in the gutter down to the Pier Head, escorted by a phalanx of scornful policemen, not quite demonstrating but not quite walking either. I found this a particularly excruciating experience. I had grown up going on demonstrations, and as far back as I could remember they had mostly felt ridiculous and stupid. The chanting, the folk-singing, the empty, sloganising speeches all made me squirm inside, and I was certain that girls were not impressed by a boy walking in the gutter with a placard on a stick.

In 1968 the Merseyside Marxist-Leninist Group gave their support to the secessionist Biafran movement in Nigeria. I remember on a hot summer day walking down Princes Road in Liverpool 8, a shabby but once elegant tree-lined street. Feeling like frauds, we were the only white people amongst several hundred Africans, all of us chanting, 'We are Biafrans . . .' (clearly not true in our case) '. . . fighting for our freedom. With Ojukwo leading, we will con-quer.' (No, they didn't.) I think we then changed sides and gave our support to the Nigerian government.

I was on a Vietnam demonstration in '68 or '69 when I noticed the rainbow flag of the Woodcraft Folk flying above the throng. The Woodcraft Folk had embodied so much of the ramblin', folk singin', knitted jumper-wearin' kind of social-ism, but on going closer I saw that many of those marching under their banner were wearing leather gimp masks, fluores-cent leotards or rubber ballerina outfits and were dancing about in a very sensuous way blowing whistles and shaking maracas. Perhaps here was a sign that the socialist left was finally getting more in touch with the spirit of the age. It seemed that the Woodcraft Folk had loosened up quite a lot since my time and I regretted letting my membership lapse until I realised what had happened. The gay movement had stolen the Woodcraft Folk's flag, the rainbow banner, and were now claiming it as their own.

This demonstration at the Pier Head ended with the tradi-tional occupying of the US consulate. Nigel Morley Preston Jones came up to me and said, 'Man . . . you should come with us on this Vietnam demo in London in May. We've got like paint bombs and I've got marbles to roll under the police horses and there's going to be all kinds of trouble.' Unfortunately Molly was standing next to me when he told me this and she wouldn't let me go despite all my pleading, and so I missed out on the biggest riot in post-war Britain – the famous Grosvenor Square demo of '68. Nigel told me afterwards that it had been bril-liant, though he hadn't used his marbles because he found he didn't want to hurt the horses.

Molly did finally let me go on the one in October 1968, which was very tame. Tariq Ali, a student radical and former President of the Oxford Union, was accused by many on the left of betraying the cause because he had agreed with the authorities to avoid Grosvenor Square this time. So there wasn't much violence but I did manage to get caught up in a brief outbreak of fighting when I attached myself to a breakaway group of anarchists who were attempting to storm the square, throwing themselves against the police lines. Breathless, I found myself exhilarated by the violence. The charging, then the running away, the shouting and the drama, the thrill of seeing people being taken away in ambulances, their heads dripping with blood, the self-righteousness you felt, were all fantastic. Up until that point I hadn't understood the Mod kids at school who got caught up in football riots, but now I could totally see what they were getting out of it. And you could tell that the police were having as good a time as we were – after all, they were young men too and they wanted to have a fight as much as we did.

For many people 1968 was a year of upheavals, highs and lows, tremendous excitement and catastrophic disillusionment. For me one of the most shocking things was to find out that I had only passed four O-Levels: a low Grade Three in English lit and art and a lousy Grade Four in history and English language. More than anything else, I was astounded to get only a Grade Eight, a calamitous fail, in French.

It had always been a core belief in our family that the Sayles were really good at foreign languages. So confident was I in my natural linguistic ability that for five years I had paid hardly any attention in French classes – I refused to hand in any homework and as the exam grew nearer did no revision, instead relying on my genetic inheritance to see me through. It was only when I was met with complete incomprehension during the oral part of the exam that I began to suspect that things were not going to go well. '*Quoi?*' the examiners kept asking me with puzzled expressions on their faces and '*Je ne comprends pas.*' I, on the other hand, thought I was eloquently and fluently conveying complex ideas of political philosophy in perfect, slightly Marseilles-accented French.

When the results came through the door they confirmed that this idea of our polyglotism had been a collective delusion. After that shock, when I thought back to our overseas holidays there arose several uncomfortable and long-suppressed memories of foreigners staring in stunned bafflement at one or both of my parents as they talked at them. Now those incidents began to make sense. The more I reflected on it the more memories surfaced of perplexing incidents that had happened abroad which were now understandable – why, for example, we were served boiled cod in Stuttgart when we thought we were getting an ice cream. I began to suspect that Joe, rather than being fluent in any foreign language, got others to understand him and do what he wanted simply out of sheer niceness, while people did what my mother wished because they were frightened of her.

Highway 61 Reevoosottid

It was during the 1967 NUR AGM which was held in Inverness in the Scottish Highlands that I resolved never to go on holiday with my parents ever again. Me, Molly, Joe and Bruno had been due to stay in a caravan in the surrounding hills for two weeks. After about five days I had demanded to be allowed to go home. The caravan was like our boat except that at least on a canal cruise the landscape changed, whereas outside the steamed-up window of the caravan there remained day after day the same glowering, alien and unsettling pine forest. The city of Inverness was on a broad flat river and surrounded by a huge amount of more wooded nothingness. It was disconcerting to be in a place that was musty, cold and wet but where you still were continually bitten by insects. We were given the usual privilege passes for entry to all council-run facilities, but as far as I can remember there was nothing that I wanted in Inverness even at half price. One memory I have is that up in the wooded secret hills we visited some people who were painting hundreds of plaster figures of Mickey Mouse by hand in a long shed. That was it for me, I said, 'I can't take any more of this.'

The journey from the Highlands took the whole evening and night and it was just before dawn the next day when we crawled into Lime Street Station. The buses hadn't yet begun running, so I walked all the way from town to Anfield through early morning streets slick with rain.

To have a whole house to myself brought a tremendous sense of liberation. For seven days I lived on small tins of chicken in jelly, Fray Bentos pies where you cut the top off the tin and then cooked it in the oven so the crust rose and packets of Vesta Chop Suey where you fried a curly little crispy thing to put on top of your meal. In my mind I watched myself doing these things and thought I saw a sophisticated and independent young man.

One night some friends of mine and Cliff's from the sixth form came back to my empty house with some girls. While they were upstairs I found myself sitting in the living room frustrated that I didn't have a girlfriend. Turning on the TV, I came in about a third of the way through the most extraordinary film I had ever seen. The movie was shot in jagged black and white, and in the first scene I saw there were girls in black leather biker jackets who had boys' haircuts and they were menacing a more feminine woman who was tied up to a bed in a motel and the biker women were smoking marijuana, in the fifties! The tale was of a big fat corrupt sweaty policeman in a neon-lit city that looked like Venice but without any canals. Dennis Weaver from the cowboy series *Gunsmoke* kept running into the seedy motel where the boyish girls were tormenting the woman and smoking the joints, shouting, 'It stinks in hayah!' Charlton Heston was pretending to be a Mexican and Marlene Dietrich played a fortune teller. Even when it finished I didn't know what it was I had seen, and it was years before I realised that I had watched two-thirds of Orson Welles' *A Touch of Evil*. All I knew right there and then was that I wanted a leather jacket like those bad girls and I wanted to smoke marijuana.

* * *

In '68 Molly and Joe had booked themselves a cruise on a
Russian ship named after Lenin's wife, the *Krupskaya*. The
Soviet Union possessed a whole fleet of these boats, enormous
white vessels that cruised the Baltic and the Black Sea calling
in at various ports of the Eastern Bloc, from where Western
tourists would be shown the wonders of the Soviet world. Then
they were whisked back to their ship for running buffets that
always featured a huge glazed salmon as their centrepiece and
displays of folk dancing in the evening. While I, on the eve of
my sixteenth birthday, planned to travel to a city that only three
months before had been rocked by some of the most violent
riots in its history during which several people had been killed,
where there had been massive factory occupations, the seizure
of universities by students and an unofficial general strike
involving eleven million workers which had succeded in bringing down the government. You could never tell with my parents
what they would object to – especially Molly. Though Molly
wouldn't let me go on the May Vietnam demo she did, without
any argument, allow me to travel to Paris, abroad alone for
the first time in my life. She didn't even express mild concern
about me travelling to a city where the riot police were still
attacking people months after the main event, whereas a few
weeks before when she found out I had been eating chips from
the chip shop up the road from school rather than a nutritious
lunch she started screaming that I was going to give myself
stomach cancer and tearfully begged me to stop.

My parents may have felt reassured because I had told them I
was going to take the train to Paris – and why wouldn't I seeing
as it was fast and in my case completely free? But I had told

them a lie. Actually my plan was to hitch-hike. There was an almost mystical significance to hitch-hiking. It was free, so that appealed to hippy stinginess, and according to the mythology you were guaranteed to meet all kinds of really 'cool' people and enjoy all kinds of freaky adventures. As soon as Molly and Joe were on the train to Harwich to join their cruise ship I took the bus to a roundabout at the beginning of the East Lancashire Road, which I vaguely thought led to London. I stood on the edge of the road and stuck out my thumb . . . and I waited on that roundabout for the rest of the day and right throughout the whole of the following night. The next morning I got the same bus back into town and took the train to London and onward to Paris. As I ate a meal in the dining car on the train from the French coast the ticket collector, seeing my free pass, saluted me, proletarian to proletarian.

In all the time over the next couple of years that I spent trying to hitch-hike I think I only ever got about five lifts. Two of those drivers were drunk and one thought he was Jesus. It was my appearance that was mostly to blame – my clothes, my hair and the tortured expression of doubt and embarrassment that I wore permanently on my face. The front cover of the album *Highway 61 Revisited* showed Bob Dylan dressed in a white T-shirt with a drawing of a Triumph Bonneville motorcycle printed on it. The Triumph logo was placed above the picture of the motorbike and the word 'Motorcycles' ran below. I desperately wanted a T-shirt like that but, having no idea where to buy one, I produced my own version drawn with a felt-tip pen on an old and yellowing scoop-necked T-shirt from the Co-op. When attempting to create my own drawing

I hadn't really been able to stretch the T-shirt flat on the living room table and so the image came out all crazy-looking, as did the lettering. Rather than saying 'Triumph' it looked more like 'TrUmP' and 'Motorcycles' had come out as 'momoMymy-cles'. As I stood on the roundabout at the beginning of the East Lancs Road I looked like a wild man who had been writing mad incoherent words on his shirt, or possibly somebody who had tried to commit suicide by repeatedly stabbing himself with a magic marker. And I was still wearing my toy hat.

And I wasn't intending to stay in small hotels or youth hostels as I had told my parents – I was planning to sleep rough. After hitch-hiking, sleeping rough was another experience that was supposed to give you all kinds of insights into the human condition. I had bought myself an olive green sleeping bag from the Army and Navy stores in Lime Street and I travelled with this rolled up, tied with straps and supported by another strap that went over my shoulder. All the clothes I had with me were inside the bedroll, and it was very inconvenient to get anything because you had to undo all the straps. Typically, I was far more interested in looking like Woody Guthrie than in having anything practical to carry my luggage in.

Along with a few pairs of baggy underpants and some T-shirts with mad drawings on them was an enormous, double-edged commando dagger in my bedroll. I don't quite know when the thing with me and knives started. Travelling through France when I was quite young, I had seen in shop windows some wooden-handled penknives called Opinel which had entranced me. These simply made objects exuded a powerful kind of utilitarian beauty: they embodied the idea of peasants hacking off a chunk of rough *saucisson sec* for their lunch or a philosopher sharpening his pencils prior to composing a stinging diatribe against some other philosopher. By contrast British penknives, with their clumps of pathetic, tiny blades, were fussy things you associated with boy scouts. So on one early trip through France I bought myself an Opinel, and then on a subsequent holiday I bought myself a bigger one, then I bought one with a locking ring so that it could be held open and wouldn't close if you stuck it in something, at which point I couldn't deny to myself that, though I did like the idea of cutting up sausage and sharpening pencils, I also very much liked the idea of having a weapon tucked in my back pocket. Then somebody gave me the commando dagger and I thought I might as well take that on my holidays too.

As I walked from the Gare du Nord to the Left Bank, there were riot police everywhere – the notorious and feared CRS. The city was hot and humid under the afternoon sun. The buildings, like huge storage heaters, gusted wet air into the cobbled streets. I felt lonely. Down a side street carpeted with vegetable peelings I came upon a row of Citroën vans full of men in padded suits, helmets on and visors down. They looked at me with my long hair and my bedroll as a hawk might look at a fieldmouse.

From its high point in May the street protests and occupations had declined, partly due to the connivance of the Communist Party and their trade union federation, the CGT, with the right-wing government. The students, intellectuals and anarchists who had rioted had been as opposed to the French CP and the conventional trade unions as they had been to the de Gaulle government, seeing them all as part of the same old-fashioned corrupt system. The *Morning Star*, taking its line from the British party leadership, came out and condemned the '68 protests; and Pif the dog, who after all was at the centre of things, had several strident points to make about the intellectual narcissism of the protest's leaders.

o 47 o
Beneath the Pavement, More Pavement

On the posters outside the Gaumont cinema that advertised the coming attractions there would always be a strapline designed to express the essence of the film. There was one movie incongruously starring method actor Rod Steiger and blowsy, blonde, Swindon-born bombshell Diana Dors, whose caption read, 'You're not afraid of the jungle, so why are you afraid of me?' Beneath the title of the movie of our family's life, which might be called 'Von Sayle's Express', the legend would read, 'Holidays were overly important to them.' Consequently when I tried to devise my first independent holiday I over-reached myself catastrophically.

I had the idea that Paris '68 would be my Aldermaston march, that like Glen Cocker I would encounter a girl who was so aroused by the political upheaval, so excited by the throwing off of all bourgeois morality, that she would have sex with me, even if she didn't want to, as part of her revolutionary duty.

Going to Paris alone was a huge mistake. I should have known that if the prospect of spending an evening in Liverpool by myself brought on feelings of existential dread so severe I had to go running around town until I met somebody to talk to, then travelling to an alien city where I knew no-one and where the streets were full of out-of-control riot police was likely to open up a pit of desolation in me so terrible that each second was an agony that seemed to go on for hours. Especially since I was truly awful at striking up the superficial friendships you needed if you were going to go on a holiday like this. I would hear other hitchers say to each other, 'Man, I got talking to this guy outside Athens, man, and he just like invited me to his sister's wedding on this Greek island and I ended up playing the bouzouki all night for all these chicks, man, and then. . . .' Whereas my story would go, 'This bloke started talking to me in Victoria Station but he seemed to be saying how sealions were tapping his phone, so I ran away.' I would have liked to ask somebody to come with me but, fearing rejection, I lacked the confidence to do so.

As I lay in my sleeping bag under the Pont Neuf, whimpering with loneliness and occasionally, as I turned over, getting stabbed in the back by my commando dagger, all around me pretty girls were humping groovy, handsome-looking guys who played Beatles songs on the guitar. Thus I learned the lesson that, even after the revolution, cool, handsome and confident is always going to beat weird-looking and needy.

*   *   *

After a few days in Paris I was running short of money. I had only brought thirteen pounds' worth of travellers' cheques, which really was a tiny amount – but then I had no idea how much holidays cost. On previous trips my parents or the Czech government had paid for everything. Travellers' cheques were what Molly and Joe had carried with them when they journeyed abroad, and back in Liverpool I had been very excited to be buying my own. Emptying my post office account I went to the Thomas Cook office in the centre of Liverpool. 'How would you like your cheques?' the girl behind the counter asked. Being aware that travellers' cheques came in denominations that were sometimes different from conventional currency and trying to act like the world-weary globetrotter I said to her, 'Oh, I dunno . . . just give me two threes and a seven.'

I was down to my last few Francs but I'd hatched a plan to get by. Though I was constantly finding myself in confusing situations through my own stupidity I also possessed an eccentric survival instinct. In times of distress, just as Joe would go look for communists when there was a problem, I would turn to politics, politics and drawing, for my salvation.

Though the May uprising had not reformed society or even made sex with lonely boys compulsory, there had been a significant improvement in the quality of political graffiti. Up until that point activists has simply scrawled straightforward slogans on walls: 'Smash the state', 'End the war in Vietnam' – that sort of thing. In London I had a particular favourite on a wall at Hyde Park Corner which I passed regularly on the way to shout at the US embassy. It read, 'Free all political pris~~~~', the words trailing off in a long jagged line of red paint. Obviously whoever had been writing it had been grabbed by the police before they had the chance to finish.

The reason the graffiti in Paris was so much better than anywhere else was because it had been strongly influenced by the thinking of one particular group known as the Situationists. The Situationists were inspired by both Marxism and Surrealism, and the most obvious results of their theories were the puzzling and thought-provoking slogans which remained on the walls of the Sorbonne and surrounding area after the riots had ended. 'Be realistic, demand the impossible,' read one. 'If God existed it would be necessary to abolish him,' read another, and 'Live without dead time.' The most famous of all was 'Under the paving stones, the beach.'

Eager to try and make some money I bought a box of chalks from an art shop and, securing a little strip of pavement on the Boulevard St Michel where there were many incompetent buskers, I began sketching. I drew the likeness of a revolutionary hero such as Che or Mao with a speech bubble emerging from their mouth saying something I thought was Situationist and cryptic like 'The revolution is for fish' or 'Underneath the pavement, more pavement'. This might not sound like much but the standard of street art in those days, before the invention of the silver robot statue was terribly low. So, in a couple of days passing tourists were throwing a decent amount of money into my toy cap, certainly enough to pay for bread and rough red wine. Though I still didn't really have anybody to talk to, I was at least drunk in the evenings.

Towards the end of the week I was in a park, a little triangular patch of trees and grass just off the Boulevard Montparnasse where I was thinking of sleeping that night, when somebody got in a dispute with a park official (I think it might have been me). The man blew a whistle and immediately the park was full of riot police who scooped up all the backpackers and took us to a police station near the Sorbonne, where we were locked in a cage for a few hours while gendarmes glared at us in a threatening fashion. Luckily they didn't search me or my bedroll, but they did get my parents' phone number out of me with a minimum of threats. A sergeant tried to call Valley Road, but of course the phone just rang and rang because while I was in this French police station Molly and Joe were halfway up the Kiel Canal.

In the early morning the gendarmes let us out of the cage and herded us down a corridor and into the back of a van. Not knowing what was going to happen next, the whole smelly group were taken to the outskirts of the city where the police let us out on to the side of a busy ring road. They informed us that we were all barred from Paris – we had an hour to leave town and never return. Then the van drove off.

All the other hippies walked to the slip road of the motorway to begin hitching, but I said, 'Oh, I'm, erm . . . going to another good hitching spot that I know.' Then I took the Métro back into Paris to the Gare du Nord and, ducking round a corner every time I saw a policeman, got on the first train to the coast and was back in London by the afternoon.

I decided I didn't want to go back to Liverpool as that would have been admitting defeat – the importance of holidays was so great that they couldn't under any circumstances be abandoned but had to be endured at all costs. Maybe I was hoping that if I held on long enough Ladislav would come and rescue me with a fleet of Tatra limousines. Some English hippy I had spoken to while in the cells had said, 'There's a cool scene in Brighton, man.' So, taking the word of a drug-addled idiot, I caught a train down to the south coast of England.

On the beach front at Brighton things seemed to be improving. Amongst the druggies hanging around the deck chairs and ice cream vans I was delighted to see a guy who I vaguely knew from O'Connor's pub in Liverpool. I went up to him and said, 'Hi, Eric!'

Eric, however, didn't seem so pleased to see me. 'Hey,' he replied in an unfriendly manner, looking around to see if anybody else had heard our exchange. Then, dropping his voice to a whisper, he said, 'They call me Moose down here, man.'

By this time I was so desperate for company that I chose to endure hanging out with a guy named Moose rather than be on my own. He told me he knew an empty house where we could crash for the night, so me and Moose walked a little way out of town until we came to a suburban villa with boarded up windows. By now darkness had fallen, so our actions were hidden from the street as we prised back the rough wooden shutters and climbed in through one of the windows. Breathing heavily from our exertions, we stood in the derelict room for a few moments, the only illumination filtering in from the sodium lamps outside. Then suddenly our eyes were dazzled by half a dozen powerful torches shining in our faces. The police had been waiting in the house, expecting a teenage runaway to turn up, but they took me and Moose to the police station anyway. I had now been arrested twice in two countries within twenty-four hours and this time I was searched. The desk sergeant took my Opinel number 8 with the 8.5cm blade out of my back pocket and said, 'I'm not happy with this.'

'Well,' I replied, 'if you're not happy with that, you're definitely not going to like what's in my bedroll.'

He looked at the commando dagger where it lay on the padded sleeping bag. 'I'm going to have to take this off you,' he finally said.

I wasn't going to argue, but they did give me a receipt written on the back of an envelope. These police too tried to ring Molly and Joe, but by then they would have been docking at the port of Rostock and so once more there was no answer. This time I was kept in a cell until about 6 a.m., after which me and Moose were given the now familiar speech about leaving town and never returning. Amazingly, a very young constable offered to take us back into town in his own car. The desk sergeant gave him a wry and weary look as he did so, and once we were on the move it became apparent why. With ridiculous faux casualness the young policeman turned to us and asked, 'Er, I hear, like, that there are . . . like people selling drugs in Brighton.'

'Are there?' me and Moose asked with apparent shock.

'Yes. You don't know who they are, do you?'

'No, we don't, officer, honest. We never knew such things went on, but we'd certainly tell you if we did.'

Pulling up on a road, still a fair way out of town, the ambitious young constable said, 'You two can fucking get out here.'

Me and Moose-slash-Eric stood on the grassy verge as he

drove away in his little red Ford Escort. Below us across the Downs the English Channel sparkled in the early morning light and I experienced for the first time something liberating and empowering, a sensation I would feel many times over the coming years – the wonderful release of giving up. Completely and utterly I gave in to the reality that my hitch-hiking holiday was a disaster and, feeling lighter in spirits than I had for weeks, I headed home.

The house was cold and on the doormat under a stack of letters were my extremely poor O-level results, but I remained happy to be home. That night I caught the bus into town. It took a while for me to find anyone to have a drink with, but when I did something else remarkable occurred. Naturally I related what I had been up to over the last few weeks, and in the telling my catastrophic hitch-hiking holiday gained a coherence and a vitality it hadn't had while it was actually happening. In previous years I had recounted various incidents from my holidays to the kids at school, but this was the first time I had been able to fashion a complete saga that was entirely centred on my mishaps and adventures – everything and everyone were merely a backdrop to the doings of me. People listened fascinated as I told it in the Philharmonic, and then I went to O'Connor's and told it there, and then I went to the Crack and told it there, and then I went back to the Phil and told it again to some different people, each time adding detail, dropping bits, altering the sequence of events and mostly making myself appear much less of a dick, until by the time I got to Kavanagh's I was a modern-day Scouse Odysseus. Up to that point I had thought that when things happened it was the end of them, but it turned out that if you could tell a story that was only the beginning of their life. In the right hands events could be chopped and shaped and filleted until they came out exactly as you wanted them to come out, just like election results in the Soviet Union.

I had a whole new audience for my story when I returned to school a week later as a member of the sixth form, studying for three A-Levels: Art, History and English. Then everybody in the political world came back from their summer holidays and I told it to them too. One night I was at a meeting in Liverpool University and afterwards, sitting around, I was relating the story of my summer holiday, which was by now almost as long as the holiday itself, to a group who hadn't heard it before. One particular girl with long auburn hair and a round pretty face seemed to be regarding me with rapt attention. I thought to myself, 'Why is that girl looking at me like that?' Then I thought, 'Oh, yeah!'

She was a couple of years older than me, a student at a teacher training college on the edge of Liverpool. I went back with her to her hall of residence that night and stayed until the early hours, when I had to climb out of the window to avoid the prowling authorities. It was a misty morning as I waited for the first bus back into town, giddy with the thought that finally I had found somebody who liked me enough to let me do that to them.

But it might have been that I hadn't got it quite right, because as the bus moved off I began to feel this tremendous pain in my groin. Then a few seconds later the bus hit somebody with a thump. We had to wait for about a quarter of an hour before an ambulance arrived and I did think of asking them to take me to the hospital, but then we moved off. I got home about an hour later and spent the rest of the day in bed like some Victorian lady who had been violated for the first time, while Molly kept bursting into my bedroom shouting, 'Lexi! Lexi! What's wrong? Are you all right? Oh God! Oh Christ, are you ill? Shall I phone Cyril Taylor? What's wrong? Tell me what's wrong!' I didn't mind – in the end my disastrous holiday had got me a girlfriend.

Molly and Joe brought me a balalaika, a three-stringed folk instrument with a triangular body, as a souvenir of their cruise. While my parents had been on the high seas the Soviet Union had invaded Czechoslovakia, bringing to an end Dubcek's Prague Spring. The first Molly and Joe knew of it was when a group of Italians on the *Krupskaya*, having heard the news on the BBC World Service, demanded that they be landed at the nearest port and allowed to go home right away.

Ladislav never mentioned the upheaval in his letters, but a little while later he wrote to say that Prukha, the Minister for Trade Union Affairs who had hosted many dinners for us and had come to our home several times, was dead, apparently murdered during a street robbery. Which always seemed a bit unlikely in such a rigorously policed country.

⹀ 48 ⹀

Allen Ginsberg's Whippet

One evening the local BBC TV news programme, *Look North*, ran a feature on a Japanese performance artist who was appearing at the Bluecoat Gallery, one of Liverpool's oldest buildings, situated behind Woolworth's in the town centre. This extremely odd-looking woman wrapped herself in toilet paper and conducted her side of the interview, composed of various cryptic pronouncements, in a high, squeaky voice. The presenters in turn treated her as if they were talking to some-one in the novelty slot usually reserved for harmonica-playing livestock or batty, hundred-year-old men who had fought in the Boer War. They said the woman's name was Yoko Ono. 'That's the last we've seen of her,' I said to my dad.

To live in Liverpool in those days it might have seemed as if you were a citizen of some magical city. Every day was a pulsat-ing stew of music, art, poetry and theatre. Twenty-four hours a day you might see avant-garde performers from outside town, such as Yoko or Bob Dylan. At a hundred venues you could witness home-grown talent, poets, painters and musicians of enormous ability. I had very little to do with any of it.

Largely this was due to my disorganised nature. I knew things were going on from the TV and newspapers and sometimes I would try and attend an event but would either get there on the wrong night or go to a pub that had the same name as the pub where history was being made so

I would spend all evening in some grimy bar down by the docks, sipping on a half of bitter in a smeared glass and wondering if the old bloke in the plastic mac talking to his whippet was in fact the American beat poet Allen Ginsberg in disguise.

It was probably the only time in the history of a northern city you could impress people by saying you were a poet. In imitation of Adrian Henry, Brian Patten and Roger McGough I began composing verse and managed to have one poem published in the school magazine, a corruscating account of my life as the black inhabitant of a Chicago slum, which ended, 'Rats in the basement . . . sniper on the rooftops.' I did a reading at the Library on Walton Road which was run by two librarians who wore matching black polo-necked jumpers and thought of themselves as the Ted Hughes and Sylvia Plath of Liverpool but it didn't lead anywhere. I also began attending the Merseyside Youth Theatre but though we rehearsed for a couple of years we never managed to put on a play.

Two people however who had managed to insert themselves into the very heart of Liverpool's pulsating artistic scene were Joe and Molly Sayle. As secretary of Merseyside Medical Aid to Vietnam, Molly organised several blood drives that I failed to contribute to, as well as fund-raising events and petition-writing campaigns. There was a Vietnamese woman called Lin Qui, who was officially a journalist based in Paris but was known by everybody in left-wing circles as the main representative of both the Vietcong and the North Vietnamese Communist government in Europe who when I got home from school often seemed to be sitting in our front room, silent and enigmatic in her black tunic staring at the Secatrol.

Now because Molly was mixing in the same radical circles as I was she and Joe started turning up in the same pubs that I drank in, having got over her revulsion for these 'noisy smoky places'. I would see my mother coming down Hope Street striding along while Joe, in his trilby hat and belted raincoat, ran to keep up with her. Bearing down on me like a destroyer in the Mediterranean ramming a midget submarine, no matter how I twisted and turned Molly was always there in my periscope. The only other fifty-year-olds the young clientele of these places knew were their mums and dads, their aunts and uncles, quiet and self-effacing souls in cardigans and slippers. Now, here in their midst, was this red-haired woman who was the same age as their parents but was shouting fuck as loudly as she could, arguing endlessly, hitting them when they disagreed with her and expressing deliciously inflammatory opinions, noisily calling Princess Margaret a prostitute and vehemently defending Stalin's show trials. Joe they liked for his gentleness and good humour. In the pubs where I knew perhaps eleven people to say hello to all the young drinkers thought Molly was amazing so that often my mother would be surrounded by a fawning crowd of admirers, who would look at me like an interloper if I ever tried to join them.

One of the artists Molly became friendly with was a sculptor called Arthur Dooley. It's hard to imagine that Arthur could have become a celebrity in any other age than the 1960s. This was an era when churches had forgotten what their purpose was so when new ones were occasionally built they resembled tortured collisions of blockhouse and circus tent or Wimpy Bar and airport control tower. Arthur specialised in figures of Christ, Joseph or Mary that were commissioned to stick on the outside. A pudding-faced, garrulous man with a thick Scouse accent he was a former apprentice at Cammel Lairds shipyard who managed to somehow combine being both a devout Catholic and a committed Communist. Unlike the deformed structures in which his work was displayed Arthur's sculptures – tortured, skeletal figures rendered in fibreglass, rags and scrap metal – were eloquent and powerful works of art. Bizarrely Arthur was also a fixture on the TV chat show circuit, a regular guest on 'Parkinson' and celebrities, most notably the drag artist Danny La Rue, were collectors of his work, though its hard to know what Danny La Rue did with a seven foot high scrap metal Jesus.

That's who Molly was mixing with now, members of the Vietcong and people off the telly. Arthur Dooley's studio was in a former pub in the village of Woolton on the edge of Liverpool. Together he and Molly organised an art exhibition in support of Medical Aid for Vietnam. I sold one of my pictures for ten shillings and immediately lost the cheque.

49

Someone Else's Sandwiches

Everybody was in a state of high excitement when the United States landed a man on the surface of the moon. The next day I told my class-mates that though they might have stayed up all night to watch the TV coverage I'd gone to bed early. I said that everyone I knew agreed with Gil Scott Heron of the Last Poets. As far as heroin-addicted black men from the ghetto like me and Gil were concerned, the lunar landings were just 'Whitey on the Moon'. Today the staff would have had a big case conference about me and afterwards I would have been booked twice weekly sessions with the school psychologist and proscribed heavy doses of some stultifying drug but then they conspired against me, which only served to increase the messianic sense of my own significance. Of all the pupils in the sixth form I was the only one who wasn't made a school prefect. Then a few weeks after the beginning of term the head-master announced at assembly that the school was going to have a student council with a representative drawn from each year. Clearly this institution would have as much power as the North Korean parliament, but still my classmates chose me as their representative. There was a pause of a day or two while the votes were counted; then the word came back that our class had to hold the election again. Again they voted and again they picked me. When their choice was rejected once more my class-mates got the idea and elected somebody else. I think if the school had only reached out to me at that crucial point, then like a trade union firebrand given a life peerage or a troublesome journalist awarded a well-paid seat on the board of an arts organisation they might have been able to buy me off and make me their most enthusiastic advocate out of gratitude. Instead they drove me further into the arms of rebellion.

Yet despite, or perhaps because of, the persecution by the school I considered this a very happy time. Me and my mates would play football every lunchtime in Walton Hall Park over the road from school, and sometimes we would go to one of the pubs on Rice Lane in Walton and get mildly sozzled. I would spend all my lunch money on drink, then go to the cloakroom where the little kids ate their packed lunches and extort them into giving me one of their sandwiches. There seemed no greater taste in the world than somebody else's sandwich when slightly drunk.

In spite of getting a lot of detentions I loved being in the sixth form. We sat not at desks like schoolchildren but in chairs with little swivel tables like students probably had.

The subject I was particularly drawn to was English. This was because, like a paranoid schizophrenic who thinks that the TV newsreaders are addressing him directly, the syllabus seemed to have been devised by the Oxford and Cambridge examination board with the sole purpose of highlighting crucial aspects of my life. The Dickens novel we were studying was *Hard Times*, set in a fictionalised version of nearby Preston, it concerned the terrible working conditions of industrial towns – conditions that had given rise to the theories of Marx and Engels. The Shakespeare play was *Coriolanus*, at the heart of which is the relationship between an overpowering mother and her son, allied to a debate over whether 'the plebeians', have the right to govern themselves or if they can only be ruled by a stern and cruel leader.

But it was *Animal Farm* that affected me the most. I felt like I had a personal relationship with George Orwell; over the years he had been condemned in our house with great bitterness, as if he was some errant relative who had stolen the family silver and run off to Australia. Now I was being forced to read one of his books, and this book really, truly was all about me and my family and the thing that we believed in.

While my classmates struggled, I was aware of exactly who all the characters represented. The pig Napoleon represents Stalin, and Snowball, Napoleon's rival and original leader after the farmer is thrown out, was clearly Trotsky. The horses Boxer and Clover are the honest proletariat. The vicious puppies are the KGB. Moses the raven, with his tales of a place in the sky called Sugarcandy Mountain, symbolises the Russian Orthodox Church and so on. I half expected a delegation of trade union mice to come trooping through at some point with a little mouse translator, to be given presents and made honorary pigs at lavish banquets.

Still, it was terribly hard to take in this fairytale allegory of the corruption and cruelty that descended on Russia in the two decades after the Bolshevik revolution.

If it had been written as a conventional novel I might have been able to dismiss it, but written like this it seemed undeniably true. It was both disturbing and moving. I thrilled to the revolution when the animals overthrow the cruel farmer, and I was upset as I had never been before when towards the end the brave horse Boxer tries at the last minute to break out of the van taking him to the knacker's yard.

Animal Farm had such an effect on me that I had to construct a way of coping. I scoured the book to find a character I could identify with, a figure who would represent some kind of personal salvation for me, the animal I would be in that situation – and I found it in the cat. The cat represents what Marx called the *Lumpenproletariat*, by which he meant, generally speaking, the criminal classes. The criminal classes broadly share with the working-class their social attitudes, their accents and of course their neighbourhoods, but they differ in their motivation. While the worker slaves to earn an honest living, the *Lumpenproletariat* merely cares about itself. It is only at the last minute that the cat joins in the revolution, sinking her claws into Mr Jones the farmer. Later on she is seen telling the birds that they are all comrades now and it's perfectly safe for them to land on her paw. I understood that in *Animal Farm* she personifies those who insincerely adhere to ideology for personal gain, but I hoped that perhaps I could be a slightly better version of the cat. I was telling myself that whatever happened I would make sure I looked after me first, that I would always hold some secret part of myself back from politics.

But there was another lesson I took from the novel and its author. When I mentioned to Molly how I felt it was a great book and I was really grateful we were doing it for 'A' Level she just kept shouting 'Orwell's a bastard! Orwell's a bastard!' which typified not just her opinion but how most on the left regarded any art form. Like fundamentalist Christians who have to believe that every word of the Bible is true and those holy words were written by people who had no human foibles, so it was with Marxists like my mother. They only wanted to listen to messages that confirmed the things they already believed in written by authors who were ideologically pure. From then on I was eager to listen to all the competing voices I could get my hands on, even though such liberality was disapproved of in our house. While I could leave pornography or alcohol lying around my bedroom I was forced to hide my copy of *Brideshead Revisited* in a secret compartment at the back of the wardrobe.

This happy year at school began to come crashing down thanks to my nemesis 'the Abe', Bill Abrahams, the Jewish, cricket-loving, Everton-supporting, Communist maths teacher. He had not taken us for maths since the first year, but he continued to dislike me and took every opportunity to put me in detention if I was caught misbehaving. I quite liked having a nemesis: it played into my sense of me being an especially dangerous person whose ideas, style of dress and manner were more than the straight world could take.

Then it all went a bit too far. At Alsop, in another imitation of a public school, we had a 'tuck shop' – a little cupboard-sized place where pupils could buy chocolate, drinks and biscuits at break-time. I was in the queue one day when the Abe came in and started yelling, accusing me of being rowdy. I was particularly agitated by this because for once he was wrong and I was just standing there quietly. So we argued, and at some point he shoved me, so I punched him and we ended up having a bit of a tussle – nothing too much, but as soon as I got away from him I legged it home without waiting to be sent and told my parents what had happened. It was Joe who went down to Alsop that same day to talk to Bill Abrahams, seeing as they'd known each other since the 1930s. I was worried that he wouldn't be up to it but between them a perfectly sensible deal was worked out, indeed considering I'd hit a teacher what Joe achieved was pretty remarkable. The only condition was that I wasn't allowed back until I'd written a letter of apology to Mr Abrahams. I did it grudgingly but I never accepted that I'd done anything wrong and I never really appreciated how much my dad had done for me and how much the negotiation had taken out of him.

I got into more and more trouble with the teachers and at the end of the school year the headmaster called me into his office which always smelled of furniture polish and sitting behind his desk in the dusty gown that made him look like a third rate wizard, he told me not to bother coming back in September. I couldn't believe it, I'd got away with so much for so long but now my smart arse ways had got me expelled from school! I realised with a thumping heart that without some kind of academic qualifications I couldn't get to college and if I didn't get to college I could imagine myself at the age of sixty, still living with Molly and staying in on a Saturday night to do her hair.

⌐50⌐

Alexei's Complaint

Then my girlfriend left me for an anarchist. I didn't really blame her – I was a useless boyfriend. In theory the idea of me having a girlfriend held tremendous appeal – someone who by law had to keep me company whenever loneliness and panic crept over me. After that, though, I was pretty much out of ideas.

My problems over what you were actually supposed do (did you always give flowers after sex?) were merely a much more complicated version of the difficulties I had had over the years with best friends such as Tubby Dowling and Peter Pemberton. At least in Mao's China young people were too busy destroying factories, stopping the traffic and beating their teachers to death to concern themselves with the bewildering complexity of human sexual relations.

My efforts to find another girlfriend were hampered by Molly and Joe, having begun drinking in the same pubs as me, they now started to go to the same parties. I would climb the fetid stairs to some student flat in Liverpool 8 trying to act all cool and hard when, looking across the room, I would see Molly telling a group of pretty anarchist girls some anecdote about my potty training or how as a child I used to think that I might be kidnapped by bananas. 'That's him over there in the leather jacket,' Molly would say, pointing in my direction, and the pretty anarchists would look at me with an expression you never want to see on the face of a good-looking girl.

I decided I didn't just need to go to college, that college needed to be in London. It wasn't an original idea – when I went round the pubs, especially the Crack, I would often come across guys sitting at a table who had spent some time in the capital. They would relate their experiences to a horrified crowd as if they were telling tales of the Somme in 1916. 'It's terrible down there,' they would say, staring with faraway eyes at an un-nameable horror. 'I paid three shillings for a pint of bitter in a pub in Clapham', or 'You don't get rice with your sweet and sour pork', or 'You're completely anonymous down there.' Which seemed as good a reason as any to emigrate right away.

But even if you weren't somebody who was known to many only as 'Molly Sayle's son', there were other reasons to leave. On the surface Liverpool was booming. The pubs and clubs were packed and, though the Beatles had moved to London, there was still a vital music scene. The *Mersey Sound* poetry anthology had recently been published by Penguin, selling hundreds of thousands of copies, Adrian Henry, Roger McGough and Brian Patten reigned like pashas over Liverpool 8 and the two football teams were winning everything in sight – yet if you sniffed the wind you could smell a storm coming.

Towards the mouth of the river at Seaforth work was almost completed on a massive container terminal. When it opened, the numbers working in the docks would drop from tens of thousands to a few hundred. A Marxist historian would say that industries grew up and remained in an area because there was a plentiful supply of a certain necessary item. The existence of coal and steel in the Midlands led to the engineering industry being based there, a humid climate meant cotton was woven in Lancashire, and finance was located in the City of London because of a plentiful supply of hard-hearted and cruel individuals. But all the new factories on the outskirts of Liverpool were founded with massive government grants. Ford and Triumph at Halewood, English Electric and Otis Elevator on the East Lancashire Road, were hundreds of miles from where they should have been. When the orders dried up they were the first to close.

Liverpool's most iconic edifice, the Liver Building, had originally been planned as an office block in Chicago and adapted to Liverpool by chopping off the top fifty floors of the design. There was a similar chopped-off Chicago feel to Liverpool civic politics – the same boss culture, the same dynastic corruption, the same insularity. The police patrolled in dark blue Land Rovers like an occupying army rather than genial bobbies. As Marxist-Leninists we were constantly predicting that chaos was on the way, but for once, we were right and the city's rulers were ill suited to cope with it.

In some ways it was not just a Liverpool phenomenon. There was a notion that had been growing in every section of British society, certainly since the Second World War, that the provinces weren't worth anything. All the things that had been considered important about towns and cities outside the metropolis – substantial Victorian buildings, homely regional cooking, shipbuilding and making things in factories – were now deemed to be hopelessly naïve and old-fashioned. A comedian could get a big laugh just by saying 'Leicester'.

51

A New Revolutionary Era Dawns

In early 1969, reflecting the consolidation that was taking place in the automobile industry, banking and retailing, the Merseyside Marxist-Leninist Group ceased to be independent and became the Liverpool Branch of the Communist Party of Britain (Marxist-Leninist). The CPB (ML) had been founded in 1968 by Reg Birch, an angry, grey-haired little man in a suit, along with other leading members of the engineering union, all of them disillusioned by the Soviet-aligned Communist Party of Great Britain. At the time it had maybe three hundred members, which made it a giant amongst left-wing groups.

In China Jung Chang, the author of *Wild Swans*, a young student whose parents had been accused of being 'capitalist roaders' and horribly tortured during the Cultural Revolution, was being taught English at Beijing University. The only foreign publication available to the students was a newspaper from a tiny Maoist group in Britain, and even this was kept under lock and key. Jung Chang was allowed to look at a single copy of this paper only once, and was disappointed to discover how dull it was and how slavishly and tediously it reproduced the Chinese Communist Party line. As she was staring at it a lecturer walked past and said, 'That paper is probably read only in China.' Well, that paper was our paper! It was *The Worker*, the official journal of the CPB (ML).

But Jung Chang's lecturer was wrong. How could he know that, even though Chinese students hungry to read almost anything at all in the English language found it too insipid to bother with, me and a couple of comrades could sell twenty or thirty copies on a Saturday morning outside Central Station to people who had access to the whole of Western literature? Admittedly some of those sales went to elderly lefties who mistook *The Worker* for the old *Daily Worker* and bought a copy for the racing tips, but there were a small number of men and women, not members of any group or party but simply out shopping with their wives or on their way to the football or buying clothes at Lewis's, who would on an impulse purchase a copy of our paper and then read it thoroughly, occasionally coming back the next week to discuss some arcane point of Marxist theory.

If there was any criticism over the quality of the newspaper, Reg Birch would say that it had fewer mistakes, mis-spellings and typos than the *Guardian*. What he failed to point out was that the *Guardian* came out every day and had seventy pages, while *The Worker* came out once a month and had four pages. There was also a problem of subject matter in the party newspaper due to an imbalance in the organisation's make-up. The majority of the members of the CPB (ML) were teachers, bank workers and students but the largest single group were in the Engineering Union, while the next largest group, due to a couple who were enthusiastic and persuasive recruiters, worked in a warehouse owned by Penguin Books near Wembley. So the stories in *The Worker* often tended to be about either the manoeuvrings for power in the Engineering Union or the problems of working in a big book warehouse near Wembley.

In Liverpool the membership had changed. Nigel Morley Preston Jones, the city's first Maoist, had left the group to join the Anarchists, but he let us keep our bookstall in the Simon Community Hostel. Nigel had never quite seemed to have the right dour spirit for a Marxist-Leninist anyway. Once we had been on a demonstration about housing in Birkenhead and, handing me the megaphone, he suggested I chant, 'Build bombs not houses!' Without thinking I yelled the slogan into the mouthpiece and then wondered why everybody suddenly turned round and started staring and making angry faces. Once I had realised from Nigel's sniggering what he had made me do, the thing that really surprised me was that anybody actually listened to these chants. I certainly didn't, even when I was shouting them into a megaphone. It was a shock to be reminded that most of the people on the left wholeheartedly believed this stuff, that they thought shouting these slogans and going on these demonstrations might actually make a difference to something. Whereas I generally looked on it as, at best, a nice day out with friends with the possibility of a fight at the end of it.

The Merseyside Marxist-Leninist Group voting to become a branch of the CPB (ML) caused the first split in our little band of revolutionaries. You were nobody in left-wing politics until you had been involved in a split, so I felt that the huge and acrimonious argument over joining the larger party in London was some sort of initiation ceremony or rite of passage. There was a Syndicalist group based in Birkenhead, who we would occasionally see at meetings and demos; the creed they followed stated that social justice and equality would only be attained when every worker in the world belonged to a single gigantic trade union. They had four members. This group, who were not wealthy, saved up for ages to go to a Syndicalist conference in London but unfortunately they had a split over some fine point of doctrine on the way there and attended the conference as two separate groups, one with three members and the other with one.

Barry and Ingrid, the couple from Yorkshire, were the main members who left us to join a completely different organisation called the Communist Federation of Britain (Marxist-Leninist). The CFB (ML) soon became our deadliest enemies. The difference between the party and the Federation was that according to Marxist ideology you were only supposed to form a party once the revolution was imminent and the capitalist system on the verge of collapse. This did present our party, the CPB (ML), with a problem in that we had to see the embers of insurrection and the seeds of destruction in every minor glitch of the economic or social order. Any late train or the sacking of a woman from a cake shop was pointed to as a sign that we would all be at the barricades by the end of the week.

In those days everything in Britain seemed to be grey apart from the cars. Tiny, simple things coloured bright red, yellow, green and blue like children's building blocks they tick-tocked around the streets running people over with great jollity. Chris Walker had bought a pea soup-coloured Minivan with bare metal all round and toggles on a string to open the doors. In it, in a time before the M1 and the M6 were joined up, we would travel down to London for introductory meetings at party headquarters.

Those journeys were like a joke about how many Marxist-Leninists you could fit into a Mini. Chris and Ian sat in the front while there would be another four of us folded up in the back, in a space no bigger than a bathtub. Bouncing around in the fetid dark, we would only be allowed to emerge into the light, feeling like hostages in Beirut, once the Minivan was parked outside the CPB (ML)'s base of operations. The Bellman Bookshop was a dark and forbidding former bank on Fortess Road in Tufnell Park, north-west London, a depressive Irish neighbourhood of gloomy pubs, grey rooming houses and cash butchers. There were at least two other Maoist book-shops in the area owned by competing sects – one, in Camden High Street, was nearly as big as a Woolworth's. These other places had proper Marxist-Leninist names such as the London Workers' Bookshop, but bizarrely the Bellman was named after a character in Lewis Carroll's nonsense poem 'The Hunting of the Snark' who says, 'What I tell you three times must be true' and possesses a map of the ocean which is a blank piece of paper. What sort of message was that sending?

I thought to myself that this huge, undulating city was the place that I would soon be living and the London members would, before too long, be my new comrades, except they all seemed crazy.

The party bookshop was overseen by Reg's wife, Dorothy. The daughter of a vicar who looked like the daughter of a vicar in a play, she smoked constantly and would tap the ash from her fag into the pocket of the long grey cardigan she inevitably wore. Occasionally she would begin smouldering, wisps of grey smoke curling from her hips. Comrades were frequently too frightened of Dorothy to tell her she was on fire. Mrs Birch was always spectacularly rude to anybody who ever came into the shop – partly it was because of her abrasive character, but also perhaps she knew the stock to be so dreary that anybody browsing must be a member of the Special Branch or a rival group.

Around the corner from the Bellman Bookshop was the only colourful spot in the entire district, a London-Italian café called the Spaghetti House. If they weren't in the pub this was where all the members would go in the few breaks allowed in the day-long meetings. The Spaghetti House was the first eating place of its type I had encountered as there wasn't anything like it in Liverpool – an ebullient collision of Italian and British cooking mixing bacon sandwiches, spaghetti bolognese and jam roly-poly with custard. Though the party hierarchy were obsessed with security and were continually excommunicating innocent people for being suspected police spies, the staff in the Spaghetti House always seemed to know a lot more about the affairs of the CPB (ML) than the actual members. They would say as they served you, 'Hokay, here's your mixed grill, extra toast no tomatoes and I hear that the executive committee is planning to discipline the Brighton Branch for incorrect thought on Comrade Birch's Crumbs of Imperialism Theory.'

52

I Wouldn't Call This Paradise

Suddenly over the summer, after being expelled from school, I was thrown into a scramble of applying for college places long after everybody else had put in their bid. It turned out that the London School of Economics wasn't impressed by four poor O-Level results, but many nursing schools and teacher training colleges also didn't want me. A few months earlier I thought I had a dazzling number of options, but now my future had narrowed to a tiny dot. My exam results told me university wasn't a choice open to me, despite my previous delusions I wasn't a genius at languages, and I knew I didn't have what it took to go to drama school. I was still convinced that I was a brilliant performer, but all the same couldn't imagine myself attending classes in fencing, ballet dancing and mime. In order to brighten the empty summer months, while rejection letters fluttered daily on to the doormat, I decided to repeat the wildly unsuccessful hitch-hiking holiday experiment of the year before – except this time I planned to go to the Netherlands since I was still technically banned from France.

My aim was to go and stay with Cliff's brother Glen, who had moved to London to work in an advertising agency, then after a few days take a ferry to Ostend and from there travel to Amsterdam. While I was in London my intention was also to pay a visit to Julie, the cute girl from Ealing I had met in

Bulgaria, I thought it might be a good idea to have a girlfriend in London for when I went to college there.

I thought I'd really got my look together. Apart from the lesbians in *Touch of Evil* I had also been very impressed by the Buñuel film *Belle de Jour*, in which Catherine Deneuve plays a woman named Séverine who decides to spend her days as a prostitute while her husband is at work. Séverine becomes involved with a young gangster, Marcel, who ends up shooting her husband before being shot himself. Throughout the film Marcel is dressed totally in black, wearing a long leather over-coat that I thought looked totally ace and carrying a stick that had a knife in it, which also was totally cool. While a whole generation of pretentious teenage boys became obsessed with Catherine Deneuve, that's what I took from the film.

My other influence was a guy called Zbigniew Cybulski, sometimes referred to as the Polish James Dean. He had starred in Andrzej Wajda's 1958 film *Ashes and Diamonds*, completing the trilogy *A Generation* and *Kanal*, all three of which I had seen either on the TV or at Unity Theatre. Cybulski wore these really stylish tinted sunglasses all the time. I had read some-where that they were his own – he had to wear them because he had fought in the Warsaw Uprising, the three-month-long insurrection against the Nazis, when the resistance used the sewers to move about in (the subject of *Kanal*) so he couldn't now take bright light. Which, even if it wasn't true, was a bril-liant excuse to wear shades after dark. In *Ashes and Diamonds* Cybulski not only wore cool sunglasses but also got to carry a German 9mm MP 38 sub-machine gun around all the time.

So this was me on my way to London. Long black hair parted

in the middle, beard with the middle shaved out of it to make it look a bit different, dark glasses, black leather biker's jacket with lots of zips that my mum had bought me in a shop in Southport, black leather gloves and black trousers. By tucking them into my trousers I was able to disguise the different lengths of the legs and the weird pouchy bits around the thighs tucked into sheepskin-lined black motorcycle boots. It was a very hot summer, 1969.

When Julie opened the door of their large semi-detached house she was more beautiful than I remembered, with the air of being a proper grown-up rather than the pretend one that I was. That she should look so lovely was not a good start to the evening, because unfortunately not only did I dress like a man who had spent three months in the Warsaw sewers but I had begun to act like one too. Julie and her mother treated me with great kindness and had even invited over some other young people to provide entertainment, but throughout dinner and afterwards I remained silent for long periods, staring at the floor, then uttered a single harsh laugh or said something weird like 'Clown time is over, man.' The truth was that I was nervous and feeling terribly out of my depth. I wanted Julie to be my girlfriend but she seemed in a such a different league – not just glamorous but metropolitan too. For the whole night I behaved abominably. I imagine that those nice young teenagers cannot have had a more excruciating evening in all their young lives.

As I lay in my bed in their spare room I heard Julie and her mum talking about me on the landing outside. 'He's awful,' her mum said. 'He's got a chip on his shoulder about something.' I shrivelled like a punctured balloon, ashamed at hearing the pain and confusion in their voices and realising the chaos I had caused. Then I inflated with pride for exactly the same reason.

The next morning I slunk away and, collecting my bedroll from Glen's flat, caught the train down to Folkestone and from there took the four-hour ferry trip to Ostend.

I can remember hanging around at the Belgian seaside in the late summer sunshine, which all seemed so familiar from my childhood holidays. The flags of all the nations of Europe flapped in the breeze, pedal cars filled with laughing families trundled up and down the esplanade and the outside terraces of bars advertising their English beers teemed with holidaymakers. And I thought about how much I hated being by myself and yet I seemed to find myself over and over again in some remote foreign spot feeling awful.

With this thought in mind I caught the train to Amsterdam – I don't think I even bothered going through the masquerade of hitching, so despondent did I feel. My parents had dug out the address of their old friends Ank and Ayli, and once in the city I walked to where I thought they lived. Except that I didn't do anything as sensible as buy a street map or ask anybody if this was the right place and I don't think we'd actually told them I was coming either. The result was that late at night I found myself, a man with long hair and a beard dressed entirely in black with a bedroll over his shoulder, hammering on a beautifully polished wooden door set with bevelled glass windows in an Amsterdam suburb. Through the glass, inside the house, I could see shapes moving about and heard high-pitched frightened voices whispering to each other as I banged over and over on what was almost certainly the wrong door.

After a while I gave up and went back into the centre of town. Somehow I found my way to Club Paradiso, a famous hippy counter-culture place inside an old church. Typically for Holland, Paradiso had been opened by the city authorities, was publicly subsidised, and the sale and consumption of dope and acid were allowed. Outside, the building was dark and creepy, and in some ways was even worse inside. The only thing I found more unpleasant than being on my own was being with hippies and listening to their endless talk, yet this too was something which I seemed to find myself doing all the time. The self-pity and sense of entitlement of these people repelled me – all their tales were either about how they had taken advantage of somebody else or how they had been done out of something that they felt was rightfully theirs. In a balcony overlooking the stage area, with three large illuminated church windows behind me, I bought some dope so strong that it left me drooling, shivering and sweating, propped up against a wall throughout the night. In the morning I decided, even quicker than the previous year, to cut my holiday short and go home.

Just before I left I saw a shop selling flick-knives, which were illegal in the UK, so with the last of my Dutch money I bought one and hid it inside my jacket. I thought it one of the most lovely things I had ever seen. Its handle was inlaid with bone and the blade, chromed stainless steel, sprang out from the side at the click of a button. Suddenly there was a knife in your hand where there had been nothing a split second before. Because of my knife I was very nervous as the ferry approached the south coast of England, so I got chatting with some random guy until we were through customs. I realised right there that I didn't have the nerve to be a criminal, so there was another career opportunity gone.

One unique contribution Liverpool had made to the counter-culture was a character I never encountered anywhere else, and that was the Hard Hippy. The Hard Hippy was some-body who had the same qualities of self-pity and narcissism as the normal hippy but was also capable of kicking your head in. During that long summer I sometimes used to hang around a ramshackle art gallery in the centre of Liverpool where a Hard Hippy used to hold court. He had long blond hair and his muscular torso was only ever covered by faded denim dungarees as worn by US hillbilly farmers, except that in his case he wore them with the legs cut off high up on his bulging hairy thighs. Dotted around the gallery were various house plants that ranged from fairly well through sickly to dead. One day the Hard Hippy was discoursing to a group of us about how he was planning to name the child he was having with his chick Fluoride when a mild-mannered guy in glasses who had been wandering around looking at the terrible art on the walls inadvertently interrupted the Hard Hippy's monologue.

'Er . . . does anybody mind if I take a cutting from one of these plants?'

The whole room fell into a nervous silence as the muscular blond stopped talking and, sensing the change, the mild-mannered guy began to shift nervously from foot to foot realising that he had made a bad mistake.

After an uncomfortable thirty seconds during which we all fidgeted anxiously the Hard Hippy finally said in a calm but icy voice, 'I dunno, man. Why don't you ask the plant?'

'What?' said the visitor.

'I said, "Why don't you like get on your knees and ask the plant if you can take a cutting?" After all, it's like you're taking like one of its babies or something, man.'

'Erm . . . OK, yes,' said the mild-mannered man, and bending down to the ill-looking spider plant he said to it, 'Erm . . . hi. Erm, do you mind if I take a cutting from one of your shoots?'

Nothing happened.

'What did it say?' asked the Hard Hippy.

'It doesn't seem to mind.'

'Well, go ahead, then.'

With trembling hands the visitor took a tiny sprig of the plant and quickly left.

'Fucking straights, man,' the Hard Hippy said.

★☆☆53

Molly Gets into Art School

That summer really did seem to go on for ever. Even Maoism had been suspended for the months of July and August and on into early September, so there weren't even any dull meetings or screenings of *The East Is Red* to go to. Either side of my trip to Holland I reverted to what I used to do, which was to wander about aimlessly. One day towards evening, just before my trip to Amsterdam, I was standing on Everton Brow, a high ridge running north–south above a slope that curved down to the Mersey a mile and a half away and which in the early nine-teenth century had been lined with substantial villas. In the late afternoon between where I stood and the languid water there was virtually nothing but rubble, as if farmers were being paid to cultivate fields and fields of broken bricks between the occasional fifteen-storey slabs of vertical housing. The old neighbourhoods, the narrow cobbled streets of terraced housing, the corner shops, the wide boulevards of stores, the cinemas and pubs had been obliterated as thoroughly as a Czech village that had resisted the Nazis. Here and there the isolated stump of a building remained – a library with Arts and Crafts detailing or a High Victorian pub – but these only served to emphasise the desolation. From my vantage point the city was like somebody with a beautiful smile who had had their teeth kicked in. All the buses had lost their conductors and no longer carried the city's coat of arms on the sides, but rather an unattractive logo that appeared to have been designed as a class project in a school for troubled children, and were now run by something called 'Merseytravel'. It was as if an instruction had gone out from some centralised office saying, 'Make everything ugly'.

Nearer to home, along Oakfield Road the Gaumont cinema had closed down, Peter Pemberton's house had been bulldozed, Eric Savage's house was scheduled to go the same way, the Co-op store had gone, a lot of the little shops were derelict, boarded up or burned out, and the two Dickies had long ago abandoned their delicatessen. On the other side of the city Liverpool University had bought up all of Crown Street and then flattened the entire neighbourhood. This was what Joe had promised in his election literature in 1938: '. . . the demolition of slums and every insanitary house, large-scale replanning of built-up areas with provision of open spaces, children's playgrounds and school development'. There had certainly been demolition and there were now open spaces, but there was nothing in them except mud.

Coming towards me, bright against the gloom, was a shock of blond hair. It was Sid, my former drinking buddy – Sid, who had been on probation and got drunk and been chased round and round the Everyman Theatre. He hadn't gone into the sixth form with the rest of us but had left school the year before at fifteen. I was enormously relieved to see a familiar face in this wasteland and waved the startled young man down with an extravagant smile on my face. He reluctantly stopped and, once he recognised who it was, told me how he was getting on. He was now, he said proudly, an office junior at an insurance company in town. But as we talked Sid kept glancing uneasily about him, and after a few minutes of strained conversation he said a quick goodbye and scuttled off, leaving me standing alone on that long and bleak escarpment.

I knew that Sid had been nervous in case somebody from his neighbourhood saw us talking together. He lived in one of those bleak tower blocks down the hill whose populations were intolerant of anybody who acted, thought or dressed in even the tiniest way different from the norm. So for him to be seen chatting to a man resembling a Cossack who had become detached from his regiment meant he was at the very least risking having his sexuality questioned and being mercilessly mocked for months about having weirdy friends. Still, I found it sad that somebody who had once been so wild had been that easily tamed by a weekly wage and a shiny suit.

On the other hand, at least he was getting on with things. What was I going to do with my life? The only offer I had got, even of an interview, was at Southport College of Art for a place on a two-year foundation course. If I impressed at the interview and got on the course, then passed A-Level art, it would mean I could eventually apply for a place at a London art school. It had come down to this – only my skill at drawing was likely to save me.

Unfortunately, when the letter came informing me of the date of my interview it coincided with my planned journey to Holland. So sacrosanct were holidays that nobody contemplated for a second the idea that I should delay or cancel my intended trip. Instead, we decided that Molly would attend the most important interview of my life for me. On 11 September

1969, while I was still coming down from the dope I had smoked the night before, my mother took the portfolio of work I had done at school with her on the train to Southport. Fearing she might be late for my interview she took a taxi from the station to the art school, which was maybe four hundred yards away.

Molly must have done well in the interview, because a few days after my return from Amsterdam they offered me a place. I had the feeling when I turned up for classes on my first day that they were expecting a Jewish lady with red hair and glasses.

What might have swung Molly's interview was that she'd actually once been in the same room as Picasso and had watched him create a work of art. On a cold and blowy Monday in November 1950 fleets of coaches departed from every major city and town in Britain heading to Yorkshire for 'the Sheffield World Peace Congress'. My parents, recently married, were on one of the many coaches that left from Liverpool. They were in the massive crowd who cheered and cheered as Pablo Picasso, speaking from a stage decorated with yellow banners proclaiming 'Ban All War Propaganda' in big red letters, related how he and his father used to paint doves together and how he was allowed to paint the legs. Then he declared. 'I stand for life against death. I stand for peace against war!' Picasso sat down to thunderous applause.

Oddly enough my mother was as excited at hearing Hewlett Johnson, a Christian Marxist, the so-called 'Red Dean' of Canterbury Cathedral speak, as she was at seeing the world's greatest living artist in the flesh. Perhaps that is why my parents failed to make a bid for a sketch of a dove that they watched Picasso draw, a sketch which he then signed and later in the evening was auctioned to raise funds. Instead it was bought by an American businessman for twenty guineas.

The term at Southport Art College began a week later than that at Alsop, so one lunchtime I decided to go back to see my old school mates, who I knew would be playing football over the road in Walton Hall Park, just as we had done the year before. Somehow I hadn't managed to see any of them during the summer holidays. After spending all morning choosing my outfit, in the end the only change I made was that in place of the ragged denim jacket lined with rabbit fur I was wearing when I met Sid I put on my black leather biker jacket. I suppose when you have a look that works you should stick with it, though when I wore my black leather boots on the bus, sarcastic people kept asking me where my motorbike or occasionally where my horse was.

One of the television programmes that the entire Sayle family was happy to watch together was *The Saint*, starring Roger Moore and broadcast on Granada TV. Molly felt it was ideologically safe because a lot of the writers and cast were Unity Theatre alumni and therefore socialists. Alfie Bass and David Kossoff regularly turned up in supporting roles, as did Warren Mitchell who would always be cast as the swarthy Moroccan.

What I liked most about *The Saint* was that when the hero, Simon Templar, visited somewhere impossibly exotic on a case (distant locations such as Marseilles, Salzburg or Tangier, faraway places whose streets, even to a teenager, looked suspiciously like the back end of Elstree Studios) whatever he needed for his mission – guns, plans of the main post office, a hot air balloon – was always available via some old pal who lived there. All kinds of helpful and exotic folk in towns and cities all over the world – jittery safe-crackers, sexy dancing girls and world-weary police inspectors – were happy to help Simon out without giving it a second's thought. In the world of the Saint, friendship was a fixed and simple thing that lasted for ever. None of these people ever told Simon that they didn't want to help him solve a murder, rob a bank or let him play a game of football with them.

The day was hot and cloudy as I walked across Stanley Park, then on through Anfield Cemetery past rows of collapsing tombs and tilting angels. It suddenly struck me that this was the last time I would do this familiar walk – I wasn't a schoolboy any more. Arriving at the park opposite Alsop just after the lunch break had begun, I saw my former classmates in their school uniforms kicking a ball about across the grass. Crossing the worn turf towards them I thought they looked like children, shouting, swinging at the ball and rushing around. As I got closer they stopped one by one, turned and looked at me, as if they didn't know what I was doing there. And I for my part, sensing their hostile attitude, may then have laid it on a bit thick about where I would be going next week – telling them that at art school you could come in at any time of the day that you wanted and there would be sexy girls and drugs and you called the lecturers by their first names and went to parties at their flats and they gave you lifts home in their sports cars and they treated you as an equal. Unlike at school where they were.

Nobody invited me to stay and have a kick-about with them,

so I turned and strode away like I had somewhere else to be. It seemed to me that they would have liked to be different and I would have liked to be different but there was a script that we were following, a script that we didn't have the wit to rewrite. Or maybe I was just being a git.

Acknowledgements

For their invaluable help I'd like to thank Harry Jackson, Chris Walker, Ian Williams, Nigel Preston Jones, Sylvia Thomas and as ever Linda.